J. Wiesenfarth

GEORGE ELIOT'S ORIGINALS AND CONTEMPORARIES

George Eliot's Originals and Contemporaries

Essays in Victorian Literary History
and Biography

GORDON S. HAIGHT

Edited by

Hugh Witemeyer

Ann Arbor
The University of Michigan Press

Published in the United States of America by
The University of Michigan Press

1995 1994 1993 1992   4 3 2 1

Printed in Hong Kong

Library of Congress Cataloging-in-Publication Data
Haight, Gordon Sherman.
   George Eliot's originals and contemporaries : essays in Victorian
literary history and biography / Gordon S. Haight : edited by Hugh
Witemeyer.
      p. cm.
   Includes bibliographical references and index.
   ISBN 0–472–10264–8 (alk. paper)
   1. Eliot, George, 1819–1880—Characters.   2. Eliot, George,
1819–1880—Contemporaries.   3. English literature—19th century—
–History and criticism.   4. Characters and characteristics in
literature.   5. Authors, English—19th century—biography.
I. Witemeyer, Hugh.   II. Title.
PR4689.H27   1992
823'.8—dc20   91–28045
                                                          CIP

Contents

Introduction

This volume contains a selection of essays in literary history and
biography by Gordon Sherman Haight (1901–85). Their author is the
founder of modern George Eliot studies and, according to Kathleen
Tillotson, 'the outstanding scholar of his generation in the Victorian
field'.[1] A gathering of his occasional essays is one of the few projects
Haight left unfinished at the time of his death. The present edition
seeks to fulfil his aim by bringing together a group of writings in
which information of lasting interest is conveyed in prose of enduring grace.

Haight is best known as the authoritative biographer of George
Eliot and the editor of her correspondence. But he was also an
accomplished essayist who contributed scores of well-crafted short
pieces to periodicals, *Festschriften* and works of reference. Many of
these items have to do with Eliot's life and work, but the range of
Haight's interests extended well beyond the Eliot circle. Thus he also
wrote on the poetry of Tennyson, the journalism of George Meredith,
the sculpture of G. F. Watts and the problem of male chastity in the
nineteenth century. The essays, in other words, reveal new and
unexpected facets of Haight's indefatigable investigation of Victorian literary culture. They also present fresh information based upon
meticulous archival research among unpublished documents,
thoughtful insights into the sensibility of the period and many drily
humorous turns of phrase.

Before we consider these previously uncollected writings, we
may briefly turn the tables on the biographer. Gordon Haight was
born in Muskegon, Michigan, on 6 February 1901. He enrolled at
Yale University in the autumn of 1919. In the following year he
discovered the works of George Eliot in a class taught by Professor
Robert James Menner. Chauncey Brewster Tinker was another important influence upon the future scholar's development at Yale.
After graduating in 1923, Haight taught for one year at the Kent
School in Kent, Connecticut, and for five years at the Hotchkiss
School in Lakeville, Connecticut, both of them private preparatory
schools for boys. During this period, he also worked on his first
biography of a nineteenth-century woman writer, the American poet

Lydia Huntley Sigourney (1791–1865). The Yale University Press published *Mrs Sigourney: The Sweet Singer of Hartford* in 1930.

In 1931 Haight returned to Yale for graduate work. Two years later, he completed his doctorate and joined the University's faculty as a member of the Department of English and a fellow of Calhoun College. The subject of his dissertation was Francis Quarles, the seventeenth-century maker of English emblem books. The young scholar later published half a dozen articles and notes on Quarles. Then, in the spring of 1933, Haight's attention was diverted from the Renaissance to the Victorian period. The Yale University Library had recently acquired some 600 unpublished letters by George Eliot. At first, Haight determined to write a life of Eliot. But he soon realised that he could not do so without first editing her correspondence.

These two projects – the editing of George Eliot's letters and the writing of her biography – became the principal work of Gordon Haight's life, occupying him steadily for the next 50 years. His researches led him to many of the major libraries in the United States and Great Britain, and won him no fewer than three Guggenheim Fellowships. The first fruit of his efforts was a volume entitled *George Eliot and John Chapman, with Chapman's Diaries*. Published by Yale University Press in 1940, this was a lively account of Eliot's personal and professional relationship with the unorthodox publisher of the *Westminster Review*.

Haight's own life, in the meantime, remained agreeably orthodox. On 24 June 1937 he began a happy, lifelong marriage to Mary Treat Nettleton, with whom he eventually settled in a handsomely situated, rural home in Woodbridge, Connecticut, just north of New Haven. During the war years, Haight kept the pot boiling by editing a number of English and American literary classics for a New York publisher named Walter J. Black. The titles of these works reflect the range of the editor's interests: Francis Bacon's *Essays* and *New Atlantis*; Daniel Defoe's *Robinson Crusoe*; Edward FitzGerald's *The Rubaiyat of Omar Khayyam*; Benjamin Franklin's *Autobiography*; Ralph Waldo Emerson's *Essays*; Henry David Thoreau's *Walden*; and Walt Whitman's *Leaves of Grass*. Haight's interest in American literature was also evidenced in his work on Civil War novelist John W. DeForest; he edited DeForest's *Miss Ravenel's Conversion from Secession to Loyalty* for Harper in 1939, and later wrote the chapter on DeForest, William Dean Howells and other nineteenth-century realists for the *Literary History of the United States* (1948).

The 1950s were years of achievement and recognition. At Yale Haight was made Master of Pierson College in 1949, serving in that role until 1953. In 1950 he was promoted to the rank of Professor. To students he was accessible, urbane and unobtrusively helpful. To fellow scholars he gave generously of his time and his vast store of precise knowledge.

The crowning development of this decade was the publication by Yale University Press in 1954–5 of the first seven volumes of *The George Eliot Letters*. They were immediately hailed as a monumental work of scholarship, of inestimable value to students not only of Victorian literature but of the Victorian period in general. According to Lionel Trilling in the *New York Times*, 'intelligence and tact mark Mr Haight's editing at every point. . . . His notes are as succinct and modest as they are pertinent. They answer every question, great or small, that any reader might ask, and they represent – as needs they must, George Eliot's mental range being what it was – a mastery of the whole intellectual history of the nineteenth century.'[2]

In addition to Eliot's letters, Haight edited several of her novels in these years. His paperback editions of *Adam Bede* (1949), *Middlemarch* (1956) and *The Mill on the Floss* (1962) were widely used in American colleges and universities. He later compiled a selection of critical essays by divers hands entitled *A Century of George Eliot Criticism*; it was published by Methuen in 1966. In the same year, Haight was appointed to an endowed chair at Yale, the Emily Sanford Professorship in English.

The long-postponed and eagerly awaited *George Eliot: A Biography* was published by the Oxford University Press in 1968. It immediately became the standard biography, and seems likely to hold that position for many years to come. Kathleen Tillotson has called it 'a masterpiece of accurate record, sympathetic insight, and narrative impetus'.[3] The book won the Van Wyck Brooks Memorial Award in the United States; in Great Britain, it received both the James Tait Black Memorial Prize and the Heinemann Award of the Royal Society of Literature. Haight was elected a fellow of both the Royal Society of Literature and the British Academy. He carried these honours into retirement from active service to Yale in 1969. To them, the Yale Graduate School added the Wilbur Cross Medal in 1977.

'The only thing wrong with being retired,' Haight's colleague René Wellek once remarked, 'is that one gets no vacations.' It must have seemed so to Haight during the next fifteen years. In the 1970s, he edited *The Portable Victorian Reader* for the Viking Press (1972) and added two volumes (VIII and IX) of newly discovered correspondence to his edition of *The George Eliot Letters* (1978). He also served as General Editor of the Clarendon Edition of Eliot's novels, a major undertaking for which he himself prepared the text and apparatus of *The Mill on the Floss* (1980). In addition, he continued to write reviews of current scholarship in the Victorian field; more than 45 of his thoughtful assessments appeared in British and American journals during his lifetime.

In 1980 came the centenary of George Eliot's death. On 21 June both the author and her editor-biographer were honoured. A tablet commemorating George Eliot was unveiled in Poets' Corner at Westminster Abbey, and Gordon Haight was invited to present the dedicatory address. His remarks were published in the *London Review of Books* for 17 July–6 August 1980. With Rosemary T. VanArsdel, Haight also edited a volume of essays entitled *George Eliot: A Centenary Tribute*; it was published by Macmillan in 1981.

He worked steadily into the eighty-fifth year of his life. In that year the Yale University Press brought out a volume of *Selections from George Eliot's Letters*, and Viking-Penguin issued a paperback edition of *George Eliot: A Biography*. Thus the two major projects of his long and productive career sustained him to the end. He died on 28 December 1985.

* * *

In all, Gordon Haight published some 57 essays, notes, letters to editors and book chapters. A checklist of these is appended to the present volume, which reprints fourteen of the most important pieces.

For the sake of unity, my selection includes only essays on George Eliot and other Victorian authors. This emphasis excludes two substantial groups of essays in other literary fields which interested Haight deeply: the English Renaissance and the seventeenth century, and the American nineteenth century. Likewise excluded are book reviews and book introductions, whether to Haight's own editions or to works by other scholars. Substantive essays, based upon original research, have been given preference over topical and polemical pieces.

The fourteen essays selected according to these criteria fall into two groups. The first six items all have to do with George Eliot's fictional characters. These studies hold a special place in Haight's *oeuvre*, because in them he applies his biographical research to the novels and stories, often developing his interpretive arguments in greater detail than was possible in *George Eliot: A Biography*. He aims both to evaluate the *dramatis personae* and to search out their 'originals', this being the term he himself favoured to designate the living people who were models for Eliot's created figures. The opening essay, 'George Eliot's Originals', is a classic of Eliot scholarship, and several other pieces in the set are also cited regularly by students of the novelist and her work. These influential analyses are here gathered in one volume for the first time.

The second group of essays has to do with George Eliot's Victorian contemporaries. The principal figures include George Henry Lewes, Thomas and Jane Carlyle, Charles Dickens, George Meredith, Alfred Tennyson, Robert Browning and George Frederic Watts. Some of these pieces grow out of Haight's research on Eliot and Lewes, but others are independent studies which reflect the range of his interests in the period. The two groups of essays are linked not only by their common focus upon the Victorian period but also by a consistent, biographical–historical methodology best described as resolutely empirical.

Each of the essays is reprinted in its entirety. A number of additions, deletions and corrections made by Haight himself before his death have been silently incorporated. Otherwise, the texts of the essays have not been changed except in their styling. This editorial policy preserves the author's final intentions, but its limitations should also be acknowledged.

Here and there Haight's statements are subject to correction or qualification.[4] No scholar can always be right, though few, probably, have come nearer that goal than Gordon Haight. Yet I have not attempted systematically to verify all his assertions and conclusions. Even if such a procedure were practicable, it would be intrusive, distracting and inevitably dogged by errors of its own. By the same token I have not eliminated Haight's repetition of phrases, sentences and groups of sentences in several of the essays on George Eliot's 'originals'. Deletion would break the flow of the argument, and emendation would raise a new set of problems. It seems preferable to solicit the reader's toleration of these redundancies, the most prominent of which comprises but three sentences. Such echoes are not uncommon in writings originally published far apart in time and place.

The texts of the essays have been uniformly restyled according to Macmillan house rules. The annotations have been standardised in form and grouped as endnotes, each set following the essay to which it pertains. The unnumbered notes which give the dates and places of original publication of the essays have been provided by the editor. The numbered notes are Haight's own.

For permission to reprint the essays, the editor is grateful to Mary Nettleton Haight and to the presses and periodicals in which they first appeared. Essays 2 and 7 are reprinted by permission of the Duke University Press; essay 3, by permission of the University of Toronto Press; essay 5, by permission of Methuen Ltd; and essay 8, by permission of the Modern Language Association of America, from *PMLA*, vol. 71 (1956). The editors of the following periodicals have also allowed items to be reproduced from their pages: *Victorian Newsletter* (essay 4), *Nineteenth-Century Literature* (9), *Modern Language Review* (10), *Studies in Philology* (11), *The Times Literary Supplement* (12), *Yale University Library Gazette* (13) and *Contemporary Review* (14).

The editor wishes above all to thank Mrs Haight, without whose active co-operation this book could not have been completed. I am also indebted to the following people for advice, encouragement, and material assistance: Frances Arnold, William Baker, Linda Berauer, Margaret Cannon, Virgil D. Duff, LeAnn Fields, Donald Gallup, Amy Ghaemmaghami, Barbara Hardy, Ward Hellstrom, U. C. Knoepflmacher, George Levine, Stephen Parks, Thomas Pinney, Sarah Roberts-West, Leonard Skipp, R. H. Super, Jeremy Treglown, R. M. Walker, Adrienne Marie Ward and Margaret Wimsatt. These friends and colleagues have helped the book come into being, but none of them is responsible for its errors and omissions. I would like to dedicate my editorial work to the memory of my father, Benton Diehl Witemeyer (1911–91).

Notes

1. Kathleen Tillotson, 'Professor Gordon Haight', *The Royal Society of Literature: Reports for 1985–86 and 1986–87* ([December] 1987) p. 43. For a concise summary of Haight's life and work, see John Mulryan, 'Gordon S. Haight', *Dictionary of Literary Biography* (Detroit, Mich.: Gale Research Inc., 1991) vol. 103, pp. 146–50.

2. Lionel Trilling, 'A Victorian Woman's World and Way' (review of *The George Eliot Letters*, vols I–III), *New York Times Book Review*, 22 August 1954, p. 1.
3. Tillotson, 'Professor Gordon Haight', p. 43.
4. For example, in his essay on 'The Carlyles and the Leweses', Haight suggests that the Carlyles never received George Eliot in their home on Cheyne Row (pp. 105, 111–12). Yet there is contemporary evidence to the contrary; see Thomas Adolphus Trollope, *What I Remember*, 2 vols (London: Richard Bentley and Son, 1887) vol. II, p. 305.

Part One
Originals

1

George Eliot's Originals

The passion for realism – as George Eliot defines it, 'the faithful representing of commonplace things' – led the Victorians to strive in all the arts for meticulous imitation of original models. With Ruskin's approval the Pre-Raphaelite painters spent whole weeks rendering in photographic detail a brick wall, a weedy bank or an old wagon. The novelists fell easily into the habit of transcribing particular scenes and characters from life. Though Dickens boasted of Boythorn as 'a most exact portrait of Walter Savage Landor', he seemed surprised that Leigh Hunt was hurt by his equally unmistakable caricature as Skimpole, and was embarrassed when Mrs Seymour Hill, a deformed manicurist, protested against his using her as Miss Mowcher. The emotional force of the early part of *David Copperfield* came largely from the painful memories of his own childhood woven into it. Thackeray too, as Professor Gordon Ray shows in *The Buried Life*, took characters from the members of his own family and others to whom he was bound by emotional ties. Trollope's *The Three Clerks*, Meredith's *Evan Harrington* and Hardy's *A Pair of Blue Eyes* offer further examples of the practice. Nor was it an exclusively English phenomenon. Tolstoi and Dostoevski, George Sand and Balzac, most of the Continental novelists of the time, drew portraits of people they knew. 'In the last analysis', Professor Ray declares, 'all fiction is inevitably autobiographical, for no novelist can transcend the limits of his personality and experience.'

George Eliot's fiction began with the description of episodes that had occurred in the neighbourhood of Nuneaton during her girlhood. The original of Amos Barton, her first hero, was John Gwyther, the curate of her parish of Chilvers Coton, where through years of Sundays she had had ample opportunity to study him; she was seventeen in 1836 when his wife (the Milly Barton of the story) died. Like Amos, Mr Gwyther also moved regretfully to the North, first to a dreary parish in Sheffield, and then to Fewston, Yorkshire, where he died in 1873. When the first part of 'Amos Barton' appeared in *Blackwood's Magazine* for January 1857, his eldest daughter Emma (the Patty of the story) asked him, 'Who in the world could have written this – have you, Papa?' so certain was she that it was an episode from his life. Succeeding instalments confirmed the opinion that it must have been written by someone intimate with him. The only person he could suspect was the Reverend William Hutchinson King, a former curate at Nuneaton, who figures in the story as Mr Ely. And in 1859, when speculation about the identity of George Eliot still ran high, Mr Gwyther asked Blackwood 'to make my kind remembrances to our gratuitous Historian' and assure him that, 'now the pain I felt at the first publication is past off – although I thought it unkind and taking a great liberty with a living Character – yet I fully forgive for old acquaintance sake. For we are as assured that I am intended by Amos Barton as I am of the Truth of any Fact soever.' His curious letter illustrates the accuracy of George Eliot's description: like Amos's it was 'not *very* ungrammatical'. Twice Mr Gwyther wrote 'it was him' and then changed the offending pronoun to *he*.

George Eliot at once wrote a note of apology for *Blackwood's* to copy and send him:

> The author of the 'Scenes of Clerical Life' and 'Adam Bede' begs me to inform you that he is not the Rev. W. H. King, but a much younger person, who wrote 'Amos Barton' under the impression that the clergyman whose long past trial suggested the groundwork of the story was no longer living, and that the incidents, not only through the license and necessities of artistic writing, but in consequence of the writer's imperfect knowledge, must have been so varied from the actual facts, that any one who discerned the core of truth must also recognize the large amount of arbitrary, imaginative addition.
>
> But for any annoyance, even though it may have been brief and not well-founded, which the appearance of the story may have caused Mr. Gwyther, the writer is sincerely sorry.

Mr Gwyther was not the only one to confound the imaginative additions with the core of truth in 'Amos Barton'. Lists giving a key to all the characters mentioned were soon circulating about Warwickshire. In one or two of the less clearly defined minor figures they show some variation, but on at least a score of names there is complete unanimity. No one near Nuneaton could fail to see Mr Newdigate in Mr Oldinport, Mr Harpur in Mr Farquhar, or Mr Bellairs and Mr Hake thinly disguised as Fellowes and Carpe.

For 'Mr Gilfil's Love-Story', the second of the *Scenes of Clerical Life*, George Eliot turned back to a generation she had never known. Sir Christopher Cheverel is based on things she had heard about old Sir Roger Newdigate (1719–1806), founder of the Newdigate Prize at Oxford, whose transformation of Arbury Hall from Elizabethan to magnificent Gothic antedated and in some ways surpassed Horace Walpole's better-known alterations at Strawberry Hill. George Eliot had slight childhood recollection of the Reverend Bernard Gilpin Ebdell, the original of Mr Gilfil, who was presented by the Crown in 1786 and lived on as Vicar of Chilvers Coton till she was nine years old; he had baptised her a week after her birth. His wife Sally Shilton had been (like Caterina) a protégée of Lady Newdigate, and died when George Eliot was only four. The outline of the story had been picked up from local legend, perhaps in the housekeeper's room at Arbury, and embellished with such romantic inventions as Caterina's Italian birth, her love affair with Sir Christopher's nephew and heir, and her early death a few months after marrying the faithful Mr Gilfil. The original of Caterina lived to enjoy twenty-two years of matrimony.

For the third of the *Scenes*, 'Janet's Repentance', George Eliot returned to events within her own memory. Janet Dempster is drawn from Mrs Nancy Wallington Buchanan, whose mother owned the school in Nuneaton, where George Eliot boarded from 1828 to 1832. The central incident of the tale, the persecution of Mr Tryan, records an actual experience of the Reverend John Edmund Jones, curate during most of those years at Stockingford (Paddiford) parish, where his earnest Evangelicalism provoked similar disorders. Mr Tryan's chief tormentor is Janet's drunken husband Lawyer Dempster, who brutally mistreats her too and finally turns her out of doors in her nightdress. This violence is soon followed by his death in delirium tremens after he has been thrown from his carriage and broken his leg. Janet, who had taken to drink and been saved by Mr Tryan, survives, wealthy and sober, to ease the decline of her rescuer, who soon dies of consumption.

The real facts in the case were somewhat different. When she married James Williams Buchanan in 1825, Nancy Wallington, then a teacher in her mother's school, was thought to have made a good match. Her husband was one of the leading lawyers of Nuneaton, the agent of several insurance companies, a trustee of the Leicester Turnpike Company, a man accustomed to lead – even in such misdi-rected affairs as ridiculing the innovations the Evangelicals had begun introducing into the Church, which as clerk of Nuneaton parish he felt it was his peculiar responsibility to oppose. There is no evidence that her marriage was particularly unhappy or that, like Janet, Mrs Buchanan sought relief in the brandy bottle. After the death of Mr Jones in December 1831 she had two children, one born in 1832, the other in 1834. She continued 'in her usual busy style' to take an active part in civic affairs. When Queen Adelaide passed through Nuneaton in 1839 on her royal progress to Warwick Castle, we see Mrs Buchanan rehearsing the children of the various schools to sing the national anthem in the market place. Soon after this great day she fell ill, and in July 1840 she died. A week later her husband suffered the accident that George Eliot inflicts on Mr Dempster a decade earlier. The Coventry *Standard* says:

> J. W. Buchanan, Esq., solicitor, of Nuneaton, met with a severe accident last week. While driving towards Coventry, one of the wheels of his carriage came off, near the second milestone, and in dismounting he fell, and the vehicle passed over his legs, one of which sustained a compound fracture, and the other was severely lacerated. Mr. Ball, surgeon, of Foleshill, set the broken limb, and he was removed home, where he lies in a very precarious state. The circumstance is rendered more distressing by the decease of Mrs. Buchanan, who died after a short illness at Margate, on Sunday last. She will be a serious loss to her poorer townsfolk, to whom her kindness and charity were unlimited.

Unlike Lawyer Dempster, Mr Buchanan recovered and survived his wife for nearly six years.

The blackened portrait of him in 'Janet's Repentance' may perhaps be explained by the influence on George Eliot of Maria Lewis (1800?–87), principal governess at Mrs Wallington's School. An Evangelical of the strictest sort, she inculcated in her impressionable ten-year-old pupil a painful piety that frowned on every kind of worldly amusement and dominated her mind for nearly a decade. Miss Lewis doubtless took the darkest view of Mr Buchanan's 'intemperance', which, in those heavy-drinking days, may have been nothing remarkable, and probably gossiped about his 'mistreatment' of her friend and colleague Nancy, whom she later accompanied to Margate and nursed in her last illness. The shadows in the Buchanans' married life were seen at their blackest through Miss Lewis's eyes. In 1831 she was one of the Reverend Mr Jones's most ardent adherents; and the indignation she felt at the public insults offered him was surely imparted to the trembling Marian Evans, kneeling beside her on a bench at the window to watch the noisy crowd in the street below.

On first reading the manuscript of 'Janet's Repentance' John Blackwood protested against the stark realism and urged George Eliot to soften the picture as much as possible.

The story [she replied] so far as regards the *persecution*, is a real bit in the religious history of England that happened about eight-and-twenty years ago. . . . Everything is softened from the fact, so far as art is permitted to soften and yet to remain essentially true. The real town was more vicious than my Milby; the real Dempster was far more disgusting than mine; the real Janet, alas! had a far sadder end than mine, who will melt away from the reader's sight in purity, happiness, and beauty.

Mr Tryan was recognised as quickly as Amos had been. After the first two numbers appeared in *Blackwood's*, the Reverend William Pitman Jones wrote to the editor to say that they alluded to his deceased brother and that he was 'utterly at a loss to conceive who could have . . . revived what should have been buried in oblivion'. Of the parties alluded to, he added, most, if not all, 'have long been in Eternity'. John Blackwood sent the note to George Henry Lewes to be passed on to George Eliot, saying: 'I hope . . . that our friend has not in his love of reality said anything to identify his story with living characters.' George Eliot herself replied:

Mr. Tryan is not a portrait of any clergyman, living or dead. He is an ideal character, but I hope probable enough to resemble more than one evangelical clergyman of his day. If Mr. Jones's deceased brother was like Mr. Tryan, so much the better, for in that case he was made of human nature's finer clay. I think you will agree with me that there are few clergymen who would be depreciated by an identification with Mr Tryan. But I should rather suppose that the old gentleman, misled by some similarity in outward circumstances, is blind to the discrepancies which must exist where no portrait was intended. As to the rest of my story, so far as its elements were suggested by real persons, those persons have been, to use good Mr. Jones's phrase, 'long in Eternity'. . . .

I should consider it a fault which would cause me lasting regret, if I had used reality in any other than the legitimate way

common to all artists who draw their materials from their observation and experience. It would be a melancholy result of my
fictions if I gave *just* cause of annoyance to any good and sensible
person. But I suppose there is no perfect safeguard against errone-
ous impressions or a mistaken susceptibility. We are all apt to
forget how little there is about us that is unique, and how very
strongly we resemble many other insignificant people who have
lived before us.

On the last day of February 1858, Mr Blackwood was finally told
that the mysterious unknown George Eliot, whose stories he had
been publishing for more than a year, was really Marian Evans, the
Mrs Lewes he had met several times when calling on Lewes at
Richmond. Sensitive to the proprieties, as the editor of a family
magazine must be, he agreed that on all accounts it was desirable to
keep the secret. However, it was becoming increasingly difficult.
Some months before a newspaper on the Isle of Man had attributed
the authorship of the *Scenes of Clerical Life* to a certain Joseph Liggins,
a baker's son at Nuneaton, who in the absence of other candidates
was accepted; and though he would neither affirm nor deny the soft
impeachment, he declared that the publishers had never paid him a
penny. In May when John Blackwood was smoking his cigar in front
of the stand at the Derby, he was accosted by C. N. Newdegate, MP
for Warwickshire, who told him that the capital series of stories, the
Clerical Scenes, were 'all about my place and County', and that he
knew the author, whose name was Liggins. Blackwood lost no time
in sending the fascinating news to George Eliot.

> You were right in believing that I should like to hear Mr.
> Newdegate's opinion of the Stories [she replied]. His testimony to
> the spirit in which they are written is really valuable, for I know
> he deserves the character you give him.
>   As to details, he seems, from what you say, as likely to be
> mistaken about them as he is about the authorship; but it is
> invariably the case that when people discover certain points of
> coincidence in a fiction with facts that happen to have come to
> their knowledge, they believe themselves able to furnish a key to
> the whole. That is amusing enough to the author, who knows
> from what widely sundered portions of experience – from what a
> combination of subtle shadowy suggestions with certain actual
> objects and events, his story has been formed. Certain vague

traditions about Sir Roger Newdegate (him of 'Newdigate-Prize' celebrity) which I heard when I was a child are woven into the character of Sir Christopher Cheverel, and the house he improved into a charming Gothic place with beautiful ceilings, I know from actual vision – but the rest of 'Mr. Gilfil's Love Story' is spun out of the subtlest web of minute observation and inward experience, from my first childish recollections up to recent years. So it is with all the other stories. It would be a very difficult thing for me to furnish a key to them myself. But where there is no exact memory of the past any story with a few remembered points of character or of incident may pass for a history.

To avoid the dangerous ground she had trodden in the *Scenes* George Eliot chose more private materials for her next book. The germ of *Adam Bede* was a story told to her by her aunt Mrs Samuel Evans, a Methodist, who in 1802 at Nottingham had softened the heart of a girl named Mary Voce, about to be executed for child-murder. They were the originals of Dinah Morris and Hetty Sorrel. The character of Adam was based on what she knew of her father, Robert Evans, who was once a carpenter and later agent for several great estates, including that of the Newdegates at Arbury. Unlike the affairs in the *Scenes*, these were hardly known outside George Eliot's own family, from whom she was now quite alienated. Her illegal union with Lewes so outraged her brother Isaac Evans that he had the family solicitor answer her letter announcing the news and forbade her sister Chrissey to communicate with her.

The phenomenal success of *Adam Bede* in 1859 revived curiosity about George Eliot's identity. Liggins's supporters pressed their claim, publishing indignant letters in *The Times*, which Blackwood and the real George Eliot instantly denounced. A foolish busybody, a Warwickshire magistrate named Bracebridge, a Liggins champion, went scouring about the countryside for the original of Mrs Poyser and discovered one who resembled her – in nothing but the name. Through Florence Nightingale's father he heard of a daughter of the original Dinah Morris and found himself interviewing a Mrs Walker, the wife of Nightingale's tailor, who recalled that when George Eliot visited her mother she occupied some hours in writing down Mrs Evans's experiences from her own lips 'and was hardly ever seen in Wirksworth without a notebook and pencil in her hand'. Dinah's sermon, Mrs Walker added, was copied from one of Mrs Evans's manuscripts. Alas for the truth! both notebook and sermon are as imaginary as George Eliot's visit. By the end of June the secret of George Eliot's identity was beginning to leak out in literary circles; and since *Adam Bede* had sold five printings in as many months and had been universally acclaimed, there was no longer much reason to preserve anonymity. Mr Bracebridge in Pickwickian fashion continued his researches all summer among George Eliot's Staffordshire cousins. To the irritation caused by his findings, which were obligingly passed on by her friend Charles Bray, we owe George Eliot's best statements about the originals:

> One of the scenes in my books that many people have pitched on as peculiarly *true* is the conversation of the clergy at the Clerical Dinner, in *Amos Barton*. It is needless to say, that I was never present at a Clerical Dinner party. Mr. Bracebridge is quite right in saying I was too young to witness and judge, when the events that suggested my stories occurred – the inference of a little wisdom and a little modesty would be, that the events are *not* precisely what happened, as people with dim confused memories imagine them to be, because they see a few particulars which they *do* remember. I've no doubt there are people who think that Dempster really spoke from a window just as I have described – if he did, *I* never heard that he did, and I was a child kneeling on a form at a school-room window at that date.

George Eliot admits that there are two portraits in the *Scenes of Clerical Life*:

> first, *Amos Barton*, who however is made a much better man than he really was, and far more unimpeachable in conduct. The affair of the 'Countess' was never fully known to me: so far as it *was* known, it is varied from my knowledge of the alleged fact. 2nd *Dempster*, whose original has been dead twenty years or more, (I thought 'Amos' was dead) and was by no means so witty, I imagine, as his representative in 'Janet'.

But in *Adam Bede*, George Eliot insists, 'There is not a single portrait'.

> I could never have written Adam Bede if I had not learned something of my father's early experience: but no one who knew my father could call Adam a portrait of him – and the course of Adam's life is entirely different from my father's. Again, Dinah

and Seth are *not* my aunt and uncle. I knew my aunt and uncle and they were Methodists – my aunt a preacher; and I loved them: so far only they resembled Seth and Dinah. The whole course of the story in Adam Bede – the descriptions of scenery or houses – the characters – the dialogue – *everything* is a combination from widely sundered elements of experience. . . . I remember very well the moment of writing that speech of Mrs. Poyser's in which she says Dinah provokes her because she's 'like the statty outside Treddles'on church – a-staring and smiling whether it's fair weather or foul'. But I never remember seeing any statue outside any church, that suggested the image. It was the only place where Mrs. Poyser could have seen anything like a statue – that was the reason why the statue was 'outside Treddles'on church'. Treddleston is *not* Ellastone. Hayslope is, with a difference.

One reader of *Adam Bede*, a Derbyshire woman, thinking she recognised the dialect of the country people she knew in her child-hood, was convinced that the book must have been written there. But, George Eliot continues,

I never knew any Derbyshire people, or Staffordshire either, ex-cept my father and his brothers. His brothers I never saw so many times as I could count fingers, and my visits to those counties were not more than four or five altogether – none of them for more than a few days. Yet, I imagine, no one will go to the length of saying that the dialect was put in for me.

The suggestion that she had copied Dinah's sermon from notes in her aunt's journal George Eliot repudiates indignantly:

I never knew my aunt *had* a journal – and I hear it with some surprise – incredulity, rather. Some one said they thought Mrs. Poyser's sayings must have been collected for me!! It is happy for me that I never expected any gratification of a personal kind from my authorship. The worst of all this is that it nauseates me – chills me and discourages me in my work.

In a letter to her friend Sara Hennell a few weeks later George Eliot describes her aunt more minutely:

Although I had only heard her spoken of as a strange person, given to a fanatical vehemence of exhortation in private as well as public, I believed that [when she came to visit at Griff in 1839] we should find sympathy between us. She was then an old woman – above sixty – and, I believe, had for a good many years given up preaching. A tiny little woman, with bright, small dark eyes, and hair that had been black, I imagine, but was now grey – a pretty woman in her youth, but of a totally different physical type from Dinah. The difference – as you will believe – was not *simply* physical: no difference is. She was a woman of strong natural excitability, which I know, from the description I have heard my father and half-sister give, prevented her from the exercise of discretion under the promptings of her zeal. But this vehemence was now subdued by age and sickness; she was very gentle and quiet in her manners – very loving – and (what she must have been from the very first) a truly religious soul, in whom the love of God and love of man were fused together. . . .

As to my aunt's conversation, it is a fact, that the only two things of any interest I remember in our lonely sittings and walks, are her telling me one sunny afternoon how she had, with another pious woman, visited an unhappy girl in prison, stayed with her all night, and gone with her to execution, and one or two accounts of supposed miracles in which she believed – among the rest, *the face with the crown of thorns seen in the glass.*

Mrs Evans was more interested in the work of divine grace than in details of Mary Voce and her unhappy end.

In her account of the prison scenes, I remember no word she uttered – I only remember her tone and manner, and the deep feeling I had under the recital. Of the girl she knew nothing, I believe – or told me nothing – but that she was a common coarse girl, convicted of child-murder. The incident lay in my mind for years on years, as a dead germ, apparently – till time had made my mind a nidus in which it could fructify; it then turned out to be the germ of 'Adam Bede'. . . .

You see how she suggested Dinah; but it is not possible you should see as I do how entirely her individuality differed from Dinah's. How curious it seems to me that people should think Dinah's sermons, prayers, and speeches were *copied* – when they were written with hot tears, as they surged up in my own mind!
. . .

As to my aunt's children or grandchildren saying, if they *did* say, that Dinah is a good portrait of my aunt – that is simply the

vague easily satisfied notion imperfectly instructed people always have of portraits. It is not surprising that simple men and
women without pretension to enlightened discrimination should
think a generic resemblance constitutes a portrait, when we see
the great public so accustomed to be delighted with *mis*representations of life and character, which they accept as representations,
that they are scandalized when art makes a nearer approach to
truth.

Regarding her indebtedness to facts and locale of Staffordshire
and Derbyshire, George Eliot continues,

I never remained in either of those counties more than a few days
together. . . . The details which I knew as facts and have made use
of for my picture were gathered from such imperfect allusion and
narrative as I heard from my father, in his occasional talk about
old times.

Hayslope, as she had told Mr Bray, was Ellastone, but 'with a difference'. That is, Hayslope was rather more like Chilvers Coton. The
wonderful background of *Adam Bede* in which contour of land, subtle variation in the foliage, the sounds of domestic animals, as well as
the countryman's attachment to the soil and the almost instinctive
rites of seed-time and harvest – these were never culled from a
notebook kept during a hurried visit to a strange county. They were
the recollections of a sensitive mind, turning nostalgically back to
the world of childhood from which Marian Evans was now cruelly
and unjustly excluded.

The same nostalgic feeling permeates the first two volumes of *The
Mill on the Floss* (1860). The flood that ends Maggie Tulliver's life
could not take place in Warwickshire, but it was not, as careless
readers often think, a crude melodramatic device to extricate the
author from an impossible and unforeseen dilemma. The flood was
the first thing George Eliot determined about the story. In January
1859 she began to look out accounts of inundations in the *Annual
Register*, and in September she and Lewes spent ten days in
Dorsetshire searching for a suitable setting. At Radipole near Wey-
mouth they discovered a mill that pleased her so much they tried to
rent a labourer's cottage so as to live near it for a week. A few days
later they went to Dorchester to see whether the Frome would be an
adequate river. Neither Wey nor Frome seemed right for the cata-
strophic flood she needed, and off they dashed to the north to study

the Trent. At Newark, where the Avon joins it, the Trent was hardly deep enough. Farther downstream, however, at Gainsborough, where the Idle flows in, she found just what she wanted for the Floss and the Ripple. On the course that Maggie was to follow they rowed down to the Idle, ascended some way on foot, and then walked back to Gainsborough. There one can still see vestiges of St Ogg's with its 'aged, fluted red roofs and the broad gables of its wharves'.

But Dorlcote Mill was never on the Trent or the Idle. The old mill of Marian Evans's childhood at Arbury supplied the few details we are given. More clearly than the mill itself we see the wagoner coming home with a load of grain, his horses

> strong, submissive, meek-eyed beasts . . . looking mild reproach at
> him from between their blinkers, that he should crack his whip at
> them in that awful manner as if they needed that hint! See how
> they stretch their shoulders up the slope towards the bridge, with
> all the more energy because they are so near home. Look at the
> grand shaggy feet that seem to grasp the firm earth, at the patient
> strength of their necks, bowed under the heavy collar, at the
> mighty muscles of their struggling haunches! I should like well to
> hear them neigh over their hardly-earned feed of corn, and see
> them, with their moist necks freed from the harness, dipping their
> eager nostrils into the muddy pond.

This team was not caught on a two-day excursion in Lincolnshire; they are horses Marian Evans knew well in her childhood, and they shed the gleam of reality on the shadowy mill behind them. The background of the scenes drawn from her own memories has a density of realisation not achieved in the third volume. Think of the Round Pool, where Maggie fishes with Tom, framed in with willows and tall reeds with purple plumy tops, and then compare the vaguer, more general views of 'the silent, sunny fields and pastures' where she drifts along the river with Stephen Guest. The Round Pool was near Griff House, and the details flashed spontaneously from her memory; the banks of the Trent had to be recalled with conscious effort, perhaps even with the help of map and notebook.

The Mill on the Floss is George Eliot's *David Copperfield*, shot through in the early parts with autobiography. In 1859 her brother Isaac Evans was heard to say that *Adam Bede* had 'things in it about my father'. One would give a good deal to know what he thought of *The*

Mill, which is full of things about *him*. The dead rabbits, the new fishlines, the jagged cropping of Maggie's unruly hair are too real to have been invented, and Tom's harshness toward his misjudged sister must have spoken eloquently against the barrier Isaac's stern rectitude had raised between them. He had all of Tom's proprietary feeling about his sister. More than once in the 1840s, when Marian was living at Coventry with her father, he had called to 'school' her about her conduct and her unconventional friends. According to Mrs Bray he

> thinks that his sister has no chance of getting the one thing need-
> ful – i.e. a husband and a settlement, unless she mixes more in
> society, and complains that since she has known us she has hardly
> been anywhere else; that Mr. Bray, being only a leader of mobs,
> can only introduce her to Chartists and Radicals, and that such
> only will ever fall in love with her if she does not belong to the
> Church. So his plan is to induce his father to remove to Meriden
> where being away from us and under the guardianship of her
> sister she may be brought back to her senses.

Tom Tulliver talks much like Isaac:

> I wished my sister to be a lady, and I would always have taken
> care of you, as my father desired, until you were well married. But
> your ideas and mine never accord, and you will not give way. Yet
> you might have sense enough to see that a brother, who goes out
> into the world and mixes with men, necessarily knows better
> what is right and respectable for his sister than she can know
> herself.

Isaac acted on Tom's high but rigid principles in rejecting Marian after her union with Lewes.

Maggie's love for Philip Wakem also came from a germ in George Eliot's own experience. Her first biographer, knowing only that he was a painter and deformed, suggested as the original François D'Albert-Durade, in whose house at Geneva she had boarded in the winter of 1849. The parallel is not close. D'Albert-Durade was not merely a hunchback; he was a dwarf, 'not more than four feet high', whom it is impossible to cast effectively in the love scenes with Maggie in the Red Deeps. But another candidate has lately come to light, another painter, whom Marian Evans met in 1845 at her half-sister's house in Baginton. To Mrs Bray's letter to her sister Sara Hennell we owe the account of this affair:

> She says she was talking to you about a young artist she was going to meet at Baginton. Well, they did meet and passed two days in each other's company, and she thought him the most interesting young man she had seen and superior to all the rest of mankind; the third morning he made proposals through her brother-in-law Mr. Houghton – saying 'she was the most fascinating creature he had ever beheld, that if it were not too presumptuous to hope etc., in short, he seemed desperately smitten and begged permission to write to her. She granted this, and came to us so brimful of happiness; – though she said she had not fallen in love with him yet, but admired his character so much that she was sure she should: the only objection seemed to be that his profession – a picture-restorer – is not lucrative or over-honourable. We liked his letters to her very much – simple, earnest, unstudied. She refused anything like an engagement on so short an acquaintance, but would have much pleasure to see him as a friend etc. So he came to see her last Wednesday evening, and owing to his great agitation, from youth – or something or other, did not seem to her half so interesting as before, and the next day she made up her mind that she could never love or respect him enough to marry him and that it would involve too great a sacrifice of her mind and pursuits. So she wrote him to break it off – and there it stands now.

Since there is no suggestion of deformity in the young picture-restorer, it is possible that two widely separated sources have combined here. But I believe we are more likely to find the germ of Maggie's love for Philip in the emotional experience of this affair than in her relations with a Swiss dwarf old enough to be her father, whose wife she always affectionately called Maman.

The Dodson sisters – Jane Glegg, Sophy Pullet and Susan Deane – were immediately recognised about Nuneaton as Mary, Elizabeth and Anne Pearson, George Eliot's aunts Mrs John Evarard, Mrs Richard Johnson and Mrs George Garner. There is a portrait of Mrs Evarard in a lace cap and her best 'front' of glossy curls over a handsome face that one sees instantly to be Mrs Glegg's. Like Maggie, Marian Evans was both 'niece and legatee', and the property bequeathed her by a codicil to Mrs Evarard's will in 1844 was the last item proved in George Eliot's own will. Beneath the touches of caricature her gratitude can be read in Aunt Glegg's rebuke of Tom for admitting the worst of his sister before he was compelled. Clanship was as strong a motive with her as equity in money matters. 'If you were not to stand by your "kin" as long as there was a shred of honour attributable to them, pray what were you to stand by?' Of Aunt Pullet there are fewer traces in George Eliot's biography. Both Mr and Mrs Johnson died in 1833, and the few references to them concern prolonged illnesses, which perhaps explain the medicine bottles Mr Pullet preserved so carefully:

> 'He won't have one sold. He says it's nothing but right folks should see 'em when I'm gone. They fill two o' the long store-room shelves a'ready – but,' she added, beginning to cry a little, 'it's well if they ever fill three. I may go before I've made up the dozen o' these last sizes.'

The Garners, originals of the Deanes, were more cheerful folk living comfortably at Sole End, the Garum Firs of the novel, and the brief allusions to them in Robert Evans's journal mention family dinners rather than funerals. Their daughter Bessie seems a more likely prototype of Lucy Deane than George Eliot's sister Chrissey, who is traditionally assigned the part.

Chrissey appears in *The Mill on the Floss*, I believe, in the very different guise of Mr Tulliver's sister Gritty Moss. Christiana Evans, to give her her proper name, was married in 1837 to Edward Clarke, fifth son of Robert Clarke, Esq., of Brooksby Hall, Leicestershire, whose earnings as a country surgeon were never adequate to maintain the family. In January 1842 his father-in-law bought from him for £250 the little house at Attleborough that her uncle John Evarard had bequeathed to Chrissey, his favourite niece, and a few months later lent him £800 more, which, if not repaid, was to be taken out of her share of Mr Evans's estate. In spite of these measures, by October 1845, shortly after the sixth of his nine children was born, Mr Clarke was bankrupt. When he died suddenly in December 1852, he left Chrissey with scarcely any resources. Isaac was kind to her, George Eliot said, 'though not in a very large way'. He allowed her to live in the house, once her own, which he had inherited, but did little to provide for her children. George Eliot shuddered at talk of an orphanage and once considered going with them all to Australia – 'to settle them and then come back'. Overworked and undernourished, Chrissey came down with tuberculosis, and in 1859, two months after *Adam Bede* appeared, she died. Isaac Evans could hardly have read the chapter describing Mr Tulliver's visit to his sister Gritty Moss without recalling his own less generous treatment of his late sister Chrissey Clarke.

Edward Clarke appears plainly in *Middlemarch* as Tertius Lydgate, who was not unwilling to have people know that he was better born than the other country doctors and who also had debts of £1000 when bankruptcy threatened him. Seven other candidates have been mentioned as originals. Sir Clifford Allbutt differs too widely from Lydgate in birth, education and medical career, even during his early days at the Leeds Infirmary, to be considered. I find a likelier prototype in Bray's friend Charles Benjamin Nankivell, who studied medicine abroad (MD, Pisa, 1828) and came to Coventry in 1831 as the first physician at the new Provident Dispensary. But there are many sides to Lydgate, and possibly Nankivell, Allbutt and Clarke all contributed toward George Eliot's conception of him. By no stretch of the imagination, however, can I accept Oscar Browning's assumption that *he* was 'the man from whom in some measure she had drawn the character of Lydgate'.

The other character in *Middlemarch* for whom several originals have been proposed is Casaubon. In most cases the resemblance is reduced to the fact that they married much younger wives. On no better ground than this Miss Cobbe suggested the shy, kindly Robert William Mackay, a scholar of real distinction. Sir Sidney Lee had 'no doubt' that Casaubon was drawn from Mark Pattison. But how is one to compare the ignorant pedantry of the Key to All Mythologies with the profound and admirable scholarship of the Rector of Lincoln College? The publication of his great *Life of Isaac Casaubon* in 1875, four years after *Middlemarch*, prompted the identification as much as the fact that Mrs Pattison, like Dorothea, was nearly thirty years younger. John Morley rightly characterises the suggestion as 'an impertinent blunder'.

I find a closer parallel to Casaubon in Dr R. H. Brabant, with whom George Eliot had an unfortunate experience in her youth. Dr Brabant, the father of her friend Mrs Charles Hennell, was a pompous and rather foolish gentleman who was engaged for years on a never-finished book that was to dispose forever of the supernatural elements in religion. In 1843, when Marian Evans was invited to visit him in Wiltshire after his daughter's wedding, we are told by a rather malicious gossip that 'she knelt at his feet and offered to devote her life to his service'. But the story ended there. Mrs Brabant, a rather formidable old lady, though blind, was well enough aware of her husband's silliness about the ardent young lady reading German and Greek with him, and after a shorter visit than was at first contemplated, arrangements were made for her return to Coventry. When pressed to say from whom she had drawn Casaubon, George Eliot pointed to her own heart. There in the pain and humiliation of this episode lay the venom that gave Casaubon his horrible vividness.

Though no original has been indicated for Mr Brooke, it is tempting to think that he may owe something to the scatter-brained Mr Charles Bracebridge, who had also traveled in Greece and gone into a great many things, at one time, you know. It is a mistake to consider his niece Dorothea an autobiographical projection of George Eliot, who resembled her in little more than the common Victorian urge to be useful, and had neither her birth, fortune nor beauty, and certainly not the lack of humour that caused most of Dorothea's trouble. If, like Alfred Hitchcock, she must appear somewhere in each of her novels, we should look for her rather in Mary Garth, a land agent's daughter, whose earnest desire to do good was combined with prudence, sound common sense, an omnivorous appetite for reading, and the lively sense of humour that is too often forgotten by critics of George Eliot.

Most of the convincing parallels to real persons are found in the early novels. Apart from the historical figures in *Romola* only the heroine herself has been given an original: Mme Belloc saw in her 'an immortal portrait' of the face and bearing of their friend Barbara Leigh Smith, Mme Bodichon. In *Felix Holt* the dissenter Rufus Lyon was thought by some to resemble Mr Francis Franklin, the Baptist minister in Coventry, and the Meyrick sisters reminded them of the Hennells. John Churton Collins's statement that George Eliot 'made no secret' of having drawn the portrait of Felix from Gerald Massey, though unsupported by evidence, was repeated by Sir Sidney Lee in his article on Massey in the *Dictionary of National Biography*. I see a closer resemblance between Felix and John Chapman, who was also the son of a druggist, a student of medicine, and a watchmaker.

Of the later novels *Daniel Deronda* has attracted most hunters of originals with its Jewish characters. There are several claimants for the title role. Leslie Stephen, who gave George Eliot advice about Daniel's life at Cambridge, fancied that she drew some touches from handsome young Edmund Gurney, whom she met there. According to Beatrice Webb, Edward Bond (1844–1920) was said to be the original. And Theodor Herzl's diary for 1895 recounts a conversation in which Col. Albert Goldsmid told him, 'I am Daniel Deronda.' Born in India and brought up a Christian, Goldsmid went over to Judaism while a lieutenant in the army – and compelled his reluctant wife to follow him. There is nothing to show that George Eliot knew of this. She was acquainted with Phoebe Sarah Marks, later Mrs Ayrton, the physicist, who was often called the original of Mirah, though she saw no resemblance herself. The original of Mordecai is usually said to be the watchmaker Cohn, described by Lewes as the expounder of Spinoza to the club of students in Red Lion Square in 1836, though both Lewes and George Eliot repeatedly declared the identification entirely wrong. Cohn, in direct contrast to Mordecai, was a 'keen dialectition and a highly impressive man, but without any specifically Jewish enthusiasm'. For that element of the character a closer comparison might be drawn with George Eliot's friend Emanuel Deutsch of the British Museum, who died in 1873. Klesmer the musician, with his tall thin figure, his great mane of hair floating backward, his well-modelled features, powerful clean-shaven mouth and chin, probably owes something in appearance to Liszt, whom George Eliot had met in Weimar in 1854, when he was living there with his mistress the Princess Caroline Sayn-Wittgenstein; but aside from genius and talent, their characters are not similar.

Gwendolen Harleth is the only one in *Daniel Deronda* whose origin can be documented from George Eliot's papers. At Homburg in 1872, where she watched the gamblers crowded about the table, 'The saddest thing to be witnessed', she wrote, 'is the play of Miss Leigh, Byron's grand-niece, who is only 26 years old, and is completely in the grasp of this mean, money-raking demon. It made me cry to see her young fresh face among the hags and brutally stupid men around her.' Here is the germ of the opening chapter at Leubronn. It illustrates the change in George Eliot's method since the early novels. 'Was she beautiful or not beautiful?' it begins. The question is never answered in the direct way in which Hetty Sorrel's spring-tide charms were described. Gwendolen remains to the end somewhat elusive; we get less external detail and more impression of her mind – her mood, in the Old English sense. It is something like the change that came about in painting between the 1850s, when Landseer was at the peak of his vogue, and the 1870s, when Whistler was painting his Nocturnes.

Except in the *Scenes of Clerical Life*, which are in a sense *romans à clef*, few of George Eliot's characters are modelled closely on real people. They are, as she told Blackwood, 'a combination of subtle shadowy suggestions with certain actual objects and events'. A list jotted down on the back of a calendar for 1876 shows her turning over in her mind people she had known twenty or thirty years before. There is Dr B., surgeon's assistant at K[enilworth?]. There is a 'widow supporting herself by keeping a school [like Mrs Wallington]: imperfectly instructed: dominated over by her head teacher [Miss Lewis?]'. There are names of acquaintances at Geneva: Mrs Lock, the Baronne de Ludwigsdorf and her Cousin Rosa, M. Maunoir [the oculist] and Mme Courier. There are a good many others. Such 'widely sundered portions of experience', if she had lived, might have become the germs of another *Middlemarch*.

Note

This essay first appeared in *From Jane Austen to Joseph Conrad*, ed. Robert C. Rathburn and Martin Steinmann Jr (Minneapolis: University of Minnesota Press, [1958]) pp. 177–93.

2

Poor Mr Casaubon

Every teacher of *Middlemarch* has encountered the disgust that undergraduates feel at the marriage of nineteen-year-old Dorothea Brooke to 'loathsome old Edward Casaubon'. Though he was only 48, they never hesitate – despite a generation of sex-education – to describe him as 'impotent'. Victorian novels supply many other examples of such marriages. Dr Strong in *David Copperfield* was 62 when he married his nineteen-year-old Annie. Charlotte Brontë created Mr Rochester twice the age of Jane Eyre, and in *Villette* married Augusta Fanshawe to a man 'much older than papa'. Even in real life these disparate matches were not at all uncommon. Sir James Hope was 50 when in 1858 he married Victoria, the nineteen-year-old daughter of the Duke of Norfolk. Sir Charles Murray at the age of 56 married a daughter of George Eliot's friend Lord Castletown, who was three years younger than his son-in-law. In 1863 the second Earl of Wilton at the age of 64 took as his second wife a girl who was younger than her step-children. According to Greville's Diary the third Viscount Melbourne had the good fortune 'at sixty years old, and with a broken and enfeebled constitution, to marry a charming girl of twenty'. Most of these matches were made to provide heirs, and (as the records show) often with success. Faced with a class of undergraduates particularly vociferous on the subject of Casaubon's impotence, I once pointed out the window to a statue of President Woolsey of Yale, the youngest of whose dozen children was born when he was 71 years old; and I might have cited the contemporary example of Charlie Chaplin, who at the age of 54 married Oona O'Neill and had eight children by her. Viewed in the light of these examples there was nothing unusual in the Casaubon marriage.

George Eliot had always been fascinated by the theme. In her Journal, 2 December 1870, noting the beginning of 'Miss Brooke', she wrote that the subject 'has been recorded among my possible themes ever since I began to write fiction'. In a notebook kept when she was a pupil at Miss Franklin's school in Coventry, the earliest work we have in her hand, she copied a poem by Thomas Haynes Bayly entitled 'The Unwilling Bride':

> The joybells are ringing – oh! come to the church
> We shall see the bride pass if we stand in the porch;
> The bridegroom is wealthy; how brightly arrayed
> Are the menials who wait on the gay cavalcade. . . .
>
> Yon feeble old knight the bride's father must be
> And now walking proudly, her mother we see;
> A pale girl in tears, slowly moves by her side;
> But where is the bridegroom, and where is the bride?

The answer comes in the next stanza:

> A Bridal like *this* is a sorrowful sight
> For *that* pale girl is bride to the feeble old knight.

In 'Silly Novels by Lady Novelists', which she wrote for the *Westminster Review* in 1856, George Eliot comments on some of these ill-assorted matches. The brides are sometimes learned young ladies, who

> read the Scriptures in their original *tongues*. Greek and Hebrew are mere play to a heroine; Sanscrit is no more than *a b c* to her; and she can talk with a perfect correctness in any language except English. She is a talking polyglott, a Creuzer in crinoline.

More often than not she will marry the wrong person to begin with. But, though she suffers terribly from the mistake, in the end 'the tedious husband dies in his bed, requesting his wife, as a particular favour to him, to marry the man she loves best, and having already dispatched a note to the lover informing him of the comfortable arrangement'.

George Eliot is a little kinder to her own heroines. Romola, for example, longed to become as learned as Cassandra Fedele, the famous young philosopher of the fifteenth century, 'and then perhaps some great scholar will want to marry me' (ch. 5). The recurrence of this trait in Dorothea was noted by Harriet Martineau; in commenting on the 'prodigious' advance George Eliot had made between *Romola* and *Middlemarch* she wrote: 'Nobody seems to realise the likeness – almost identity – of the leading conceptions in the two books: e.g. old Bardo and Casaubon – and Romola and Dorothea'.[1] In a passage near the end of the Finale George Eliot wrote:

> Among the many remarks passed on her mistakes, it was never said in the neighbourhood of Middlemarch that such mistakes could not have happened if the society into which she was born had not smiled on propositions of marriage from a sickly man to a girl less than half his own age.[2]

In revising for the one-volume edition this passage was deleted, possibly to eliminate the repetition of 'a fine girl who married a sickly clergyman, old enough to be her father' in the previous paragraph. Both passages emphasise Mr Casaubon's sickliness. Chapter 5, containing his letter of proposal, takes for its epigraph a sentence from the famous digression on the misery of scholars in Burton's *Anatomy of Melancholy*:

> Hard students are commonly troubled with gowts, catarrhs, rheums, cachexia, bradypepsia, bad eyes, stone, and collick, crudities, oppilations, vertigo, winds, consumptions, and all such diseases as come by over-much sitting: they are most part lean, dry, ill-coloured . . . and all through immoderate pains and extraordinary studies.

Besides his sallow complexion and leanness the only defect on this repulsive list found in Mr Casaubon is bad eyes. He shows no obvious signs of sickliness. And the difficulty with his eyes is a definite attraction for Dorothea, since it provides her with opportunities to read to him. The deep eye-sockets in which they are set are perhaps the only resemblance he bears to the familiar portrait of John Locke. Dorothea herself suffers from short-sightedness and had never noticed the two white moles with hairs in them which so troubled Celia. Though Mr Casaubon was 'fastidious in voices' of those serving him as readers, his own voice was an unpleasant singsong, in which he delivered his balanced periods with occasional nodding movements of the head. He disliked music. 'I never could look on it in the light of a recreation to have my ears teased with measured noises', he said (p. 48). Yet he never seemed to hear the noise of his spoon scraping the bottom of the dish, which so annoyed Celia when he was eating his soup.

The harshest opinion of his physical deficiencies comes, naturally, from Sir James Chettam, the suitor Mr Casaubon has displaced: 'He is no better than a mummy' (p. 43), 'a dried bookworm' (p. 17), with 'no good red blood in his body' (p. 52). At each stage of Sir James's indignation, Mrs Cadwallader, whose plans for Dorothea have been shattered by the preposterous engagement, caps his gibes: 'A great soul. – A great bladder for dried peas to rattle in!' she exclaims (p. 43); under a microscope his blood would be all semicolons and parentheses; he dreams footnotes, and they run away with all his brains (p. 52). She wishes Dorothea joy of her hairshirt, and comforts Sir James, by declaring that he is well rid of 'a girl who would have been requiring you to see the stars by daylight. Between ourselves, little Celia is worth two of her, and likely after all to be the better match. For this marriage to Casaubon is as good as going to a nunnery' (p. 43).

Mrs Cadwallader's shrewd eye and sharp tongue distinguish the sexual inadequacy in Casaubon, at which Sir James can hardly hint. Yet it is not due entirely to his age. Lydgate, conscious of his own large and energetic frame, watches Casaubon walking slowly with bent shoulders and thin legs and thinks: 'Poor fellow, some men with his years are like lions; one can tell nothing of their age except that they are full grown' (p. 309). Sir James believed that at any age Casaubon would never have been 'much more than the shadow of a man. Look at his legs!' (p. 50). Weakness of body does not always correspond with weakness of sexual passion. In Casaubon's case, however, we infer that he never felt a strong sexual interest in women. He assures Dorothea in his letter that he can offer her 'an affection hitherto unwasted' and (in a most characteristic metaphor) a life with no 'backward pages whereon, if you choose to turn them, you will find records such as might justly cause you either bitterness or shame' (p. 32). Despite his conventional allusions to 'bloom of youth' and 'feminine graces', he is clearly attracted most to Dorothea's mental qualities, which are 'adapted to supply aid in graver labours and to cast a charm over vacant hours'. What he wants is a secretary for the graver labours in that row of notebooks for his Key to All Mythologies. Courtship proves a sad hindrance to its progress.

But he had deliberately incurred the hindrance, having made up his mind that it was now time for him to adorn his life with the graces of female companionship, to irradiate the gloom which fatigue was apt to hang over the intervals of studious labour with the play of female fancy, and to secure in this, his culminating age, the solace of female tendance for his declining years. Hence he determined to abandon himself to the stream of feeling, and perhaps was surprised to find what an exceedingly shallow rill it was. As in droughty regions baptism by immersion could only be performed symbolically, so Mr Casaubon found that sprinkling was the utmost approach to a plunge which his stream would afford him; and he concluded that the poets had much exaggerated the force of masculine passion.   (p. 46)

As the wedding day came nearer, he did not find his spirits rising, nor did the contemplation of that flower-bordered matrimonial garden scene 'prove persistently more enchanting to him than the accustomed vaults where he walked taper in hand' (p. 63). In discussing plans for their wedding journey to Rome he more than once urged Dorothea to take Celia with her. 'I should feel more at liberty', he said, 'if you had a companion' (p. 64).

The conventions of family reading and the circulating library, which determined what Victorian novelists could write about the marriage bed, necessarily relegated details of the Casaubons' honeymoon to the reader's imagination. For Dorothea with her 'enthusiastic acceptance of untried duty' it was an experience of 'dreamlike strangeness':

the dimmer but yet eager Titanic life gazing and struggling on walls and ceilings; the long vistas of white forms whose marble eyes seemed to hold the monotonous light of an alien world: all this vast wreck of ambitious ideals, sensuous and spiritual, mixed confusedly with the signs of breathing forgetfulness and degradation, at first jarred her as with an electric shock, and then urged themselves on her with that ache belonging to a glut of confused ideas which check the flow of emotion. Forms both pale and glowing took possession of her young sense, and fixed themselves in her memory even when she was not thinking of them, preparing strange associations which remained through her after-years. . . . In certain states of dull forlornness Dorothea all her life continued to see the vastness of St Peter's, the huge bronze canopy, the excited intention in the attitudes and garments of the prophets and evangelists in the mosaics above, and the red drapery which was being hung for Christmas spreading itself everywhere like a disease of the retina.   (p. 144)

This red drapery 'spreading itself everywhere' is particularly interesting as a clue to Dorothea's experience.[3] Through the turbulent imagery in which Dorothea clothes her thoughts a sympathetic reader perceives that her initiation into matrimony had been violent and painful. To have done it differently called for more tact and tenderness than the novice Casaubon possessed. 'No one would ever know what she thought of a wedding journey to Rome' (p. 204).

'Dorothea – but why always Dorothea?' George Eliot asks at the beginning of Chapter 29. What were poor Mr Casaubon's feelings on this disastrous honeymoon?

> In spite of his blinking eyes and white moles objectionable to Celia, and the want of muscular curve which was morally painful to Sir James, Mr Casaubon had an intense consciousness within him, and was spiritually a-hungered like the rest of us. He had done nothing exceptional in marrying – nothing but what society sanctions, and considers an occasion for wreaths and bouquets. It had occurred to him that he must not any longer defer his intention of matrimony, and he had reflected that in taking a wife, a man of good position should expect and carefully choose a blooming young lady – the younger the better, because more educable and submissive – of a rank equal to his own, of religious principles, virtuous disposition, and good understanding. On such a young lady he would make handsome settlements, and he would neglect no arrangement for her happiness: in return, he should receive family pleasures and leave behind him that copy of himself which seemed so urgently required of a man – to the sonneteers of the sixteenth century. (p. 205)

Whether Dorothea would find his 'family pleasures' equally agreeable it was not in him to inquire. He is one of George Eliot's prime egoists.

As with Dorothea we must guess at Casaubon's experience from the imagery. Sigmund Freud, to whom *Middlemarch* appealed very much because 'it illuminated important aspects of his relation with [his wife] Martha',[4] taught the world that the mind masks painful sexual experiences in symbolic terms. How else can we read this sentence?

> Mr Casaubon had never had a strong bodily frame, and his soul was sensitive without being enthusiastic: it was too languid to

thrill out of self-consciousness into passionate delight; it went on
fluttering in the swampy ground where it was hatched, thinking
of its wings and never flying.   (p. 206)

He lived at Lowick – and names are never negligible in George
Eliot's novels – spending most of his time in the gloomy library and
taking his exercise only in the walk to the shady summerhouse, lined
with dusky yews. Though he had a trout stream on the Lowick
estate, he never fished in it. Strong light always bothered him; almost
the first remark he made to Dorothea is, 'We must keep the germi-
nating grain away from the light' (p. 16). His life was full of pigeon-
holes, locked drawers, small closets, winding stairs, labyrinths, mines,
catacombs, museums. In the dark regions of mythology he was
'carrying his little taper among the tombs of the past', at work on 'a
ghastly labour producing what would never see the light' (p. 348).
Here George Eliot tosses in without comment the remark that Celia
'had lately had a baby'.

On the last night of his life Casaubon allows Dorothea to read to
him from the table of contents of his Key to All Mythologies and at
each point where he said 'mark' to make a cross with her pencil.
'After she had read and marked for two hours, he said, "We will take
the volume upstairs – and the pencil, if you please – and in case of
reading in the night, we can pursue this task. It is not wearisome to
you, I trust, Dorothea?"' (p. 349). The reading in the night did come.
There is something grimly comic in the spectacle of the bridegroom
of fifteen months awakening his bride to take down notes on the
fertility rites of Crete for his Key to All Mythologies, which Dorothea
now saw as

> shattered mummies, and fragments of a tradition which was itself
> a mosaic wrought from crushed ruins – sorting them as food for
> a theory which was already withered in the birth like an elfin
> child. Doubtless a vigorous error vigorously pursued has kept the
> embryos of truth a-breathing: the quest of gold being at the same
> time a questioning of substances, the body of chemistry is prepared
> for its soul, and Lavoisier is born. But Mr Casaubon's theory of
> the elements which made the seed of all tradition was not likely to
> bruise itself unawares against discoveries . . . .   (p. 351)

Before their marriage – in one of his lighter moments – he had
pronounced the aphorism 'See Rome and die' an extreme hyperbole,

proposing to emend it to 'See Rome as a bride, and live thenceforth as a happy wife' (p. 148). Like most of Mr Casaubon's emendations this proved less true than the original.

His scholarly reputation was limited. At the first mention of his name we are told that he was 'noted in the *county* as a man of profound learning' (p. 8). Oxford, however, questioned the value of his studies. The

> pamphlets – or 'Parerga' as he called them – by which he tested his public and deposited small monumental records of his march, were far from having been seen in all their significance. He suspected the Archdeacon of not having read them; he was in painful doubt as to what was really thought of them by the leading minds of Brasenose, and bitterly convinced that his old acquaintance Carp had been the writer of that depreciatory recension which was kept locked in a small drawer of Mr Casaubon's desk, and also in a dark closet of his verbal memory.   (p. 206)

In one of his pamphlets he had published

> a dedication to Carp in which he had numbered that member of the animal kingdom among the *viros nullo aevo perituros*, a mistake which would infallibly lay the dedicator open to ridicule in the next age, and might even be chuckled over by Pike and Tench in the present.   (p. 207)

His chief purpose in the pamphlet he was writing at the time of his death was vengeance against the sneers of Carp & Company, 'for even when Mr Casaubon was carrying his taper among the tombs of the past, those modern figures came athwart the dim light, and interrupted his diligent exploration' (p. 308).

During his brief employment as Casaubon's secretary Will Ladislaw, whose schooling had gone no farther than Rugby, saw the futility of spending a lifetime correcting the mistakes of Jacob Bryant and Warburton a century before. His glib remark to Dorothea that 'If Mr Casaubon read German he would save himself a great deal of trouble' was superficial. The two most important studies by Germans were already available to him: Creuzer's *Mythologie* (1810–12) had appeared in a French translation and Lobeck's *Aglaophamus* (1829) was written in Latin. George Eliot comments, 'Young Mr Ladislaw was not at all deep himself in German writers; but very little achievement is required in order to pity another man's shortcomings' (p. 154). Yet the shortcomings were there, and Mr Casaubon was morbidly afraid of their being exposed. He had sent Will away, not because of any lack of thoroughness, but from conviction of his scorn for the futility of the Key to All Mythology. Now he 'foresaw with sudden terror' that Dorothea's blind worship of his learning might be replaced with the same sort of critical judgement. Jealousy for his reputation mingled with jealous foreboding that, if he should die, Will and Dorothea might marry and be the happier that he was gone. He prepared the codicil to his will withdrawing his estate from Dorothea if she should marry Will Ladislaw.

Casaubon's antecedents are rather shadowy in *Middlemarch*. His mother was the younger of the two ladies of Lowick Manor. When his Aunt Julia, the elder and prettier of them, was disinherited for marrying the Polish refugee Count Ladislaw, the estate passed to the younger sister, who married a Mr Casaubon and had two sons. The elder inherited the estate; Edward, the younger, became a clergyman and on the death of his brother in 1819 came to live at Lowick. No one in the novel speaks of the earlier members of the family. Casaubon told Dorothea that he had 'none but comparatively distant connections' (p. 274); we hear from Mr Cadwallader that he 'is very good to his poor relations: pensions several of the women' (p. 51), but we learn nothing further about them. Will Ladislaw's father was one of these poor relations, a first cousin, towards whom he recognised a duty. Having learned of his desperate plight, ill and starving at Boulogne, Casaubon sent Ladislaw money and, after his death, continued an allowance to his widow and son Will, whose education he paid for. As the only male in the family, of course, Ladislaw should have been the heir of the Lowick estate.

Though George Eliot was always obsessively anxious about the legal details of her novels, there is nothing in her notebooks or papers concerning the codicil to Casaubon's will. My friend Romilly Ouvry, an English solicitor and great-grandson of George Henry Lewes, who has studied the question, suggests that on her marriage Dorothea brought a dowry of about £20,000, which was comprised in the settlement. Apparently Casaubon contributed nothing to it, but, with the knowledge of Mr Brooke, made a will leaving the Lowick property to Dorothea, whether for life or absolutely is not stated. Though George Eliot was 'quite right in her law', Mr Ouvry tells me, she was 'wrong in her practice', for it was most unlikely that Mr Brooke's solicitor would have agreed to such an arrangement; he would have insisted on at least an equivalent to the £20,000 being brought into the settlement by Casaubon, and would never have been content with a will which could be torn up next day. Provision might have been made in the settlement for Dorothea's life interest in the Lowick property to cease on remarriage, but it would have been unusual to provide for such termination by will or codicil. Had Dorothea deigned to challenge it, the Court of Chancery might have set it aside, particularly since Will Ladislaw was the nearest blood relation. Until 1936, however, such a codicil could not have been challenged by a widow.

I suspect that George Eliot's treatment of the codicil was determined by the case of Branwell Brontë, who, according to Mrs Gaskell's account, was dismissed as tutor in the family of the Reverend Edmund Robinson because of the 'criminal advances' made to him in a love affair with Mrs Robinson. In her *Life of Charlotte Brontë* Mrs Gaskell declared that the Reverend Mr Robinson altered his will to bequeath his property to his wife 'solely on the condition that she should never see Branwell Brontë again'.[5] Threatened with a libel suit, Mrs Gaskell made a public apology in a letter to *The Times*,[6] retracting every statement imputing any breach of conjugal duties or 'guilty intercourse with the late Branwell Brontë', and removed the offensive passages from the revised edition. George Eliot read Mrs Gaskell's book as soon as it appeared and was deeply moved by it, but regretted her setting down Branwell's alcoholism and opium addiction as due entirely to remorse over the alleged affair with Mrs Robinson, which 'would not make such a life as Branwell's was in the last three or four years unless the germs of vice had sprouted and shot up long before'.[7] Mr Robinson's will contains no reference to Branwell, who was probably dismissed for some indiscretion with his pupil, thirteen-year-old Edmund Robinson, Jr.

The ironic echoes in the name *Casaubon* made it a happy choice for George Eliot. She had long known about the great Renaissance scholar Isaac Casaubon, who died in England in 1614 and was buried in Westminster Abbey. She had used his edition of Theophrastus, and was familiar with the part he had played in the Catholic–Protestant disputes that brought him from France as a refugee after the assassination of Henry IV. In the notebook containing extracts from her reading in the 1860s and 1870s – Sophocles, Euripides, Theocritus, Drayton, Sidney, Shakespeare, Marlowe, Donne, Browne, Milton, and most of the nineteenth-century poets – between two long passages from Spenser's *Shepherd's Calendar* she wrote: 'Spenser, born 1552, twelve years older than Shakspeare, died 1598–9. Curious to turn from Shakspeare to Isaac Casaubon, his contemporary.'[8] To use the name for the pseudo-scholar of *Middlemarch* was a touch that delighted her.

In 1875, four years after the novel was written, Mark Pattison, the Rector of Lincoln College, Oxford, published his *Isaac Casaubon 1559–1614*. He and his wife had been acquainted with George Eliot since 1869, and until her death they remained warm friends. Mrs Pattison, the daughter of an Oxford bank manager, had raised her position socially by the match, marrying him in 1861 (according to A. H. Sayce) 'from ambition rather than from love'.[9] He was 48 and she was 21. It was not a happy marriage. Fifteen years later in a letter to Pattison she spoke of her 'physical aversion' to their sexual relation and her 'fear of its renewal'.[10] But her intimacy with Sir Charles Dilke had already begun. There could hardly be greater contrast in moral character between the sophisticated worldly-minded Mrs Pattison and the serious, naïve Dorothea Casaubon – unless it was that between the foolish pedant of Lowick and the energetic and learned Rector of Lincoln. In an obituary article on him Henry Nettleship wrote:

> There have been those who judging from a very imperfect knowledge of a few facts, and from the name of the book by which he is best known, have fancied that George Eliot had the Rector's studious habits in mind to a certain extent when she drew the character of Mr. Casaubon in *Middlemarch*. There was, however, nothing in common between the serious scholar at Lincoln and the mere pedant frittering away his life in useless trivialities; nor was George Eliot, Mark Pattison's friend, at all likely to draw a caricature of one she loved and valued.[11]

In a manuscript 'Memoir of E. F. S. Dilke', later prefixed to her *The Book of the Spiritual Life* (1905), Dilke, who became her second husband, declared:

> To those who know, Emilia Strong was no more Dorothea Brooke than Pattison was Casaubon; but it is the case that the religious side of Dorothea Brooke was taken by George Eliot from the letters of Mrs. Pattison. . . . It was of Emilia Strong that George Eliot was thinking when she wrote 'Dorothea knew many passages of Pascal's *Pensées* and of Jeremy Taylor by heart'.[12]

But just what was 'the religious side of Dorothea'? A single sentence in the first chapter of *Middlemarch* alludes to her girlish notion of praying at the bedside of sick labourers and her 'strange whims of fasting like a Papist, and of sitting up at night to read old theological books'. Casaubon's fancied learning, not his clerical function, attracted her. Her asceticism was not Puseyite, like Mrs Pattison's, but sprang from Evangelical seriousness before the Oxford Tracts began. The only time Dorothea lay all night on the floor, she was impelled, not by penance, but by a paroxysm of sexual jealousy, which George Eliot had no need to study in anyone's letters. She was quoting Jeremy Taylor to her governess when Mrs Pattison was only a year old. As for Pascal, the *Pensées* were the first prize George Eliot won at school, and she had learned many of them by heart before Mrs Pattison was born.

No manuscript has ever been found to support Dilke's categorical assertion that 'Casaubon's letter to Dorothea at the beginning of the 5th chapter of Middlemarch, from what G. E. herself told me in 1875, must have been very near to the letter that Pattison actually wrote, and the reply very much the same'. Betty Askwith in her *Lady Dilke* is commendably sceptical of this story; she finds it hard to believe that any real man ever wrote that letter. Besides, she adds, the style 'is totally unlike Pattison's lucid, sinewy writing'.[13] George Eliot was always reluctant to discuss her works, even with her most intimate friends, among whom Sir Charles Dilke never figured. Indeed, in 1875 she had never met him; it was not till 1878 that Lewes first made his acquaintance at Lord Houghton's.

The most absurd hypothesis was advanced by Mr John Sparrow: that Mrs Pattison 'sanctioned and actually encouraged George Eliot to caricature her husband as Casaubon'.

> As for the Rector, George Eliot – the confidant of the suffering wife – must have meant to make him suffer in his turn, and she was shrewd enough to know that she could do so safely: Pattison was not so vain as to be blind to the odious resemblance, but he was too proud to admit by any public gesture that a resemblance existed. He had to endure seeing his own stilted proposal of marriage reproduced almost word for word and held up to ridicule, in the knowledge that his wife had repeated it *verbatim* to her friend the novelist. George Eliot could be sure both that he would suffer and that he would suffer in silence. The story, in fact, is of strong action by one high-minded woman on behalf of another.[14]

If any evidence ever existed in Mrs Pattison's or George Eliot's correspondence to support this melodramatic plot, it has vanished

under the mutilation of Sir Charles Dilke's notorious scissors; both
Mrs Pattison and Sir Charles were (according to Betty Askwith)
'uncommonly handy with the eraser and with the scissors'.[15] But to
Mr Sparrow that makes the evidence, not more dubious, but less,
suggesting only that 'Dilke took great care about the accuracy of his
text'![16] Mr Sparrow is so enthralled by his hypothesis that he dis-
covers 'parallels that George Eliot could not have been aware of,
except prophetically, when she wrote her novel'.

> Dorothea Casaubon found consolation for her husband's lack
> of sympathy in a romantic attachment formed before his death, to
> a man whom she married when she became a widow. Three years
> after *Middlemarch* was published, Sir Charles Dilke, who had
> known Mrs. Pattison slightly as a girl, resumed his friendship
> with her; he then played in her life a *rôle* exactly corresponding with
> the part played in *Middlemarch* by Will Ladislaw – a romantic
> friendship was followed, after the death of the detested husband,
> by marriage to the widow.[17]

The exactness of the parallel is somewhat blurred by the fact that
Mrs Pattison's intimacy began some years before her husband died
– an example, Mr Sparrow says, of 'life imitating art'. Even the
jealous Mr Casaubon entered into no such 'coarse misinterpretation'
of Dorothea (p. 307). The closest approach Will ever made to the
romantic in Casaubon's lifetime was going to church one Sunday to
look at her and getting nothing but a grave bow as she walked out on
her husband's arm. She was a widow more than a year before they
became engaged.

Pattison himself never betrayed the least sign that he recognised
the 'odious resemblance' – quite understandably, since there was
none, either physical or intellectual. He continued to call on George
Eliot when in London, often accompanied by that 'high-minded'
conspirator his wife. When Lewes and George Eliot were in Oxford
they usually spent an hour or two with the Pattisons. Their contemporaries were equally unaware of the alleged caricature. John
Morley, who (though not an enthusiastic admirer of George Eliot)
knew them all well, dismissed the identification as an 'impertinent
blunder'.[18] Mrs Humphry Ward, also a friend of them all, said explicitly: 'I do not believe that she ever meant to describe the Rector
. . . in the dreary and foolish pedant who overshadows *Middlemarch*.'[19]

A number of other candidates have been proposed, most of them
– like Pattison – for no stronger reason than that they had married

younger wives. Thus Frances Power Cobbe suggested the shy, kindly
Robert William Mackay, a scholar of real distinction, who bore no
other resemblance to Casaubon.[20] Eliza Lynn Linton was convinced
that he was modelled on Dr R. H. Brabant, and her evidence is
important, because, like George Eliot, she had visited Dr Brabant
during her girlhood. She describes him as

> a learned man who used up his literary energies in thought and
> desire to do rather than in actual doing, and whose fastidiousness
> made his work something like Penelope's web. Ever writing and
> rewriting, correcting and destroying, he never got farther than the
> introductory chapter of a book which he intended to be epoch-
> making, and the final destroyer of superstition and theological
> dogma.[21]

After the marriage of his daughter Rufa to Charles Hennell in 1843,
Dr Brabant invited Marian Evans, who had been a bridesmaid, to
visit him at Devizes 'to fill the place of his daughter'. The best one
can say of Dr Brabant is that he was a pompous and foolish man who
at the age of 62, thanks to an ample fortune, found leisure to impress
young ladies with his supposed learning. Naturally Marian was
gratified to have her intellectual achievements recognised, and was
eager to serve him in any capacity. According to Mrs Linton, 'she
knelt at his feet and offered to devote her life to his service'.[22] He
showed her his library, which he said she was to consider *her* room.
To her friends back in Coventry Marian wrote: 'I am in a little
heaven here, Dr. Brabant being its archangel. . . . We read, walk, and
talk together, and I am never weary of his company.' He taught her
some Greek, and after reading German aloud to him for two hours,
she was sometimes so faint as to be obliged to lie down on the sofa
till walking time.

But there was a *Mrs* Brabant, too, in this little heaven, a blind lady,
the affable archangel's wife, and her rather formidable sister, Miss
Susan Hughes, who became alarmed at the young lady's failure to
practise the required conventionalisms, made a great stir, and excited
the jealousy of the blind Mrs Brabant. Miss Evans was forced to
leave – some time before she had expected to go. Rufa Brabant
Hennell, who supplied this account years later in a conversation
with John Chapman, blamed her father for acting ungenerously and
worse towards George Eliot.[23]

Lewes used to joke occasionally about his being George Eliot's
Casaubon.[24] From the compelling realism of the character those who

did not know them sometimes imagined that she had studied Dorothea's marriage from her own. Harriet Beecher Stowe was one of these. In replying to her letter George Eliot wrote:

> But do not for a moment imagine that Dorothea's marriage experience is drawn from my own. Impossible to conceive any creature less like Mr. Casaubon than my warm, enthusiastic husband, who cares more for my doing than for his own, and is a miracle of freedom from all author's jealousy and all suspicion. I fear that the Casaubon-tints are not quite foreign to my own mental complexion. At any rate I am very sorry for him.[25]

Frederic W. H. Myers tells in his obituary article on George Eliot how

> Mr. Lewes and she were one day good-humoredly recounting the mistaken effusiveness of a too-sympathizing friend, who insisted on assuming that Mr. Casaubon was a portrait of Mr. Lewes, and on condoling with the sad experience which had taught the gifted authoress of *Middlemarch* to depict that gloomy man. And there was indeed something ludicrous in the contrast between the dreary pedant of the novel and the gay self-content of the living *savant* who stood acting his vivid anecdotes before our eyes. 'But from whom, then,' said a friend, turning to Mrs. Lewes, 'did you draw Casaubon?' With a humorous solemnity, which was quite in earnest, nevertheless, she pointed to her own heart.[26]

There in the pain and humiliation of the episode with Dr Brabant, I believe, lay the venom that was to give poor Mr Casaubon his horrible vividness.

Notes

This essay first appeared in *Nineteenth-Century Perspectives: Essays in Honor of Lionel Stevenson*, ed. Clyde de L. Ryals, John Clubbe, and Benjamin Franklin Fisher, IV (Durham, N.C.: Duke University Press, 1974) pp. 255–70.

1. To an unidentified correspondent, 29 August 1873, MS: Huntington Library.

2. *Middlemarch*, ed. Gordon S. Haight, Riverside edition (Boston, Mass., 1956) p. 612. Quotations from the novel are all from this text.
3. A perceptive analysis of this passage by A. L. French is found in 'A Note on *Middlemarch*', *Nineteenth-Century Fiction*, vol. 26 (December 1971) pp. 339–47. But Mr Little regards the 'disease of the retina' as an allusion to Casaubon's bad eyes.
4. Ernest Jones, *Life and Work of Sigmund Freud*, 3 vols (New York, 1953) vol. I, p. 174.
5. Mrs Elizabeth Gaskell, *Life of Charlotte Brontë*, 2 vols (London, 1857) vol. I, p. 226.
6. 30 May 1857, p. 5b.
7. *The George Eliot Letters*, ed. Gordon S. Haight, 7 vols (New Haven, Conn., and London, 1954–5) vol. II, pp. 319–20.
8. MS: Folger Library, M.a. 13, p. 159.
9. A. H. Sayce, *Reminiscences* (London, 1923) p. 86.
10. MS: Bodleian, 21 January 1876. Published in Betty Askwith, *Lady Dilke* (London, 1969) p. 60.
11 *Academy*, 9 August 1884, p. 94.
12. *The Book of the Spiritual Life* (London, 1905) pp. 16–17.
13. Askwith, *Lady Dilke*, p. 16.
14. John Sparrow, *Mark Pattison and the Idea of a University* (Cambridge, 1967) pp. 16–17.
15. Askwith, *Lady Dilke*, p. 10.
16. *Notes and Queries*, vol. 213 (December 1968) p. 469.
17. Sparrow, *Mark Pattison and the Idea of a University*, p. 17.
18. John Morley, 'On Pattison's Memoirs', in Morley's *Critical Miscellanies, Works*, vol. VI (London, 1921) p. 240.
19. Mrs Humphry Ward, *A Writer's Recollections* (New York, 1918) p. 110.
20. Frances Power Cobbe, *Life of Frances Power Cobbe*, 2 vols (London, 1894) vol. II, pp. 430–1.
21. Eliza Lynn Linton, *My Literary Life* (London, 1899) p. 43.
22. Ibid., p. 44.
23. Gordon S. Haight, *George Eliot and John Chapman*, 2nd edn (New Haven, Conn., 1969) p. 24.
24. See, for example, *The George Eliot Letters*, vol. V, pp. 291, 332.
25. Ibid., vol. V, p. 322.
26. Frederic W. H. Myers, 'George Eliot', *Century Magazine*, vol. 23 (November 1881) p. 60.

3

George Eliot's 'Eminent Failure', Will Ladislaw

In 1886 James Knowles, the editor of the *Nineteenth Century*, gave a dinner party which included the Prime Minister Mr Gladstone, the French Ambassador Monsieur Waddington, and the American Minister Mr Edward Phelps. During the evening when conversation turned towards the English novel, Knowles declared that George Eliot's *Middlemarch* 'would live long beyond any other – including [those of] Scott – he did not care for Scott. Gladstone upheld Scott – and *Middlemarch* too', though he felt the unsatisfactory nature of all the marriages in George Eliot's novels as compared with Scott's, which he remembered reading as a boy, lying on his stomach in the grass, 'as they came out in numbers'.[1] But the two foreign diplomats agreed that in France and in America '*Middlemarch* was scarcely known, while every one read Scott'. Monsieur Waddington was probably right about France; but Mr Phelps must have been speaking only for the older generation. Yale had just graduated Wilbur Cross, who was already beginning his work on *The Development of the English Novel* (1899), in which he declares that 'George Eliot gave prose fiction a substance which it had never before had among any people' (p. 150). In my own undergraduate days she was still being read, and I am inclined to believe the notion that her books ever lay on the shelves unopened is a vulgar error.

Few novels have borne such intensive critical scrutiny. Before his untimely death W. J. Harvey gave us admirable accounts of the contemporary reviews and of the special studies which proliferated so rapidly after 1940. One of the essays in Barbara Hardy's *Middlemarch: Critical Approaches to the Novel* (1967), J. M. S. Tompkins's brilliant 'Plea for Ancient Lights', outlined the trend of criticism in the years since it came to be treated as a 'Sacred Book'.

> If the literal and even the historical meanings of the text appeared remote and irrelevant, the allegorical and the anagogical could be

tried. In something the same way, story, character and setting – those prime data of the nineteenth-century novel – can be pushed aside with slight and sometimes imperfect inspection, while the keen analytic intellects of the modern critical scene apply themselves to elucidate the formal relations, the ideal structures, the metaphors, overt and submerged, and the key-words and phrases of the work in hand. Sometimes we are carried beyond the identification of conscious artistry and invited to discern, in sequences and recurrences of allied terms, the movements of the novelist's unconscious mind. Some of these words are no more than parts of the machinery of the language, reduced metaphors and dead symbols found in everyday talk, unrealized images with no salient meaning. But 'crumble' the text sufficiently, and there they are, and we may suppose that the unconscious is expressed through this subtle and archaic means; and since what is left of the doctrine of inspiration is now related to the activity of the unconscious, we may do well to study it *in minimis*, as early commentators studied the syllables of what they took to be the Holy Spirit. (p. 172)

Miss Tompkins's worst example of this 'shredded and crumbled' text was Mark Schorer's unhappy discovery of a 'nearly systematic Christ analogy' in Will Ladislaw, which she deftly disposed of. Her lucid summary of Will's contradictory qualities gives a more sympathetic view of the young man than most critics have bestowed on him. Henry James, for instance, wrote in 1873:

The figure of Will Ladislaw is a beautiful attempt, with many finely-completed points; but on the whole it seems to us a failure. It is the only eminent failure in the book, and its defects are therefore the more striking. It lacks sharpness of outline and depth of color; we have not found ourselves believing in Ladislaw as we believe in Dorothea, in Mary Garth, in Rosamond, in Lydgate, in Mr Brooke and Mr Casaubon. He is meant, indeed, to be a light creature (with a large capacity for gravity, for he finally gets into Parliament), and a light creature certainly should not be heavily drawn. The author, who is evidently very fond of him, has found for him here and there some charming and eloquent touches; but in spite of these he remains vague and impalpable to the end.[2]

Virginia Woolf, writing in *The Times Literary Supplement* in 1919, just two days before the centenary of George Eliot's birth, regretted that

Dorothea could not have been provided with a better mate than Will Ladislaw; Oliver Elton called him 'mere pasteboard'; to Lord David Cecil he was 'a schoolgirl's dream, and a vulgar dream at that'. F. R. Leavis in his uncompromising style dismissed him completely:

> In fact, he has no independent status of his own – he can't be said to exist; he merely represents, not a dramatically real point of view, but certain of George Eliot's intentions – intentions she has failed to realize creatively. The most important of these is to impose on the reader her own vision and valuation of Dorothea.
> Will, of course, is also intended – it is not really a separate matter – to be, in contrast to Casaubon, a fitting soul-mate for Dorothea. He is not substantially (everyone agrees) 'there'.[3]

Almost everyone, perhaps. I have recorded elsewhere my dissent from Dr Leavis's concept of Dorothea as the 'product of George Eliot's own "soul-hunger" – another day-dream ideal self'.[4] Now his contemptuous dismissal of Ladislaw prompts me to look again at that much-abused young man.

If Ladislaw is to be regarded as unrealised or non-existent, it cannot be on grounds of his appearance. George Eliot describes him indirectly, dropping details here and there and avoiding the formal introductory accounts we are used to in Scott and Trollope.[5] He is tall and slim – Miss Noble hardly comes up to his elbow, Dorothea only to his shoulder – and moves with the quickness suggested by the word 'mercurial'. In a distinctive way he is handsome. At first sight Celia, who is conspicuously sensitive to people's faces, pronounces him 'quite nice-looking'. Even the aristocratic Mrs Cadwallader twice calls him 'a pretty sprig. . . . He is like the fine old Crichley portraits before the idiots came in.' He has 'grey eyes, rather near together, a delicate irregular nose with a little ripple in it', a prominent chin and jaw, and a throat and neck reminiscent of the Romantic poets. When he was first presented to Mr Casaubon's young fiancée, his expression had a rather a pouting air of discontent, though a few moments later, when he was alone, his 'sense of the ludicrous lit up his features very agreeably'. A 'merry' smile was his usual expression, a 'sunny' smile like 'a gush of inward light illuminating the transparent skin as well as the eyes, and playing about every curve and line'. He had a light complexion – a 'girl's complexion' it is called once – that made his face and throat flush suddenly under the stress of strong feeling. His light brown hair was 'not immoderately long' – at least compared with his German artist friends' at Rome – but 'abundant and curly' and seemed to shake out light when he turned his head quickly and, with his most characteristic gesture, threw his head back.

Some of these traits annoy readers, especially those hunting for reasons to justify their dislike of Ladislaw. The way young men wear their hair has been a divisive factor at least since the days of Cavalier and Roundhead. When Lewes's son was about to leave school in Switzerland, his father warned him not to have his hair cut short as schoolboys then did. 'Let it grow nice and long', he wrote, 'so that when your mother embraces you she may embrace a good-looking chap.'[6] Today both Ladislaw's curls and his habit of stretching himself at full length on the rug are accepted more sympathetically by the young, with whom his contempt for stuffy convention ranks him as modern. They can understand, too, his experiments with fasting and with drugs, which he had tried thoroughly enough to convince him that there was an entire dissimilarity between his constitution and De Quincey's. His dress was not freakish, but there was something a little foreign-looking about him. He had lived abroad almost as long as in England: after five or six years at Rugby (before Dr Arnold's time) he declined to go up to Oxford or Cambridge, but went instead to study at Heidelberg. Though proud of his honour as a gentleman, he was quite indifferent to class. In Rome

> he was given to ramble about among the poor people, and the taste did not quit him in Middlemarch.
>
> He had somehow picked up a troop of droll children, little hatless boys with their galligaskins much worn and scant shirting to hang out, little girls who tossed their hair out of their eyes to look at him, and guardian brothers at the mature age of seven. This troop he had led out on gypsy excursions to Halsell Wood at nutting-time, and once the cold weather had set in he had taken them on a clear day to gather sticks for a bonfire in the hollow of a hillside, where he drew out a small feast of gingerbread for them, and improvised a Punch-and-Judy drama with some private home-made puppets.   (46:339)

There was something of the gypsy in him, a rebellious spirit that hated conventional restrictions. However one feels about this character, it is absurd to pronounce it vague or impalpable.

The objection most often made is that Ladislaw is a dilettante. He does not contradict his friend Naumann's accusation that he is amateurish as a painter, but insists that 'daubing a little' has taught him something about art that he could not have learned without it. A career in painting would be 'too one-sided a life' for him. Even with years of drudgery he could never hope to do well what had already been done better by others. This is clearly an oblique judgement on the futile labour of Mr Casaubon, who attributed Will's aversion to adopting a profession to dislike of steady application – a virtue which had yet to produce the first chapter of the Key to All Mythologies. Will's brief engagement as assistant in that mighty work was terminated, not by his lack of thoroughness, but by Mr Casaubon's morbid fear of being judged, which was soon to dismay Dorothea. Will's glib remark that 'If Mr Casaubon read German he would save himself a great deal of trouble' was a highly superficial criticism. The two most important books by Germans were already available to him: Creuzer's *Mythologie* (1810–12) had appeared in a French translation, and Lobeck's *Aglaophamus* (1829) was written in Latin. George Eliot comments: 'Young Mr Ladislaw was not at all deep himself in German writers; but very little achievement is required in order to pity another man's shortcomings.' Since leaving Lowick, Will had spent his time in Germany and Italy, 'sketching plans for several dramas, trying prose and finding it too jejune, trying verse and finding it too artificial, beginning to copy "bits" from old pictures, leaving off because they were "no good", and observing that, after all, self-culture was the principal point'. His apparently aimless wandering among artists and writers, among the students at Heidelberg and the poor people of Rome, had taught him a good deal about life. He is ready to give up his dependence on the allowance from Mr Casaubon and return to England to work his own way. He accepts Mr Brooke's offer to edit the *Pioneer* as much to be near Dorothea as to be independent of her husband, who banishes him from Lowick more out of jealousy than because the career of journalist was unsuited to his rank as a second cousin, or, more accurately, a first cousin once removed.[7]

'The impression once given that [Ladislaw] is a *dilettante*,' Henry James wrote, 'is never properly removed.' Careful reading, I think, reveals a slight change in Will's attitude. In Rome he had told Dorothea:

The best piety is to enjoy – when you can. You are doing the most then to save the earth's character as an agreeable planet. And enjoyment radiates. It is of no use to try and take care of all the world; that is being taken care of when you feel delight – in art or

in anything else. Would you turn all the youth of the world into
a tragic chorus, wailing and moralising over misery? I suspect
that you have some false belief in the virtues of misery, and want
to make your life a martyrdom.   (22:163)

This philosophy seems to make Will a forerunner of Pater's New
Hedonism, which has been examined so suggestively in U. C.
Knoepflmacher's *Religious Humanism and the Victorian Novel* (1965).
Later, however, at Tipton Grange, though still rebellious against
submitting to anything he dislikes, Will professes 'To love what is
good and beautiful when I see it' (39:287). Here the element of the
'good' sounds a new note, and his love for Dorothea directs his
interest more and more to the practical reforms she is concerned
with. He plans to study law to prepare himself for public service, a
phase of his career that some may feel to have been inadequately
realised. Like Lydgate's successful medical practice in the fashionable Continental bathing-place, it occurs off-stage at the end of the
novel, when the multifarious threads must be quickly drawn together.
Though it is only briefly mentioned, it is none the less genuine.

Some contemporary reviewers looked askance at Ladislaw's
morals, concurring in Sir James's opinion of him as 'a man of little
principle and light character' (84:597). Their most serious charge was
'his unworthy flirtation with his friend Lydgate's wife'.[8] Only a
censorious and evil-minded moralist would object if an attractive
bachelor of 25, unjustly excluded from the society in which he properly belongs, enjoys singing and chatting with the 'prettiest girl in
Middlemarch'. Lydgate himself, with no ear whatever for music,
had succumbed to Rosamond's other charms. He shows no sign of
jealousy, nor is there the least impropriety in Will's conduct. Twice
the Quarry states plainly (pp. 11, 26) that it is 'Rosamond's flirtation
with Ladislaw', not his with Rosamond, and George Eliot's careful
exploration of her fantasy makes the fact quite clear. Will returned to
Middlemarch, not to see Rosamond, but in hope of some accident by
which he might meet Dorothea. Ironically, he does. At the very
instant Dorothea surprises them, Will is telling Rosamond that he
loves another, that he can never love her. Even Dr Leavis concedes –
in a footnote – that Ladislaw is 'adequate' in this cruel disillusioning
of Rosamond.

But he takes particular exception to the 'presentment of those
impossibly high-falutin' *tête-à-tête* – or soul to soul – exchanges
between Dorothea and Will, which is utterly without irony or criti-

cism'.[9] Now, with all due reverence for irony, which has, perhaps, had more than its share, I think we may ask whether it has much to contribute to a love scene. Shakespeare certainly eschews it in his 'presentment' of the 'exchanges' between Romeo and Juliet. But it is simply untrue that Ladislaw's interviews with Dorothea are ever without irony or criticism. In Chapter 54, their first meeting after Casaubon's death, Dorothea assumes that Will knows about the disgusting codicil, and from his announcement that he is leaving Middlemarch concludes that he had never felt more than friendship for her. The reader knows that she is wrong on both counts. When she says that she will be glad to hear he has made his value felt, but that he must be patient, for it may be a long while, Will could hardly save himself from falling down at her feet. George Eliot here interjects: 'He used to say that the horrible hue and surface of her crape dress was most likely the sufficient controlling force' (54:396). This little touch of distancing humour Dr Leavis ignores. Again, though Will has come bitterly resolved that their meeting should not end with 'a confession which might be interpreted into asking for her fortune', Dorothea is all the while preoccupied with the hardship of his probable want of money, 'while she had what ought to have been his share' and was prevented from giving it to him. All she can ask is whether he would like the miniature of his grandmother, which Will irritably refuses: 'It would be more consoling if others wanted to have it. . . . Why should I have that, when I have nothing else? A man with only a portmanteau for his stowage must keep his memorials in his head.' Though he was 'merely venting his petulance', for Dorothea 'his words had a peculiar sting', and she replied: 'You are much the happier of us two, Mr Ladislaw, to have nothing.' But Will, without the least thought of any claim on Casaubon's property, only says that he regrets poverty because 'it divides us from what we most care for'. The whole scene is suffused with irony, which culminates in the appearance of Sir James Chettam. His mingled feelings, too, are subtly analysed. Though he had assumed that they were lovers, by entering at just that moment Sir James incorporates 'the strongest reasons through which Will's pride became a repellent force, keeping him asunder from Dorothea'. To see no irony here is sheer perversity.

Nearly two months pass before their next interview (Chapter 62). Then Will, having learned from Rosamond about the codicil and from Raffles about the scandal involving his mother's family, wrote to Dorothea, asking permission to call again at Lowick. He felt the awkwardness of asking for more last words. His former farewell had been made in the hearing of Sir James Chettam, and had been announced as final even to the butler. It is certainly trying to a man's dignity to reappear when he is not expected to do so: a first farewell has pathos in it, but to come back for a second lends an opening to comedy, and it was possible even that there might be bitter sneers afloat about Will's motives for lingering. Still it was on the whole more satisfactory to his feeling to take the directest means of seeing Dorothea, than to use any device which might give an air of chance to a meeting of which he wished her to understand that it was what he earnestly sought. (62:458)

Ironically, Dorothea did not receive his note, but met him quite by chance at the Grange, where Will had come to fetch the portfolio of his sketches; at the moment she entered the library he was thinking hopefully that he might find an answer from her awaiting him at Middlemarch and was smiling at the sketch which on the first day he ever saw her had 'a relation to nature too mysterious for Dorothea' (62:461). She had just come from Freshitt Hall with her feelings exacerbated by Mrs Cadwallader's malicious gossip (inspired by Sir James) about 'Orlando' Ladislaw's always being found lying on the rug at Lydgate's house or warbling with his wife. Though she had repudiated the report indignantly, Dorothea could not forget that the only time she went to the house she had found Ladislaw there and heard him singing. Feeling 'a strange alternation between anger with Will and the passionate defence of him', Dorothea arrived at the Grange.

Will, too, was in an angry mood. The hateful codicil had completely shattered his dream of being able to return some day to ask Dorothea to marry him, and he could not conceal his irritation:

> 'I have been grossly insulted in your eyes and in the eyes of others. There has been a mean implication against my character. I wish you to know that under no circumstances would I have lowered myself by – under no circumstances would I have given men the chance of saying that I sought money under the pretext of seeking – something else. There was no need of other safeguard against me – the safeguard of wealth was enough.' (62:462)

Throughout this brief scene their feelings are always at cross purposes, preventing their saying directly what they mean.

'What I care more for than I can ever care for anything else is absolutely forbidden to me – I don't mean merely by being out of my reach, but forbidden me, even if it were within my reach, by my own pride and honour – by everything I respect myself for. Of course I shall go on living as a man might do who had seen heaven in a trance.'

Will paused, imagining that it would be impossible for Dorothea to misunderstand this; indeed he felt that he was contradicting himself and offending against his self-approval in speaking to her so plainly; but still – it could not be fairly called wooing a woman to tell her that he would never woo her. It must be admitted to be a ghostly kind of wooing.

But Dorothea's mind was rapidly going over the past with quite another vision than his. The thought that she herself might be what Will most cared for did throb through her an instant, but then came doubt; the memory of the little they had lived through together turned pale and shrank before the memory which suggested how much fuller might have been the intercourse between Will and some one else with whom he had had constant companionship. Everything he had said might refer to that other relation, and whatever had passed between him and herself was thoroughly explained by what she had always regarded as their simple friendship and the cruel obstruction thrust upon it by her husband's injurious act. Dorothea stood silent, with her eyes cast down dreamily, while images crowded upon her which left the sickening certainty that Will was referring to Mrs Lydgate. But why sickening? He wanted her to know that here too his conduct should be above suspicion.   (62:463–4)

Will's mind was also 'tumultuously busy while he watched her', and he 'could not deny that a secret longing for the assurance that she loved him was at the root of all his words'. They both stood silent until the footman announced that her carriage was ready. Her parting words 'seemed to him cruelly cold and unlike herself'.

'I have never done you injustice. Please remember me,' said Dorothea, repressing a rising sob.

'Why should you say that?' said Will, with irritation. 'As if I were not in danger of forgetting everything else.'

He had really a movement of anger against her at that moment, and it impelled him to go away without pause. It was all one flash to Dorothea – his last words – his distant bow to her as he reached the door – the sense that he was no longer there. (62:464)

The *erlebte Rede* describing her mingled joy at realising that Will loved her and her sorrow for the irrevocable parting is richly imagined. A few minutes later, when she overtook him on the road, she longed to but could not make some sign that would seem to say 'Need we part?' She wished that she could give him the money to make things easier for him. But Will saw Dorothea driving past him as he plodded along with an increased bitterness that made his rudeness to her seem a matter of necessity. How can one read this brief, restrained episode as if George Eliot were seeing Dorothea through Will's eyes and utterly without irony?

I find nothing in the diction of these scenes to deserve Dr Leavis's quaint 'highfalutin'. Without bothering to discuss the interviews he declares:

> Their tone and quality is given fairly enough in this retrospective summary (it occurs at the end of Chapter LXXXII): 'all their vision, all their thought of each other, had been [as] in a world apart, where the sunshine fell on tall white lilies, where no evil lurked, and no other soul entered'. It is Will who is supposed to be reflecting to this effect, but Will here – as everywhere in his attitude towards Dorothea – is unmistakably not to be distinguished from the novelist (as we have noted, he hardly exists).[10]

On reconsideration Dr Leavis might soften this opinion: read in its entirety I do not think the passage in Chapter 82 can support his view that Will's valuation of Dorothea is George Eliot's. It comes immediately after Rosamond says that she has told Mrs Casaubon the truth about her relations with him.

> The effect of these words was not quite all gladness. As Will dwelt on them with excited imagination, he felt his cheeks and ears burning at the thought of what had occurred between Dorothea and Rosamond – at the uncertainty how far Dorothea might still feel her dignity wounded in having an explanation of his conduct offered to her. There might still remain in her mind a changed association with him which made an irremediable difference – a lasting flaw. With active fancy he wrought himself into a state of doubt little more easy than that of the man who has

escaped from wreck by night and stands on unknown ground in the darkness. Until that wretched yesterday – except the moment of vexation long ago in the very same room and in the very same presence – all their vision, all their thought of each other, had been as in a world apart, where the sunshine fell on tall white lilies, where no evil lurked, and no other soul entered. But now – would Dorothea meet him in that world again?   (82:589)

The language of love is highly volatile, rarely surviving through two generations. Ben Jonson dared ask, 'Have you seen but a white lily grow / Before rude hands have touch'd it?' and for earlier and later poets the lily has symbolised an ideal love. In 1870 to readers familiar with Pre-Raphaelite poems and paintings it would have seemed entirely natural for a poetic young lover to express his feelings 'as in a world apart, where the sunshine fell on tall white lilies'.

Chapter 83 follows immediately with its epigraph from Donne,

> And now good-morrow to our waking souls
> Which watch not one another out of fear;
> For love all love of other sights controls,
> And makes one little room, an everywhere,

an appropriate motto for the chapter ending with Dorothea's eager embracing of poverty. One might fear that this ultimate 'soul to soul exchange' would prove the most 'highfalutin' of all. But it does not. Dorothea's short, simple, direct sentences belie the emotion under-lying them. Derek Oldfield's splendid essay on 'The Character of Dorothea' (in *Critical Approaches to the Novel* [1967]) shows how much it is defined by her style, as plain and devoid of ornament as her dress. In this whole chapter there are not a dozen similes or metaphors, none of them in Dorothea's speech or thought. The only ones in Ladislaw's are his brief outburst: 'It is as fatal as murder or any other horror that divides people; . . . it is more intolerable – to have our life maimed by petty accidents.' All the other images occur in the author's commentary: '"You acted as I should have expected you to act," said Dorothea, her face brightening and her head becoming a little more erect on its beautiful stem.' Or 'the flood of her young passion bearing down all obstructions'. Two of them describe Will: with hat and gloves in hand he 'might have done for the portrait of a Royalist', and he started up 'as if some torture-screw were upon him'. The relative calm of the lovers' dialogue contrasts with the wild storm outside, which expresses their turbulent emotion. This is one of the most ancient romantic devices. Fires flashed in the heavens when Dido and Aeneas found themselves together in the cave; Scott, Dickens, the Brontës, Thackeray, Meredith, Hardy and many later novelists have used it, usually for melodramatic effect. It is handled with restraint in *Middlemarch*. Dorothea darted from the window when the vivid flash of lightning came, and Will, following, seized her hand with a spasmodic movement, 'and so they stood, with their hands clasped, like two children looking out at the storm'. At the very end, after Will has declared that his poverty would keep him from offering himself to any woman 'even if she had no luxuries to renounce', Dorothea says: 'I don't mind about poverty – I hate my wealth', adding 'in a sobbing childlike way',

> We could live quite well on my own fortune – it is too much – seven hundred a-year – I want so little – no new clothes – and I will learn what everything costs. (83:594)

Not even at the very climax of emotion is the irony that George Eliot has focused throughout on Dorothea's immaturity allowed to lapse.

Henry James was one of the first critics to feel that Ladislaw was lacking in masculinity. 'If Dorothea had married any one after her misadventure with Casaubon', he wrote, 'she would have married a hussar!'

> He is, we may say, the one figure which a masculine intellect of the same power as George Eliot's would not have conceived with the same complacency; he is, in short, roughly speaking, a woman's man . . . . We are doubtless less content with Ladislaw, on account of the noble, almost sculptural, relief of the neighboring figure of Lydgate, the real hero of the story.[11]

The glamour of the 'noble, almost sculptural' figure of the 'real hero' was felt by others besides James, whose homo-erotic attraction to vigorous young men Leon Edel has documented. Even before the final books of *Middlemarch* were published many readers speculated hopefully that Dorothea and Lydgate might marry as a compensation for their earlier matrimonial trials. The *Saturday Review* exclaimed: 'Poor Lydgate – ten times the better man – suffers not only in happiness, but in his noblest ambitions, and sinks to the lower level of a good practice and a good income because he marries and is faithful to the vain selfish creature whom Ladislaw merely flirts with.'[12] This opinion misrepresents Ladislaw's relations with Rosamond and assigns her more than her share of blame for Lydgate's failure. From his first appearance in the story George Eliot has indicated the major weakness in Lydgate's character: he could recognise the pink stage of typhoid fever, but was blind to his own susceptibility to blue eyes. Even the melodramatic episode with Madame Laure had not taught him much. Edith Simcox perceived that he

> is one of those men whose lives are cut in two, whose intellectual interests have no direct connection with their material selves, and who only discover the impossibility of living according to habit or tradition when brought by accident or their own heedlessness face to face with difficulties that require thought as well as resolution. There was not room in the life he contemplated for a soul much larger than Rosamond's, and it may be doubted whether the Rosamond he wished for would not, by a merely passive influence, have been as obstructive to his wide speculations. . . . On the other hand, if the scientific ardour had been more absorbing, he might have gone on his own way, crushing all poor Rosamond's little schemes of opposition, and then she would have been the victim instead of the oppressor, but his character would have been as far from ideal excellence as before.[13]

Despite his weakness Lydgate is more appealing than Ladislaw – as Samson tamed by Delilah is more appealing than Joseph resisting Potiphar's wife. But there is no blurring the tragic fact that Lydgate's failure came from his own slackening resolution. His idea of a wife's function was little better than Casaubon's: 'to cast a charm over vacant hours' (5:32). Even James's 'nobly strenuous' Dorothea might have found marriage with Lydgate disastrous. His massive frame and large white hands are in marked contrast with Ladislaw's slim figure and long thin fingers, inherited from aristocratic Polish ancestors. In spite of his girlish complexion there is nothing effeminate in Will's fiery response to Raffles, as he turns 'like a tiger-cat ready to spring on him', making that overbearing bully draw back (60:446). The notion that masculinity is proportional to bodily weight is a common but questionable male dogma.

W. J. Harvey thought that George Eliot failed with the Dorothea-Will relationship because she was 'unwilling or unable to treat fully and properly . . . romantic or passionate love between two adults'.[14] If there were such a failure, I believe it must be judged in the context of its time. Not lack of willingness or ability, but the circulating library, the shilling magazine, and the general custom of family reading imposed this reticence on all the Victorian novelists. 'The death-bed might be public, but not the marriage bed', wrote Kathleen Tillotson in her *Novels of the Eighteen-Forties* (1954, p. 54), the best account I know of that aspect of the nineteenth-century novel. Its problem was to convey the idea of passion to adult readers in terms that would not 'bring a blush into the cheek of the young person'. Neither magazine nor circulating library would countenance candid treatment of sexual relations. To compare George Eliot with Flaubert or Tolstoy, to say that one cannot imagine her 'encompassing . . . the complex intensities of Anna Karenina's passion' is hardly fair. Tolstoy read all George Eliot's novels, most of them in the year they were published. There were five editions of *Middlemarch* in Russian before 1875, when *Anna Karenina* appeared, and its influence on Tolstoy has never been adequately studied. Had George Eliot been writing in France or Russia her account of the Casaubon honeymoon would have been more explicit, and Ladislaw's thought of Dorothea might not have been screened behind tall lilies. But in England the 'troughs of Zolaism' and the conviction of Vizetelly for publishing *La Terre* were still eighteen years in the future. We ought rather to compare Dorothea and Ladislaw with Bella Wilfer and John Harmon in *Our Mutual Friend* (1864–5) or Zoë and Lord Uxmoor in Reade's *A Woman Hater* (1874) – a needless task – or any of Trollope's young lovers, or those in Hardy's early novels.

Pace Henry James, the true hero of *Middlemarch* is Will Ladislaw. A serious obstacle to Lydgate's candidacy which rarely occurs to modern readers is the wide difference in rank between a lady in county society and a surgeon. Today, when medical men enjoy perhaps a higher respect than clergymen, we can hardly conceive what a lowly position they held in 1830. In the houses of great people, then, 'if it was necessary to offer [them] a meal, [they were] entertained in the steward's or housekeeper's room'.[15] In choosing his profession Lydgate had stepped below his rank, flouting the traditions of his family, and he descended even further in marrying the granddaughter of an innkeeper. The Lydgates of Quallingham would probably have agreed with Mrs Cadwallader's generalisation that 'the people in manufacturing towns are always disreputable'. As the orphan son of a penniless military man, the younger brother of a baronet in the North, Lydgate's pretensions to rank were not imposing. We are liable to view them through provincial Rosamond's dazzled eyes.

We also tend to underestimate Ladislaw's position as a gentleman. His grandfather, bearing the name of the greatest Polish king, was a patriot who fled to the West after the first partition of Poland in 1772. Though George Eliot does not give him a title, he was obviously cultivated, 'a bright fellow – could speak many languages – musical – got his bread by teaching all sorts of things'. From him Will's father inherited the musical talent and the aristocratic hands; from his mother came the grey eyes and the 'delicate irregular nose with the little ripple in it', which he passed on to his son. Will's mother, Sarah Dunkirk, a pretty, proud-spirited lass, well educated in a fine boarding school, was, according to Raffles, 'fit for a lord's wife'. On learning the criminal character of her father's business, Sarah had run away from home and gone on the stage. Of course these low connections constitute a blemish on Will's pedigree. Yet a woman always takes her husband's rank; the peerage is studded with noblemen whose mothers had dubious origin and made their debuts in the theatre.[16]

In the English novel, where the law of primogeniture is not often set aside, the inheritance of property plays an important part in the plot. Tom Jones, illegitimate but older than Blifil, inherits Allworthy's estate and, by the hand of Sophia, Squire Western's too. In Gothic novels the hero invariably proves to be the heir to the castle. Mr Knightley in winning Emma Woodhouse for his wife returns Hartfield to the Donwell Abbey estate, of which it was originally a part. In Scott's novels a regular feature is the ultimate junction of hero with real estate, which he secures, not by killing his enemy in a duel, but through his legal right of inheritance. Alexander Welsh demonstrates in *The Hero of the Waverley Novels* (1963) how the so-called passive heroes – unlike the Fergus MacIvors, Rob Roys and Redgauntlets - abstain from violence because as English gentlemen they rely on the law, which always vindicates them. We can trace something of this pattern in George Eliot, who from childhood was nourished on Scott's novels. Many of his heroes are mild, dreamy youths, thrown by chance into adventures in which they play largely passive roles. For example, Frank Osbaldistone, the only son of an elder son, is a rebellious dilettante, interested chiefly in poetry, a drop-out from a business career with his father, who in his own youth had abandoned his rank by going into trade in London, yielding the title and the family estates in the North to his younger brother. At the end of the tale, more through the initiative of Rob Roy and Di Vernon than by his own efforts, Frank is restored to his proper place as head of the family and lord of Osbaldistone Hall.

We see a certain parallel in the case of Will Ladislaw. His grandmother, Casaubon's Aunt Julia, was the elder and prettier of the two ladies of Lowick Manor. When she was disinherited for her *mésalliance*, the estate passed to her younger sister, who married a Mr Casaubon and had two sons. The elder inherited the estate; the younger, Edward, became a clergyman and lived at Lowick parsonage until, on the death of his brother about 1819, he took possession of the manor. The history of Casaubon's family is very shadowy. He told Dorothea that he had 'none but comparatively distant connec-tions' (37:274); we hear from Cadwallader that he 'is very good to his poor relations: pensions several of the women' (8:51); but we never see any of them – in curious contrast with the presumptive heirs of Peter Featherstone. Will Ladislaw's father was one of these poor relations towards whom Mr Casaubon recognised a duty and, hav-ing learned of his desperate plight, ill and starving at Boulogne, sent him money, and after his death continued the allowance to his widow and son Will, whose education he paid for.

Dorothea, with whom generous feelings often took precedence of practical realities, regarded the disinheriting of Aunt Julia as a cruel injustice, and thought that Will – the sole descendant of the elder branch of the family – had an equal claim to the estate. With the ardour that often supplanted her tact she broached the matter at night during one of Mr Casaubon's sleepless intervals, urging Will's claim to half the property settled on her before her marriage, with an immediate provision for him on that understanding. As George Eliot points out, Dorothea 'was blind to many things obvious to others – likely to tread in the wrong places' (37:273), of which this was certainly one. Ironically, her well-meant effort for Ladislaw, who would never himself have dreamed of such a claim, precipitated Casaubon's codicil depriving them both of the estate.

In the elaborate plot of *Middlemarch*, which the Victorians so much enjoyed, Ladislaw with his relation to Casaubon and to Bulstrode, his employment by Mr Brooke, and his involvement with the Lydgates provides the only coherent focus. Through his mother Will has a similar moral claim on the Dunkirk fortune. After the death of her only son and her husband, Mrs Dunkirk, who never knew the pre-cise nature of the pawnbroker's business, tried earnestly to find

Sarah. Only after all efforts had failed did she consent to marry the confidential accountant, young Brother Bulstrode, whose piety in prayer meetings had made her trust him. But she was deceived. The daughter had been found by Raffles, whom Bulstrode bribed to silence and shipped off to New York. Except for this concealment the Dunkirk money would have been Sarah's, and Will Ladislaw might never have come to Lowick. 'But the train of causes in which [Bulstrode] had locked himself went on.' During nearly 30 years of philanthropy at Middlemarch he had striven vainly to convince himself that his good works justified the fraud by which he had got the Ladislaws' money. Then, when Raffles threatened exposure, Bulstrode asked Will to call on him and told him of the marriage to Mrs Dunkirk, which had enriched him. 'So far as human laws go, you have no claim on me whatever', he said; yet there was a claim his conscience recognised. Accordingly he offered Will an income of £500 a year and support for any laudable plan he might have in prospect. Will's rejection of the offer is merciless:

> 'My unblemished honour is important to me. It is important to me to have no stain on my birth and connections. And now I find there is a stain which I can't help. My mother felt it, and tried to keep as clear of it as she could, and so will I. You shall keep your ill-gotten money. If I had any fortune of my own, I would willingly pay it to any one who could disprove what you have told me. What I have to thank you for is that you kept the money till now, when I can refuse it. It ought to lie with a man's self that he is a gentleman. Good-night, sir.'

It is an impressive scene, quietly handled, with none of the florid rhetoric in which Dickens would have decked it. George Eliot examines the tangled feelings underlying Will's bitter words. In the rush of his impulses 'there was mingled the sense that it would have been impossible for him ever to tell Dorothea that he had accepted it'. Bulstrode's emotions are also analysed with the same sympathetic understanding that his creator extends to good and bad alike.[17]

Perhaps it is only heroes of romance who spurn offers of £500 a year so scornfully. The typical villain, like Monks in *Oliver Twist*, is usually forced in a melodramatic exposure to disgorge the hero's property and betake himself to prison or the Antipodes. But *Middlemarch* is no romance. Bulstrode is allowed to keep the money which would have made Will independent. To marry him Dorothea

gives up the Casaubon estate – possibly to those shadowy pension-
ers; we can never know. Middlemarch tradition declared that she
gave it up to marry a man 'with no property and not well-born', and
it was usually said that she could not have been 'a nice woman'.
Though Mr Brooke corresponded with the Ladislaws for a long time
he did not invite them to the Grange. He talked a good deal about
cutting off the entail so that his estate, which was worth £3000 a year,
could go to Celia's son and join Tipton with the well-kept farms of
Freshitt. But after Dorothea's son was born, Sir James advised Mr
Brooke to let the entail alone. And so the young Ladislaw will grow
up to inherit the Tipton estate and fulfil the role of fictional hero,
which in a romance would have been his father's.

> Will become an ardent public man, working well in those times
> when reforms were begun with a young hopefulness of immediate
> good which has been much checked in our days and getting at last
> returned to Parliament by a constituency who paid his expenses.
> (Finale: 610–11)

Cynics are sometimes sceptical of this career. Leslie Stephen (possibly glancing at G. H. Lewes) thought it would be easy to suggest a
living original for some of Will's peculiarities, but could not believe
that he ever got into Parliament.

> Ladislaw, I am convinced, became a brilliant journalist who could
> write smartly about everything, but who had not the moral force
> to be a leader in thought or action. I should be the last person to
> deny that a journalist may lead an honourable and useful life, but
> I cannot think the profession congenial to a lofty devotion to
> ideals. Dorothea was content with giving him 'wifely help'; ask-
> ing his friends to dinner, one supposes, and copying his ill-writ-
> ten manuscripts.[18]

Stephen's sarcasm was hardly called for. Dorothea never repented
that she had married Ladislaw. 'They were bound to each other by a
love stronger than any impulses which could have marred it' (Finale:
610). Joan Bennett sums the matter up wisely and with moderation:

> Marriage with Ladislaw is not meant to be the fulfilment of
> Dorothea's youthful dreams . . . [It] is an improvement on the first
> because its basis is an appreciation of the man as he is; their love

for each other comprises mutual sympathy, understanding and respect. . . . Dorothea invents no fiction about Ladislaw nor he about her. . . . The reader discerns faults, weaknesses or irritating tricks in Ladislaw which, he supposes, would alienate her.

But, Mrs Bennett continues tolerantly, this was not the opinion of perceptive people like Lydgate and the Farebrothers, who like him very much. And he

has certain qualities which were particularly likely to attract Dorothea after her experience with Casaubon. He is spontaneous and unselfconscious; he responds to beauty in art or nature and to nobility in human character with romantic ardour. His intelligence is quick and gay – a happy contrast to Casaubon's ponderous learning. His nature is in many ways complementary to her own. Certainly George Eliot did not intend us to share Sir James Chettam's view that their marriage was a disaster.[19]

So let us end with Dorothea's warm words: 'I will not hear any evil spoken of Mr Ladislaw; he has already suffered too much injustice' (62:460).

Notes

This essay first appeared in *This Particular Web: Essays on 'Middlemarch'*, ed. Ian Adam (Toronto: University of Toronto Press, [1975]) pp. 22–42.

1. Arthur Ponsonby, *Henry Ponsonby* (London, 1942) p. 259, and Algernon West, *Recollections* (London, 1900) p. 281.
2. Henry James, 'George Eliot's *Middlemarch*', *Galaxy*, vol. 15 (March 1873) p. 426.
3. F. R. Leavis, *The Great Tradition: George Eliot, Henry James, Joseph Conrad* (London, 1948) p. 75.
4. *Middlemarch*, ed. Gordon S. Haight, Riverside edn (Boston, Mass., 1956) pp. xii–xiii.
5. References in this paragraph are as follows: 34:241; 84:599; 9:58; 9:59; 21:152; 60:446; 19:140.
6. *The George Eliot Letters*, ed. Gordon S. Haight, 7 vols (New Haven, Conn., and London, 1954–5), vol. III, p. 274.
7. References in this paragraph are as follows: 21:153; 21:154; 46:337; 37:269; 39:286.
8. *Saturday Review*, 7 December 1872, p. 734.

9. Leavis, *The Great Tradition*, p. 76.
10. George Eliot wrote (82:589): 'had been as in a world apart'. By omitting 'as' in quoting the passage Dr Leavis blurs the metaphorical nature of Ladislaw's thoughts.
11. Henry James, '*Daniel Deronda*: A Conversation', *Atlantic Monthly*, vol. 38 (December 1876) p. 690; and 'George Eliot's *Middlemarch*', *Galaxy*, vol. 15 (March 1873) p. 426.
12. *Saturday Review*, 7 December 1872, p. 734.
13. *Academy*, vol. 4 (1 January 1873) p. 3.
14. W. J. Harvey, *The Art of George Eliot* (London, 1961) p. 167.
15. G. M. Young (ed.), *Early Victorian England*, 2 vols (London, 1934) vol. I, p. 96.
16. References in this paragraph are as follows: 62:460; 37:268; 9:58; 60:447.
17. References in this paragraph are to Chapter 61: 451, 455, 457.
18. Leslie Stephen, *George Eliot* (London, 1902) pp. 179–80.
19. Joan Bennett, *George Eliot: Her Mind and Her Art* (Cambridge, 1948) pp. 176–7.

4

The Heroine of *Middlemarch*

If we define 'heroine' as 'the principal female figure' in a novel, Dorothea Brooke seems to qualify as 'the heroine of *Middlemarch*'. She is so described in all the standard reference works today and has held the title from the beginning. Henry James, reviewing the book in 1873, regretted that she was forced to share the story with Rosamond Vincy and Mary Garth. 'Dorothea was altogether too superb a heroine to be wasted; yet she plays a narrower part than the imagination of the reader demands.' James longed to rewrite the novel to centre on Lydgate and Dorothea, who 'suggest a wealth of dramatic possibility between them'.[1] One wonders whether by subsidising Lydgate's scientific research Dorothea might have eliminated from his character those weaknesses that George Eliot took such care to endow him with. Though marriage with Lydgate may not have been beyond Dorothea's scope, it would have been a gross violation of George Eliot's fidelity to social history, ignoring the wide chasm which at that time divided the landed gentry from country surgeons. In 1830, 'in the houses of great people, they were, if it was necessary to offer a meal, entertained in the steward's or housekeeper's room'.[2] Dorothea's marriage to Lydgate would have caused a real scandal in Middlemarch.

If we enlarge the definition to include intelligence, courage, and self-sacrifice, we can make a good case for the quiet steadfast Mary Garth as the true heroine. In the manuscript of the original Middlemarch story, begun in 1869, almost a year before it was combined with the short story called 'Miss Brooke', the Garth family appear under the name of Dove. No one seems to have discussed George Eliot's reason for abandoning the earlier name. Since Noah the connotations of *dove* have related to peace and deliverance. The dove is a gentle, harmless bird, noted for its graceful form and affection for its mate. The latter trait suits Caleb Garth well; his quiet pursuit of the right, his kindness to everyone who needs help, and his loving concern for his family suggest that George Eliot may have chosen the name with Caleb chiefly in mind. As the picture of his family rounded out, the name of Garth may have seemed more suitable. *Garth*, signifying a garden, a yard, an enclosed place, comprises many ideas connected with Caleb's trade as a builder and manager of estates. It was also a happy name for his daughter Mary, whose life is centred so closely in the well-knit family group.

Mary is first mentioned in Chapter 11 at the Vincy breakfast table. Though Rosamond has refused her uncle Peter Featherstone's invitation to live with him at Stone Court, she is jealous of the opportunity that Mary's presence there gives her to see Mr Lydgate, the new doctor, who is treating their uncle. She extracts from her brother Fred a promise to take her with him when he calls at Stone Court the next day. There Mary is found administering cough syrup to old Featherstone, who has been agitated by the unwelcome visit of his sister Mrs Waule. Wanting to talk to Fred alone, he sends Mary and Rosamond out of the room.

Every reader is familiar with George Eliot's method of defining characters by contrast. In *Adam Bede* Dinah Morris and Hetty Sorrel are brought to life by parallel scenes like those in 'The Two Bed-chambers' (ch. 15). In *The Mill on the Floss* little Maggie Tulliver with her dark complexion and unruly black hair, made jealous by Tom's attention to their pretty blond cousin Lucy, pushes her into the mud, an impulsive childish action foreshadowing the conflict years later when Maggie drifts down the river with Lucy's all-but-fiancé Stephen Guest. We cannot help feeling surprised that the awkward ugly duckling we knew so well in little Maggie should have grown into the tall, dark-eyed nymph of the last two books, 'broad-chested' in the 'mould of young womanhood', with arms that recall the Parthenon marbles, a fine throat, lips full and red, brown cheeks firm and rounded under her 'coronet' of jet black hair. This miraculous transformation, accomplished offstage, accounts for some dissatisfaction with the latter part of the novel.

It seems far more likely that Maggie would have grown up looking like Mary Garth, who had also been 'a little hoyden' in childhood (ch. 23). Most people in Middlemarch agreed that Mary was 'plain' – a 'brown patch', she called herself (ch. 40). Standing at the mirror in Stone Court beside that slim blond beauty Rosamond, Mary made the strongest contrast:

> she was brown; her curly dark hair was rough and stubborn; her stature was low. . . . Advancing womanhood had tempered her plainness, which was of a good human sort, such as the mothers

of our race have very commonly worn in all latitudes under a more or less becoming headgear. Rembrandt would have painted her with pleasure, and would have made her broad features look out of the canvas with intelligent honesty.   (ch. 12)

George Eliot never blurs the lines of this initial portrait. Late in the novel at the New Year's Day party, to which Fred Vincy has insisted that his mother invite Mary with the Farebrothers, the same unflattering details occur: 'Mrs. Vincy, in her fullest matronly bloom, looked at Mary's little figure, rough wavy hair, and visage quite without lilies and roses, and wondered; trying unsuccessfully to fancy herself caring about Mary's appearance in wedding clothes, or feeling complacency in grandchildren who would "feature" the Garths' (ch. 63). All the while, across the room sat Rosamond, perfectly graceful and still, never looking at Lydgate 'any more than if she had been a sculptured Psyche modelled to look another way'.

A less obvious contrast between Mary and Rosamond is found in their minds. They had both attended Mrs Lemon's, the best school for girls in the county. Rosamond was beyond doubt the favourite pupil. She quickly mastered all the finicking refinements that passed for elegance in the provinces, excelling even in 'extras such as getting in and out of a carriage. Mrs. Lemon herself had always held up Miss Vincy as an example; no pupil, she said, exceeded that young lady for mental acquisition and propriety of speech, while her musical execution was quite exceptional' (ch. 11). This 'flower' of Mrs Lemon's School provides one of George Eliot's harshest strictures on the modes of education in the nineteenth century which 'make a woman's knowledge another name for motley ignorance' (Finale). 'Rosamond never showed any unbecoming knowledge, and was always that combination of correct sentiments, music, dancing, drawing, elegant note-writing, private album for extracted verse, and perfect blond loveliness, which made the irresistible woman for the doomed man of that date' (ch. 27). At Mrs Lemon's Mary Garth had been only an articled pupil, an apprentice, preparing (like her mother before her) to earn her living as a teacher. With Mrs Lemon's blessing she might look forward to a life of drudgery at £35 a year, eked out with 'extra pay for teaching the smallest strummers at the piano' (ch. 40). But the solid core of Mary's education had been acquired at home. Mrs Garth's grammar and accent, which were above the town standard (ch. 24), were doubtless transmitted to her children more effectually than that parroted 'propriety of speech' with which Rosamond strove to supplant her mother's hearty, vul-

gar idiom. Despite their 'living in such a small way', for which Mrs
Vincy, an inn-keeper's daughter, always pitied them, the Garths
lived in a genuinely intellectual atmosphere. While Mrs Garth cooked
the family dinner, her children followed her about the kitchen, book
or slate in hand. Thus she instilled in them the fact that one 'might
possess "education" and other good things ending in "tion" and
worthy to be pronounced emphatically, without being a useless doll'
(ch. 24). On one such occasion little Ben and his sister Letty vie with
each other in retelling the story of Cincinnatus; on another we see
the whole family gathered in the orchard under the great apple tree
while Jim reads aloud from *Ivanhoe*, by 'that beloved writer who has
made a chief part in the happiness of many young lives' (ch. 57).
Scott was the most popular novelist in 1830, and *Waverley*, *The Pirate*
and *Anne of Geierstein* also figure in *Middlemarch*. But Mary's conversation reveals an easy acquaintance with many other authors which
she would not have got at Mrs Lemon's.[3]

Another great contrast with Rosamond is found in Mary Garth's
lively sense of humour. Her brothers and sisters missed her while
she was away and wished that she would come home 'to play at
forfeits and make fun' (ch. 24). A glint of playfulness sparkles through
even her most disheartened moments. When the family's fortunes
were at their lowest ebb, she received the offer of a post as governess
in a school at York. Mary hated both teaching and the prospect of
separation from her family it would entail. Having read the letter,
she passed it without comment to her mother and picked up her
sewing again.

> 'Oh, don't sew, Mary!' said Ben, pulling her arm down. 'Make
> me a peacock with this bread-crumb.' He had been kneading a
> small mass for the purpose.
> 'No, no, Mischief!' said Mary good-humouredly, while she
> pricked his hand lightly with her needle. 'Try and mould it your-
> self: you have seen me do it often enough. I must get this sewing
> done. It is for Rosamond Vincy: she is to be married next week,
> and she can't be married without this handkerchief.' Mary ended
> merrily, amused with the last notion.
> 'Why can't she, Mary?' said Letty, seriously interested in this
> mystery, and pushing her head so close to her sister that Mary
> now turned the threatening needle towards Letty's nose.
> 'Because this is one of a dozen, and without it there would be
> only eleven,' said Mary with a grave air of explanation so that
> Letty sank back with a sense of knowledge.   (ch. 40)

One day when Fred called at Stone Court and found her laughing over Mrs Piozzi's *Anecdotes of the Late Samuel Johnson*, she looked up 'with the fun still in her face' (ch. 25).

Rosamond's lovely face never reflected any fun. She was clever, George Eliot tells us, 'with that sort of cleverness which catches every tone except the humorous. Happily she never attempted to joke, and this perhaps was the most decisive mark of her cleverness' (ch. 16). She was a perfect illustration of the principle George Meredith was to expound a few years later: that egoism is incompatible with humour. But in Mary Garth the Comic Spirit is dominant. Besides Mrs Cadwallader, whose mordantly witty epithets like 'our Lowick Cicero' impale and fix their victims, no character in *Middlemarch* has a keener sense of humour than Mary Garth. More than once George Eliot describes her remarks as made 'laughingly' (chs 14, 52). When she teased Fred about the lack of common sense in young men who have been to college, 'she spoke with a suppressed rippling under-current of laughter pleasant to hear' (ch. 14), and when she projected his future as a bachelor of forty, 'fat and shabby, hoping somebody will invite you to dinner – spending your morning in learning a comic song – oh no! learning a tune on the flute', her lips began to curl with a smile and 'her face had its full illumination of fun' (ch. 25). Mrs Garth, observing that Mary always laughed at Fred, was misled to believe it meant that she was not fond of him. As Meredith wrote: 'You may estimate your capacity for Comic perception by being able to detect the ridicule of them you love, without loving them less; and more by being able to see yourself somewhat ridiculous in dear eyes, and accepting the correction their image of you proposes.'[4]

Mary Garth has this faculty of seeing her own absurdities as well as those of others. 'For honesty, truth-telling fairness, was Mary's reigning virtue: she neither tried to create illusions, nor indulged in them for her own behoof, and when she was in a good mood she had humour enough in her to laugh at herself' (ch. 12). She readily accepted the fact that she was not good-looking because, she said, it relieved her of 'the nonsensical vanity of fancying everybody who comes near me is in love with me' (ch. 14). The most extended analysis of her mind is found at the opening of Chapter 33, where in the small hours of the night she was on duty in the moribund Mr Featherstone's bedchamber. 'Having early had strong reason to believe that things were not likely to be arranged for her peculiar satisfaction, she wasted no time in astonishment and annoyance at that fact.' George Eliot concludes that 'a vigorous young mind not overbalanced by passion, finds a good in making acquaintance with life, and watches its own powers with interest. Mary had plenty of merriment within' (ch. 33).

Truth-telling fairness supplies another contrast between Garths and Vincys in their attitude towards social distinctions. Rosamond lived in a romantic fantasy that Lydgate, being 'the nephew of a baronet', could secure her admission to that middle-class heaven, 'rank'. Lydgate himself was not entirely free from such snobbery. One of what George Eliot calls his 'spots of commonness' was his feeling 'the desirability of its being known (without his telling) that he was better born than other country surgeons' (ch. 15). In marrying Rosamond he 'had to confess to himself that he was descending a little in relation to her family' (ch. 36). As a leading ribbon manufacturer Mr Vincy was thought by Middlemarch to have come down a bit in marrying an inn-keeper's daughter. His late brother had been a clergyman and had got preferment – might have been a dean by this time if the stomach fever had not taken him off. So Mr Vincy was determined to get Fred into the Church, for, he said, '"It's a good British feeling to try and raise your family a little".... ' (ch. 13). Mrs Vincy was certain that her handsome young man was 'far beyond other people's sons: you may hear it in his speech that he has kept college company' (ch. 36), and she thought it would be a pity for him to go down a step in life by marrying that Garth girl, who, besides being so very plain, had 'worked for her bread' (ch. 40).

With such social snobbery as this Mary Garth would have nothing to do. She knew that if Fred became a clergyman it would be 'only for gentility's sake. I think', she said, 'there is nothing more contemptible than such imbecile gentility' (ch. 52). This was an opinion she found difficult to justify to old Mrs Farebrother, who was both the daughter and mother of clergymen. But married to Mr Farebrother, as she might easily have been, Mary would have been accepted as an admirable rector's wife and held the respect of everyone at Lowick. In St Botolph's parish he had 'used to the full the clergyman's privilege of disregarding the Middlemarch discrimination of ranks, and always told his mother that Mrs. Garth was more of a lady than any matron in the town' (ch. 40). But Mary was not tempted by rank; she did not marry Farebrother. She had loved Fred since they were children together and would marry no one else. Her integrity was more seriously tested by the inclination to accept him with all his weaknesses than by a chance to benefit him by letting Featherstone burn the will, which would not in any case have reinstated the earlier one.

The contrasts between Mary and Dorothea must be implied, for as far as we know they never met; if they looked at each other across the aisle of Lowick Church during Mary's long visits to the Farebrothers, we are not told. The physical contrast with Dorothea's tall calm beauty, though radically different from that with Rosamond, is just as extreme. But the greatest contrast lies in the degree of their maturity. For a girl of eighteen Dorothea, in her eagerness to marry the repulsive Casaubon, exhibits a grave deficiency of natural sexual instinct which the 'sweet dignity of her noble unsuspicious inexperience' (ch. 22) hardly extenuates. Her tragic self-delusion would set her up as a legitimate target for the Comic Spirit's volley of silvery laughter were it not muted by George Eliot's profound pity. Granting the pathetic earnestness of her zeal to share in the sterile pedantry of the Key to All Mythologies, it is very different from the intelligent honesty that guides Mary Garth's conduct at every step.

On the intellectual side there is an even more significant contrast. Dorothea's Swiss education, for all its exposure to Pascal and Bossuet, to Monsieur Liret's lectures on the Waldenses, to Jeremy Taylor and St Augustine, proves even less adequate as a preparation for life than the smatterings of elegance that Rosamond gleaned at Mrs Lemon's. Dorothea has not yet learned to see things as they are. 'I am rather short-sighted', she tells Sir James. And if she is liable to step on small dogs, she is equally blind to overtowering facts. Nor is she ever aware of her own absurdity. Apart from a faint sarcasm stirred by Celia's interest in her mother's jewels Dorothea never betrays a trace of humour. Mary Garth's practical, realistic stoicism is diametrically opposed to Dorothea's childish 'soul-hunger', her cloudy yearning for some vague, illimitable good. Caleb Garth's daughter would not have gone from the Midlands to Yorkshire looking for land on which to establish a model village till every farmhouse at Tipton had been properly restored. Yet she would have sympathised with Dorothea's defiance of the family's objections to her marrying Ladislaw in spite of the hateful codicil to Casaubon's will. In her own life Mary had faced a similar problem. With George Eliot such parallels are never accidental.

Feminists of the 1870s who hoped that the 'divine Dorothea' would turn out to be a champion of woman's rights were disappointed to find her left at the end with only the old-fashioned function of providing an heir for the Tipton estates. According to Sir Leslie Stephen she had to be 'content with giving Ladislaw "wifely help"; asking his friends to dinner, one supposes, and copying his ill-written manuscripts'. The melancholy truth seemed to be that 'a Theresa of our days has to be content with suckling fools and chronicling small beer'.[5] Such melancholy readings of *Middlemarch* spring from concentrating too intensely on Dorothea. Henry James was one of the first to make this mistake. For him even the Lydgate story seemed an unfortunate diversion from the story of Dorothea, which is 'not distinctly enough, in fact, the central one', and 'the "love problem" as the author calls it, of Mary Garth, is placed on a rather higher level than the reader willingly grants it'.[6]

A self-appointed correspondent of mine, introducing herself as a member of the National Organization of Women, took me to task for not seeing that *Middlemarch* 'begins and ends with Dorothea and her longings to be different from those around her, that is, specifically, from those women like her sister Celia and Rosamond, who typify women forced into a pattern by a male-dominated society'. I should be hard-pressed to cite anything that a male-dominated society had 'forced' on the complacent Celia; and even by readers of her own sex Rosamond is usually blamed (not altogether justly) for having destroyed her husband's career and brought him to an early grave. Indeed, T. S. Eliot declared that she frightened him 'far more than Goneril or Regan', those notorious archetypes of female domination. Like Henry James the modern feminist ignores Mary Garth, the only wife among the 'Three Love Problems' with a successful solution.

Mary Garth serves as a control, a standard of life, against which Dorothea and Rosamond must be measured. In the Finale she is the first of the three whose subsequent careers are projected.

> Marriage, which has been the bourne of so many narratives, is still a great beginning. . . . It is still the beginning of the home epic – the gradual conquest or irremediable loss of that complete union which makes the advancing years a climax, and age the harvest of sweet memories in common.
>
> Some set out, like Crusaders of old, with a glorious equipment of hope and enthusiasm, and get broken by the way, wanting patience with each other and the world.
>
> All who have cared for Fred Vincy and Mary Garth will like to know that these two made no such failure, but achieved a solid mutual happiness.

In the imperfect society of the nineteenth century, 'A new Theresa will hardly have the opportunity of reforming a conventual life, any more than a new Antigone will spend her heroic piety in daring all for the sake of a brother's burial: the medium in which their ardent deeds took shape is for ever gone.' But George Eliot reminds us that Mary and Fred, the new Crusaders, adjusting their aspirations to the inalterable, 'made no such failure'. Who can say that Dorothea's model village in Yorkshire would have been a greater achievement than Fred's contribution to theoretic and practical farming in the Midlands? His books on green crops and cattle feeding, like Ladislaw's career in Parliament, we must take on faith. Most persons in Middlemarch were inclined to believe that they had been written by his wife. But when she 'wrote a little book for her boys, called *Stories of Great Men, taken from Plutarch*, and had it printed and published by Gripp & Co., Middlemarch, every one in the town was willing to give the credit of this work to Fred, observing that he had been to the University, "where the ancients were studied", and might have been a clergyman if he had chosen'.

In putting this last stroke to the finely drawn portrait of Mary Garth, George Eliot could hardly have forgotten the incredulity of her oldest Coventry friends when Marian Evans, the plain-looking country girl they had fostered, was revealed as the author of *Adam Bede*. Lydgate, when Mr Farebrother first spoke to him about Mary Garth, said:

'She is very quiet – I have hardly noticed her.'
'She has taken notice of you, though, depend upon it.'
'I don't understand,' said Lydgate; he could hardly say 'Of course.'
'Oh, she gauges everybody' [Farebrother replied].   (ch. 17)

Critics who like to read in Dorothea 'an unqualified self-identification' with her author would do well to look more closely at plain, honest Mary Garth, sitting a little apart and observing with amusement the droll pretensions of her neighbours. For like Mary Garth, George Eliot 'gauges everybody'.

Notes

This essay first appeared in *Victorian Newsletter*, no. 54 (Fall 1978) pp. 4–8.

1. Henry James, Jr, 'George Eliot's *Middlemarch*', *Galaxy*, vol. 15 (March 1873) p. 425.

2. G. M. Young (ed.), *Early Victorian England*, 2 vols (London, 1934) vol. I, p. 96.
3. Her allusion to George Borrow's reading the New Testament to the gypsies (ch. 32) is one of George Eliot's few anachronisms.
4. George Meredith, *An Essay on Comedy and the Uses of the Comic Spirit* (London, 1877) p. 61.
5. Leslie Stephen, *George Eliot* (London, 1902) pp. 179–80.
6. *Galaxy*, vol. 15 (March 1873) p. 425.

5

George Eliot's Klesmer

The formidable musician Julius Klesmer stands out in the reader's memory among the two or three finest creations in *Daniel Deronda*. Though only a secondary character, he performs several important functions in the novel. Like Daniel he acts as mentor to both Gwendolen and Mirah, his opinions of their singing placing them in a strong contrast maintained throughout the story. His brutal dismissal of Gwendolen's dream of earning her living as a singer or actress marks the beginning of her painful effort to face reality, and provides an eloquent statement of the artist's proper place in society. Finally, in Klesmer's marriage love and mutual interests overcome the same obstacle that confronted Gwendolen in hers – disparity of wealth and social position – a happy note too often forgotten by the critics who insist on seeing *Daniel Deronda* as a melancholy book.

On his first appearance Klesmer is introduced as 'a felicitous combination of the German, the Sclave, and the Semite'. David Kaufmann sees 'a fine touch of humour' in his name. 'He is unmistakably a Jew, but he never betrays himself, although the unfortunate name Julius Klesmer is enough for the initiated' – probably because in Yiddish '*klezmer*, a player' is the less respectful of two words meaning 'musician'. The Teutonic element shows itself in his matter-of-fact reply to Gwendolen's remark that he cannot like to hear poor amateur singing: 'No, truly; but that makes nothing'. When he is brought to the archery meeting by the Arrowpoints (though 'so far out of our own set'), his foreign look makes him conspicuous among the well-bred, well-tailored Englishmen.

> His mane of hair floating backward in massive inconsistency with the chimney-pot hat, which had the look of having been put on for a joke above his pronounced but well-modelled features and powerful clean-shaven mouth and chin; his tall, thin figure clad in a way which, not being strictly English, was all the worse for its apparent emphasis of intention. Draped in a loose garment with a Florentine *berretta* on his head, he would have been fit to stand by the side of Leonardo da Vinci; but how when he presented him-

self in trousers which were not what English feeling demanded about the knees? – and when the fire that showed itself in his glances and the movements of his head as he looked round him with curiosity was turned into comedy by a hat which ruled that mankind should have well-cropped hair and a staid demeanour, such, for example, as Mr Arrowpoint's, whose nullity of face and perfect tailoring might pass everywhere without ridicule? One sees why it is often better for greatness to be dead, and to have got rid of the outward man.   (Ch. 10)

Klesmer looks plainly like 'one of your damned musicians', a 'comic fellow', and most people at the gathering would agree with the fashionable son of the Archdeacon, young Clintock, who says 'What extreme guys these artistic fellows usually are!'

Physically, however, Klesmer is quite impressive. He towers high over Mrs Arrowpoint, even when bowing to her. He has a 'massive face', 'grand features', a 'splendid profile', brown hair 'floating in artistic fashion', 'wide-glancing' brown eyes that look out through intimidating gold spectacles. Seated at the piano he would toss back the mane of hair while his hands hovered over the keys, fingers pointed down. In London drawing-rooms many knew him or knew about him, though he had not yet attained 'that supreme, world-wide celebrity which makes an artist great to the most ordinary people by their knowledge of his great expensiveness'. On the Continent, however, he was known everywhere from Paris to St Petersburg, both as a pianist and a composer.

Klesmer's playing is described several times in *Daniel Deronda*: he is first heard with Catherine Arrowpoint in 'a four-handed piece on two pianos, which convinced the company in general that it was too long'. Next, after Gwendolen had sung, he

played a composition of his own, a fantasia called *Freudvoll, Leidvoll, Gedankenvoll* – an extensive commentary on some melodic ideas not too grossly evident; and he certainly fetched as much variety and depth of passion out of the piano as that moderately responsive instrument lends itself to, having an imperious magic in his fingers that seemed to send a nerve-thrill through ivory key and wooden hammer and compel the strings to make a quivering lingering speech for him.   (Ch. 5)

In spite of her wounded egotism Gwendolen is moved by the music. The common impression, however, is probably closer to that of young Clintock, who confesses to her: 'I never can make anything of this tip-top playing. It is like a jar of leeches, where you can never tell either beginnings or endings. I could listen to your singing all day.' The third time, when Klesmer plays at Lady Mallinger's party in Park Lane, 'the torrent-like confluences of bass and treble seemed, like a convulsion of nature, to cast the conduct of petty mortals into insignificance' (ch. 45). There is no comment on this performance beyond the outburst of talk that had been interrupted by it.

Polite indifference to music constitutes part of the criticism of English philistinism for which *Daniel Deronda* is notable. Popular taste favoured the simple melodies of Rossini and Meyerbeer or the aria of Bellini's that Gwendolen sang with gratifying success. But when she had finished, Klesmer told her frankly that such music

is beneath you. It is a form of melody which expresses a puerile state of culture – a dandling, canting, see-saw kind of stuff – the passion and thought of people without any breadth of horizon. There is a sort of self-satisfied folly about every phrase of such melody: no cries of deep, mysterious passion – no conflict – no sense of the universal. It makes men small as they listen to it.

Henry James in reviewing Book I praised Klesmer's speech:

There could not be a better phrase than this latter one to express the secret of that deep interest with which the reader settles down to George Eliot's widening narrative. The 'sense of the universal' is constant, omnipresent. It strikes us sometimes perhaps as rather conscious and over-cultivated; but it gives us the feeling that the threads of the narrative, as we gather them into our hands, are not of the usual commercial measurement, but long electric wires capable of transmitting messages from mysterious regions.
(*Nation*, 24 February 1876, p. 131)

These regions were to include not only the aesthetic, but the more sensitive fields of politics, morals, social rank and racial prejudice.

Some of them are explored in the great scene in Chapter 22 between Klesmer and 'the expectant peer, Mr Bult', a man whom the world considered a suitable match for the heiress Catherine Arrowpoint. Bult, who was not only insensible to counterpoint, but could not even regard a musician 'in the light of a serious human being who ought to have a vote', was amazed to hear Klesmer's vehement after-dinner outburst on the lack of idealism in English politics, 'which left all mutuality between distant races to be determined simply by the need of a market . . . "Buy cheap, sell dear"'.

Mr Bult was not surprised that Klesmer's opinions should be flighty, but was astonished at his command of English idiom and his ability to put a point in a way that would have told at a constituents' dinner – to be accounted for probably by his being a Pole, or a Czech, or something of that fermenting sort, in a state of political refugeeism which had obliged him to make a profession of his music; and that evening in the drawing-room he for the first time went up to Klesmer at the piano, Miss Arrowpoint being near, and said –

'I had no idea before that you were a political man.' Klesmer's only answer was to fold his arms, put out his nether lip, and stare at Mr Bult.

'You must have been used to public speaking. You speak uncommonly well, though I don't agree with you. From what you said about sentiment, I fancy you are a Panslavist.'

'No; my name is Elijah. I am the Wandering Jew,' said Klesmer, flashing a smile at Miss Arrowpoint, and suddenly making a mysterious wind-like rush backwards and forwards on the piano. Mr Bult felt this buffoonery rather offensive and Polish, but – Miss Arrowpoint being there – did not like to move away.

'Herr Klesmer has cosmopolitan ideas,' said Miss Arrowpoint, trying to make the best of the situation. 'He looks forward to a fusion of races.'

'With all my heart,' said Mr Bult, willing to be gracious. 'I was sure he had too much talent to be a mere musician.'

'Ah, sir, you are under some mistake there,' said Klesmer, firing up. 'No man has too much talent to be a musician. Most men have too little. A creative artist is no more a mere musician than a great statesman is a mere politician. We are not ingenious puppets, sir, who live in a box and look out on the world only when it is gaping for amusement. We help to rule the nations and make the age as much as any other public men. We count ourselves on level benches with legislators. And a man who speaks effectively through music is compelled to something more difficult than parliamentary eloquence.'

With the last word Klesmer wheeled from the piano and walked away.

Miss Arrowpoint coloured, and Mr Bult observed with his usual phlegmatic stolidity, 'Your pianist does not think small beer of himself.'

'Herr Klesmer is something more than a pianist,' said Miss Arrowpoint, apologetically. "He is a great musician in the fullest sense of the word. He will rank with Schubert and Mendelssohn.'

'Ah, you ladies understand these things,' said Mr Bult, none the less convinced that these things were frivolous because Klesmer had shown himself a coxcomb.

Next day, when Catherine remonstrated mildly with him, Klesmer retorted:

> 'You would have wished me to take his ignorant impertinence about a "mere musician" without letting him know his place . . . Even you can't understand the wrath of the artist: he is of another caste for you.'
>
> 'That is true,' said Catherine, with some betrayal of feeling. 'He is of a caste to which I look up – a caste above mine.'

Upon this hint Klesmer speaks. Catherine's words precipitate the proposal of marriage, which comes from her in one of the finest pages of the novel. The instant hostile reaction of her parents to what they regard as a *mésalliance* parallels the racial theme in the Deronda portion of the story. Mrs Arrowpoint, the authoress of an essay on Tasso, was thrown into a pitiable state when

> what she had safely demanded of the dead Leonora was enacted by her own Catherine. It is hard for us to live up to our own eloquence and keep pace with our winged words while we are treading on solid earth and are liable to heavy dining. Besides, it has long been understood that the proprieties of literature are not those of practical life. . . . While Klesmer was seen in the light of a patronised musician, his peculiarities were picturesque and acceptable; but to see him by a sudden flash in the light of her son-in-law gave her a burning sense of what the world would say.

Mrs Arrowpoint's first suggestion on learning of the engagement is to have Klesmer horsewhipped off the premises.

'Every one will say that you must have made the offer to a man who has been paid to come to the house – who is nobody knows what – a gypsy, a Jew, a mere bubble of the earth.'

'Never mind, mama,' said Catherine, indignant in her turn. 'We all know he is a genius – as Tasso was.'

Holding firm in her most un-Victorian rebellion, Catherine finally compels her parents to acknowledge this most unEnglish husband she has chosen.

If Klesmer appears seldom after his marriage, the ethics he advocated in social relations and in the arts pervade the whole novel. He calls on Mirah to ask her to sing at a party at their house in Grosvenor Place, for which, we are told, she received £100. He also plays her accompaniment when she sings at Lady Mallinger's. From the few passing references he seems to be firmly established in London, 'a patron and prince among musical professors'. But the more vivid impression is the earlier one of the brilliant young pianist with a peppery tongue, easily stirred to defend the vocation of the dedicated artist. No character in the book is more convincing. Henry James wrote that Klesmer 'comes in with a sort of Shakespearian "value", as a painter would say'. Shakespearian characters, he explains, are 'characters that are born out of the *overflow* of observation, characters that make the drama seem multitudinous, like life'. It is a fine tribute to George Eliot's achievement.

Some critics were reluctant to believe that an author by imagination alone could create such a character and insisted on looking for an original from whom he could have been copied. Franz Liszt has been generally accepted as the model for Klesmer since 1885, when Lord Acton in his review of Cross's *Life of George Eliot* asserted that 'Liszt became Klesmer'. The opinion has been repeated and improved upon; Blanche Colton Williams in her biography of George Eliot (1936) called Klesmer 'a nearly perfect portrait of Liszt'. George Eliot made Liszt's acquaintance in 1854, when she went to live with George Henry Lewes at Weimar. Lewes, having known him in Vienna fifteen years earlier, called to renew the acquaintance, and Liszt returned the call the next day, inviting them to lunch at the Altenburg, where he lived with the Princess Sayn-Wittgenstein. During the rest of their stay at Weimar the Leweses saw him frequently. In an unsigned article entitled 'Liszt, Wagner, and Weimar' which she wrote for *Fraser's Magazine* (July 1855), George Eliot says of him:

Most London concert-goers, for whom Liszt has 'blazed the comet of a season', think of him as certainly the archimagus of pianists, but as otherwise a man of no particular significance; as merely an erratic, flighty, artistic genius, who has swept through Europe, the Napoleon of the *salon*, carrying devastation into the hearts of countesses. A single morning's interview with him is enough to show the falsity of this conception. In him Nature has not sacrificed the man to the artist . . . if Liszt the pianist were unknown to you, or even did not exist, Liszt the man would win your admiration and love. See him for a few hours and you will be charmed by the originality of his conversation and the brilliancy of his wit; know him for weeks or months, and you will discern in him a man of various thought, of serious purpose, and of a moral nature which, in its mingled strength and gentleness, has the benignest influence on those about him.

Her journal describes in greater detail the impression he made on her during their first day together:

My great delight was to watch Liszt and observe the sweetness of his expression. Genius, benevolence, and tenderness beam from his whole countenance, and his manners are in perfect harmony with it. A little rain sent us into the house, and when we were seated in an elegant little drawing room, opening into a large music-salon . . . came the thing I had longed for – Liszt's playing. I sat near him so that I could see both his hands and face. For the first time in my life I beheld real inspiration – for the first time I heard the true tones of the piano. He played one of his own compositions – one of a series of religious *fantaisies*. There was nothing strange or excessive about his manner. His manipulation of the instrument was quiet and easy, and his face was simply grand – the lips compressed and the head thrown a little backward. When the music expressed quiet rapture or devotion a sweet smile flitted over his features; when it was triumphant the nostrils dilated.

Sweetness, tenderness, gentleness, benignity – none of these are qualities one could attribute to the irascible Klesmer. Nor is there any resemblance between the long, Dantesque face of the 43-year-old Liszt, familiar to everyone from Scheffer's portrait, and the massive, square countenance and 'grand features' of young Klesmer. He is 'the German, the Sclave, and the Semite', whose Jewishness forms an important part of the novel's structure. But Liszt was a Hungarian, born a Catholic; after some scandalous decades with the countesses, he was reconciled to the Church, taking minor orders in 1865 – the year in which *Daniel Deronda* is laid – to appear, tonsured and in clerical garb, as the Abbé Liszt. That he could not have sat for Klesmer George Eliot made clear by a direct allusion in Chapter 22. As the Arrowpoints thought of him, 'Klesmer was not yet a Liszt, understood to be adored by ladies of all European countries with the exception of Lapland; and even with that understanding it did not follow that he would make proposals to an heiress. No musician of honour would do so.'

Though Lord Acton was wrong about Liszt, George Eliot did meet at Weimar a musician in whom can be seen more plausibly the germ from which the character of Klesmer grew. At the *table d'hôte* in the Erbprinz Hotel 18 September 1854 Liszt presented to the Leweses a young Russian pianist and composer named Anton Rubinstein, whose one-act opera *The Siberian Huntsmen* he was about to produce at the Weimar Theatre for the Duchess's jubilee on 9 November. George Eliot's journal mentions him only once, but there can be no doubt that she saw him frequently at the Erbprinz, where she and Lewes also took their meals, and during their visits to the Altenburg. Rubinstein fits precisely her description of 'the German, the Sclave, and the Semite'. His mother, a native of Prussian Silesia, was a Jewess named Kalèria Levenstein; his father, a Russian Jew from Berdichev. Anton, born in the Russian province of Volhynia, lived his first years on a tract of land his father farmed in the village of Vichvatinetz; when he was four or five they migrated to Moscow, where his father tried to operate a pencil factory, which was equally unsuccessful. Till he was thirteen Anton was left in the hands of his teacher Villoing, wandering about Europe as a child virtuoso, and the valuable gifts received when he played before royalty were, on his return to Moscow, pledged as collateral for the failing business. If we may believe his *Autobiography*, Rubinstein knew both 'abundance and penury, ay, even to hunger' in his early days. Klesmer's background is recalled in a single sentence. When he comes to the Meyricks' tiny house to hear Mirah sing, 'He remembered a home no larger than this on the outskirts of Bohemia; and in the figurative Bohemia too he had had large acquaintance with the variety and romance which belong to small incomes' (ch. 39).

In physique and manner there is a strong resemblance between Rubinstein and Klesmer. The portraits show him as exceedingly handsome, with the massive features given to Klesmer, blue eyes

(Klesmer's were brown), and the thick mane of hair, which he used to throw backward when he played in conscious imitation of his hero, 'the king of musicians, Liszt'. According to Grove's *Dictionary* Rubinstein could 'play a simple piece by Haydn or Mozart so as to bring tears into his hearers' eyes; on the other hand, he would sometimes fall prey to a strange excitement which caused him to play in the wildest fashion' – a mood we recall when Klesmer plays with 'the torrent-like confluences of bass and treble . . . like a convulsion of nature'. The trait in which the two most closely resemble each other is their brusqueness. The same tone of vehement, unaccommodating candour with which Klesmer pulverizes Gwendolen's hopeless plan for a career on the stage can be heard in all Rubinstein's writings. His *Autobiography* (1890), *A Conversation on Music* (1892) and his *Gedankenkorb* (1897) all bristle with tart comments on his contemporaries that rival in acerbity anything said by 'the terrible Klesmer'. Rubinstein spent a good part of his life at St Petersburg, where he had early played for the Court and in later years was Director of the Conservatory of Music. Klesmer too has connections there. After his clash with Mr Bult, resolved to leave England, he says: 'I am neglecting my engagements. I must go off to St Petersburg.'

One bit of documentary evidence confirms the relation between them. In May 1876, when Rubinstein was in London, Mrs Frederick Lehmann invited the Leweses to dine with him and stay for the evening party, at which he was going to play. George Eliot, in the midst of writing the last book of *Daniel Deronda*, was worn out and discouraged by the lack of enthusiasm readers were showing for the Jewish elements of her novel. Though she had sternly resolved to accept no invitations till it was finished and had given some offence by her refusals, George Eliot broke her rule for this occasion. Lewes wrote to Mrs Lehmann, 'We shall so like to renew our acquaintance with Klesmer, whom we met at Weimar in '54! Therefore "whisper it not in Gath" but expect us.' And in a postscript he added, 'Couldn't you bring Rubinstein here next Sunday?' The visit to the Priory proved impossible; but they met Rubinstein at the Lehmanns' dinner on 15 May 1876, after which he played Beethoven, Chopin, Schumann and some of his own compositions. 'Stupendous playing!' exclaimed Lewes in his diary. They met again at the Felix Moscheles's, where he played his sonata for violin and piano with Wieniawski, and on 27 May the Leweses went to his concert at the New Philharmonic, where he was the soloist in his *Concerto in D*. 'Rubinstein played transcendently and roused quite a storm of enthusiasm', Lewes wrote. A year later when he returned to London George Eliot was suffering from kidney stone and could not go to the Moscheles's party, where Rubinstein played while Fraülein Redeker and Max Friedländer sang two duets from his sacred opera *The Maccabees*, which were illustrated by *tableaux-vivants*. She was doubtless gratified to think that her *Daniel Deronda* had helped create the patriotic interest in Jewish history that prompted the choice of this programme.

Note

This essay first appeared in *Imagined Worlds: Essays on Some English Novels and Novelists in Honour of John Butt*, ed. Maynard Mack (London: Methuen, 1968) pp. 205–14.

6

George Eliot's Bastards

Sweeping the field for information, a biographer inevitably turns up occasional bits of scandal. Lady Colefax, who was a famous collector of gossip, once told me some fascinating anecdotes about George Eliot, which had been going the rounds at the turn of the century. Among them was one I could easily refute: that George Eliot had had a son by John Chapman, who was educated at Edinburgh. This boy, born years before she ever saw Chapman, was Lewes's son Thornton, who spent two years at the High School there. But bastards figure in all but one of George Eliot's books. In 'Amos Barton' Miss Fodge is the mother of the sniffling seven-year-old in the Shepperton workhouse. In *Adam Bede* there is Hetty's child – whether a girl or a boy we never learn. Lawyer Wakem in *The Mill on the Floss* 'had other sons besides Philip, but towards them he held only a chiaroscuro parentage, and provided for them in a grade of life duly beneath his own'. His favourite, who takes over Dorlcote Mill, is well named Jetsome. Harold Transome in *Felix Holt* is the son of Matthew Jermyn, another lawyer, whose own parentage is dubious, untraced before charity school and workhouse. In *Middlemarch* Featherstone's bastard, the frog-faced Joshua Rigg, makes an ill-matched pair with his florid step-father Raffles. Tessa's Lillo and Ninna in *Romola* and, in *Daniel Deronda*, the charming family of Mrs Glasher, whose son Henleigh inherits the Grandcourt estate, complete the list. The one exception is *Silas Marner*: the child Eppie, whose mother Molly Farren, a barmaid addicted to drink and drugs, Godfrey Cass has most improbably married, is legitimate. But his refusal to acknowledge Eppie in Raveloe makes her practically illegitimate.

George Eliot's acquaintance with bastards is revealed for the first time through the Journal of George Combe,[1] the phrenologist. Born in 1789, the son of an Edinburgh brewer, he was deformed and stunted by tuberculosis in childhood. But his mind was sharp; apprenticed to a lawyer, he was admitted Writer to the Signet at the age of 24. After hearing Spurzheim, the phrenologist, lecture, Combe abandoned the stern Scottish orthodoxy he had been brought up in for the new 'science', which taught him to believe that the bumps on the skull were a reliable index to character. Phrenology, he thought, held the key to all social and moral problems; one's genetic pattern was determined and could be read by the size of the bumps, which he supposed indicated the development of underlying parts of the brain. Morality was shaped, not by religion, but by what he called the 'Natural Laws in the Constitution of Man'. At 45 Combe married Cecilia Siddons, daughter of the famous actress, and with her fortune of £15,000 retired from business to be the apostle of phrenology. The rage for this new 'science' was as prevalent as that for psychiatry today. Prison authorities called on Combe for advice on the treatment of criminals. Prince Albert engaged him to examine the heads of the Royal children and recommend proper lines of education for them. As a champion of secular education, Combe led an active life, lecturing in Britain and America and meeting all the radical reformers of the day.[2]

Among these was George Eliot's friend Charles Bray, the son of a wealthy ribbon manufacturer in Coventry. Born in 1811, Charles, after a rebellious period of schooling, was sent to a London merchant to learn the trade, living a lonely life in the warehouse. But he found a friend near by, a highly intelligent medical man, whom he may have consulted professionally, a deeply religious Dissenter, who soon converted Bray from an indifferent churchman to a serious Calvinist Evangelical. His new religion, he wrote in his *Autobiography*,[3] enabled him 'to break away from bad habits and to withstand temptation'. So confident was he of his faith that after returning to Coventry in 1830 he undertook to convert the Unitarian minister, a learned man, who quickly showed him that some of the texts he most relied upon were mistranslations (Bray, p. 11). Bray then began a thorough study of the Bible, which ended before long in his loss of all belief in Christianity.

He fell back upon a crude postulate that 'the laws of mind were equally fixed or determined with those of matter, . . . that *everything* acted necessarily in accordance with its own nature, and that there was no freedom of choice beyond this' (Bray, p. 17). Phrenology, which he came upon by chance in Combe's books, seemed a revelation of the 'machinery' by which 'the Natural Laws of Mind' worked. Wildly excited, he went to London to have a cast made so that he could examine the skull of the man he knew best, and he purchased 100 other casts showing phrenological 'organs' large or small (Bray, p. 22). His father's death in 1835 left Bray in control of a lucrative ribbon-weaving business with a large income he could use for improving society. He established a secular Infant School, a Working Man's Club, a Co-operative Store, a Provident Dispensary, and supported every reform. In 1836 he married Caroline Hennell, a well-educated young lady from an earnest Unitarian family, and soon settled down in a lovely house called Rosehill overlooking Coventry. During their wedding tour Bray's attempts to explain his heretical religious views had only succeeded in making Cara very uncomfortable (Bray, p. 48). In distress she appealed to her brother Charles Hennell, whose careful survey of the evidence was set forth in his *Inquiry concerning the Origin of Christianity* (1838, 2nd edn, 1841). Moderate and even reverent in tone, his study forced Hennell to conclude that Christianity was not based on revelation, but was simply like other natural human histories, and its miracles merely myths (Bray, p. 49).

Marian Evans had read Hennell's book before she met Bray. His sister, who lived next door, took her to call, hoping that the Evangelicalism for which she had been conspicuous in her schooldays might correct Charles's heterodoxy (Bray, pp. 76–7). He discovered at once that Marian's mind was already turned along the same path as his, and she was soon an intimate at Rosehill. He took her to London and had a cast made of her head. Whatever we may think of phrenology, his description, written 50 years later, is interesting as that of one who knew her well:

> The Intellect greatly predominates; . . . In the Feelings, the Animal and Moral regions are about equal, the moral being quite sufficient to keep the animal in order and in due subservience, but would not be spontaneously active. The social feelings were very active, particularly the adhesiveness. She was of a most affectionate disposition, always requiring some one to lean upon, preferring what has hitherto been considered the stronger sex to the other and more impressible. She was not fitted to stand alone.   (Bray, pp. 74–5)

Charles Hennell's wife, who had begun to translate Strauss's *Das Leben Jesu*, was happy to turn it over to Marian after the first few chapters. Published in three volumes in 1846, *The Life of Jesus* had an incalculable influence on English religious thought.[4]

Combe describes his first meeting with the Brays and Marian Evans in his Journal, 29 August 1851:

We travelled from Liverpool to Coventry by rail and found Mr. Charles Bray waiting for us at the station, and went with him on a visit to Rosehill, close to the Town. He introduced us to his wife and her sister, [Sara] . . . and to Miss Evans, the daughter of a farmer. The whole party are superior and interesting persons. Mr. Bray is a Ribbon manufacturer about 40; a Phrenologist and a convert to the Natural Laws, with an excellent intellect. . . . He is proprietor of the Coventry Herald, which he uses as the organ of the new philosophy and its applications, so far as public opinion will allow him to go.

Miss Evans is the most extraordinary person of the party. She translated Strauss's work 'Das Leben Jesu' from the German, including the Hebrew, Greek, and Latin quotations in it, without assistance; and it is said to be admirably executed. She has a very large brain, the anterior lobe is remarkable for its length, breadth, and height; the coronal region is large, the front rather predominating . . . and the portion behind the ear is rather small in the regions of Comb[ativeness], Amat[iveness], and Philopro[genitiveness]. . . . She is rather tall, near 40 apparently,[5] pale and in delicate health. She is an excellent musician. . . . We had a great deal of conversation on religion, political economy, and political events, and altogether, with the exception perhaps of Lucretia Mott,[6] she appeared to me the ablest woman whom I have seen, and in many respects she excells Lucretia. She is extremely feminine and gentle; and the great strength of her intellect combined with this quality renders her very interesting.

Three weeks later the Combes stopped again at Rosehill on their way back to Edinburgh. In his Journal, 18 September 1851, Combe wrote:

Mr. Bray shewed me a cast of his head. He has an enormous cerebellum, large lungs, and strong limbs. He is far from being fond of motion: He eats largely, takes little exercise, and is afflicted by the excessive activity of the cerebellum.

This is the base of the brain, where the animal qualities were thought to reside. In his Journal at this point Combe lapses into shorthand. For fourteen years I appealed to every expert I could find for help in reading these tantalising seven lines of shorthand. In 1977 an article in *The Times Literary Supplement* by Eric Sams, a noted English cryptanalyst, and Julian Moore,[7] impelled me to send them to Mr

Sams, and he eventually deciphered them. I am most grateful to Mr
Sams for his help, and to Mr James Ritchie, Keeper of Manuscripts at
the National Library of Scotland, for permission to reproduce them.
The passage reads:

> At twelve years of age he was seduced by his father's Cook and
> indulged extensively in illicit intercourse with women. He ab-
> stained from 18 to 22 but suffered in health. He married and his
> wife has no children. He consoled himself with another woman
> by whom he had a daughter. He adopted his child with his wife's
> consent and she now lives with him. He still keeps the mother of
> the child and has another by her. I strongly objected to his being
> cooped up and recommended to him to lower his diet and increase
> his exercise and by every means lessen the vigor of his amativeness
> and be faithful to his wife.

The entry then continues in longhand:

> He has large moral organs, with large Destructiveness. Cautious-
> ness is moderate and Concentrativeness deficient. Self Est[eem]
> and Firmness are large. His family have died of apoplexy at 56
> and he says he will die then also. He is in a fair way of realising his
> prophecy. [He died at 73.]

In transcribing the passage Mr Sams noted that the word *Cook* is
written in longhand, presumably because the equivalent is unclear.

It is easy to imagine how Bray in exhibiting his cast to Combe
would have confirmed the prominence of its Amativeness with an
account of his sex life from the age of twelve. The period of abstinence
corresponds exactly with that of his conversion to Evangelicalism,
and the 'bad habits' from which he broke away are clearly defined.
Though local legend dimly held him to be something of a 'village
Casanova',[8] the fact of his mistress and children is quite new.

The earliest mention of a child at Rosehill occurs in May 1845 in a
letter from Marian Evans to the Brays, who were at Hastings while
their house was being cleaned:

> I had a most gracious reception this morning from Baby, and
> carried her to my great fatigue to pay our respects to the Cow. The
> Baby is quite well and not at all triste on account of the absence of
> Papa and Mamma, whom she invokes very lustily and shows no
> dismay that they do not come when she does call for them. Hannah

desires me to send word that the Cow has not calved and that Mr. and Miss Bray spent Sunday at Rosehill, to Baby's great delight. The young lady's smiles were abundant this morning, interspersed however with frowns which I am afraid she is taught to think as amusing as the smiles. To me they are anything but interesting. (*Letters*, I, 194)

In editing this letter 30 years ago I was puzzled by the curiously remote tone of Marian's report to the mother of an infant still in arms. Never called anything but Baby, she must have been born in 1844 or early in 1845. Though Mrs Bray's Diary[9] notes such events as the birth of the Princess Royal and the christening of the Prince of Wales, it has no mention of Baby's birth; nor would her appointments during the year have left time for such an event. The only allusion to Baby is a laconic sentence on 27 June 1845: 'Took our child back to Hampton Station' – presumably Hampton-in-Arden, about nine miles west of Coventry, halfway to Birmingham. Apparently, after two months' trial, Baby wouldn't do.

A year later on 10 June 1846 Mrs Bray wrote even more laconically: 'Brought home Elinor'. This was Bray's second daughter. Like Baby she could have been no more than a few months old; the census return for Rosehill in March 1851 lists her as 'Ellenor Mary, adopted daughter, aged 5, scholar, born at Birmingham'.[10] On Christmas Day the Brays brought her to tea with Marian in Foleshill, and she is mentioned occasionally in the correspondence thereafter. Marian wrote one charming letter to her in 1851 when she was six, thanking her for 'the nice little bag which you and Mamma sent me', signing it 'Your affectionate Auntie Pollian' (*Letters*, I. 347–8). At ten Nelly was 'a tall young lady' whom Aunt Sara Hennell is teaching to play the piano (*Letters*, II. 265). But as she grew up, Nelly's health became frail. Despite sea air and anxious watching, she fell into a decline, and after a long illness died of pulmonary consumption on 1 March 1865 (*Letters*, IV. 179). She was nineteen. 'Surely, dear Sara', Marian wrote, 'to both you and Cara there must be a sense of having tried to the utmost to give value to that young life which was brought so close to you' (*Letters*, IV. 180). The complaisance with which Mrs Bray accepted her husband's bastards is remarkable. No word of resentment from her has ever been found. During Nelly's long illness Cara looked after her as tenderly as if she were her own, and her death was a genuine grief. Marian wrote to Cara: 'There is no such thing as consolation when we have made the lot of another our own as you did Nelly's. The anguish must be borne' (*Letters*, IV. 183).

From the beginning Marian could not have been ignorant of the paternity of Bray's children. On her long walks with the 'leaky-minded fool', as Bray calls himself, after Mr Brooke in *Middlemarch* (Bray, p. 47), he probably discussed quite openly with her his way of life under the Natural Laws. How much did her knowledge of it contribute to her understanding of human passions? The tolerance and sympathy with which she treats bastards is unusual in Victorian fiction; we find in her novels none of the hypocritical reprobation that so often condemns Dickens's adulterers to distant exile or death. Compare Mrs Dombey or Lady Dedlock with Mrs Transome. This is not the time to examine each of George Eliot's bastards or to seek their originals about Coventry. Eppie Cass and Nelly Bray are both adopted by weavers – but let us leave these tangled webs to the psychobiographers.

After their first meeting Combe's admiration for Marian Evans increased during the three years while she was editing the *Westminster Review*. They corresponded frequently about articles, and she gave much time to cutting and revising his pamphlet on criminal legislation. In October 1852 she visited the Combes in Edinburgh for ten days. Though they urged her warmly to come again in 1853 and to spend the summer of 1854 with them in Switzerland, she declined all further invitations – and went instead to Germany with George Henry Lewes. When the rumour of this scandal reached Edinburgh, Mrs Combe wrote to Cara Bray for confirmation. Marian's plan to live with Lewes had been confided only to John Chapman, who forwarded her letters, and to Bray, who may have advanced funds for her journey. Cara and Sara Hennell, who had not been told, were deeply offended. But Cara rallied loyally to Marian's defence:

> We have not heard of anything dreadful happening to Miss Evans [she replied to Mrs Combe] and therefore are quite at a loss to know what has 'astounded' your friend. She wrote to us from Weimar a few weeks ago in high health and happiness. . . . I feel quite sure we should have heard if any mishap had befallen her. (*Letters*, VIII. 119)

Not satisfied, Mr Combe wrote to inquire of Bray, whose reply was no less disingenuous. After recounting the breakup of Lewes's marriage, Bray added:

> His health required that he should travel. . . . Miss Evans has long been wanting to go abroad and Mr. Lewes offered to introduce

her to friends of his in Germany and leave her there for 12 months, which is what she wished. This is all I know and all I believe and I do not see anything very serious to disapprove in it – at least I *did* not. I see now all that may and will be said about their going together and I think it would have been much more prudent to have had others of the party. I can see how necessary it was for Lewes to travel and that he should have a friend with him and that Mrs. Lewes, with her family, could not go, but I fear it was asking too much on Miss Evans part, if she sets any store by public opinion or indeed cares for that of many of her friends. She is just the person however to disregard gossip if a friend wanted her *aid* or I think even if she could go abroad. (*Letters*, VIII. 122–3)

Still not satisfied, Combe persisted, and Bray answered with quotations from Marian's letters to him. A passage from one of them is of particular interest because the manuscript of it has never been found:

She says 'I mean this letter for you alone and I beg that you will not *quote* me either in my justification or otherwise. No one has any right to interfere with my conduct – no one is responsible for me; and I beg that you will free yourself from annoyance and enquiries by stating that I am quite too old <enough> for you to be supposed in any way answerable for me. So far as my friends or acquaintances are <concerned> inclined to occupy themselves with my affairs, I am grateful to them and sorry that they should have pain on my account, but I cannot think that their digestion will be much hindered by anything that befals a person about whom they troubled themselves very little while she lived in privacy and loneliness'. (*Letters*, VIII. 128)

This was very hard for Combe, who felt that he had troubled himself a good deal about Miss Evans. He wrote again to Bray:

We are deeply mortified and distressed; and I should like to know whether there is insanity in Miss Evans's family; for her conduct, with *her* brain, seems to me like <insanity> morbid mental aberration.

I have no right to dictate to you, but I esteem you too much not to state frankly to you my convictions. . . . 'The greatest happiness of the greatest number' principle appears to me to require that the obligations of married life should be honourably fulfilled; and an

educated woman who, in the face of the world, volunteers to live
as a wife, with a man who already has a living wife and children,
appears to me to pursue a course and to set an example calculated
only to degrade herself and her sex, if she be sane. — If you
receive her into your family circle, while present appearances are
unexplained, pray consider whether you will do justice to your
own female domestic circle, and how other ladies may feel about
going into a circle which makes no distinction between those who
act thus, and those who preserve their honour unspotted? . . .
I think that Mr. Lewes was perfectly justified in leaving his
own wife, but not in making Miss Evans his mistress. (*Letters*,
VIII. 129–30)

In his Journal Combe reread his original account of Miss Evans three
years before. In the margin of his description of her Amativeness as
'rather small', he now added in pencil: 'This was written from eye-
observation. She has gone off as mistress of Mr. Lewes, a married
man with 6 children. July 1854.' It was hard for Combe to face the
fact that 'the ablest woman whom I have seen' was living with a man
who had long ridiculed and derided the claims of phrenology –
doubly bitter because it forced him to admit that he had grossly
misread her character. For him there were limits beyond which the
Natural Laws did not apply.

Notes

This essay first appeared in *George Eliot: A Centenary Tribute*, ed. G. S. Haight
and Rosemary T. VanArsdel (London: Macmillan, 1981) pp. 1–10.

1. National Library of Scotland.
2. Charles Gibbon, *The Life of George Combe*, 2 vols (London, 1878); *The
   Dictionary of National Biography*.
3. Charles Bray, *Phases of Opinion and Experience during a Long Life: An
   Autobiography* (London, [1885]) p. 9.
4. *The George Eliot Letters*, ed. G. S. Haight, 9 vols (New Haven, Conn., and
   London, 1954–78) vol. I, pp. 172–218.
5. She was 31.
6. Lucretia Coffin Mott (1793–1880), American women's rights and anti-
   slavery reformer.
7. Eric Sams and Julian Moore, 'Cryptanalysis and Historical Research',
   The Times Literary Supplement, 4 March 1977, p. 253.

8. Ernest Simpson, Librarian of the Coventry City Libraries, to G. S. Haight, 15 June 1951.
9. Mrs Bray's Diary is found on pp. 190–[203] of her Commonplace Book in the Coventry City Libraries.
10. Public Record Office, H. O. 107.

Part Two
Contemporaries

7
The Carlyles and the Leweses

On 10 October 1851 John Chapman, who had just completed the purchase of the *Westminster Review*, called at 5 Cheyne Row to ask Carlyle to write an article on the peerage for his first number. Carlyle declined, 'being clear for silence at present'. But, as soon as Chapman had gone, he sent off a letter to Robert Browning, describing Chapman as 'really a meritorious, productive kind of man, did he well know his road in these times. . .; his intense purpose now is, To bring out a Review, Liberal in all senses, that shall charm the world. He has capital "for four years' trial," he says; an able Editor (name can't be given), and such an array of "talent" as was seldom gathered before.'[1] He was reluctant to give the name of his 'able Editor' because she was a woman – Marian Evans, who had lately come from Coventry to board at Chapman's house at 142 Strand. While he interviewed Carlyle, she was wandering up and down Cheyne Walk, passing more than once the house at number 4 where she was to die in 1880.

Marian Evans had long admired Carlyle's books. In 1841 she wrote to a schoolmate: 'He is a grand favourite of mine, and I venture to recommend to you his *Sartor Resartus*. . . . His soul is a shrine of the brightest and purest philanthropy, kindled by the live coal of gratitude and devotion to the Author of all things. I should observe that he is not "orthodox".'[2] In 1848, having herself quite abandoned orthodoxy, she sympathised heartily with Carlyle's enthusiasm for the French Revolution.[3] But by the time she came to live in London, her natural conservatism was beginning to reassert itself, and she was willing to acknowledge some truth in the hostile notice of *The Life of John Sterling* in *The Times* – though it was unfair to the book, which she had read with great pleasure, 'not for its presentation of Sterling but of Carlyle. There are racy bits of description in his best manner and exquisite touches of feeling.'[4] In 1855, reviewing a volume of selections from Carlyle's works, Miss Evans carefully distinguished his ideas from his influence:

It is an idle question to ask whether his books will be read a century hence; if they were all burnt as the grandest of Suttees on his funeral pile, it would be only like cutting down an oak after its acorns have sown a forest. For there is hardly a superior or active mind of this generation that has not been modified by Carlyle's writings; there has hardly been an English book written for the last ten or twelve years that would not have been different if Carlyle had not lived. . . . And we think few men will be found to say that this influence on the whole has not been for good.[5]

In saying that 'many of the men who have the least agreement with his opinions are those to whom the reading of *Sartor Resartus* was an epoch in the history of their minds' she was glancing at her own experience.

Though Carlyle called more than once at 142 Strand while Marian Evans was living there, I have found no record of their meeting. In November 1851 he came, 'strongly recommending Browning the poet as a writer for the Review, and saying "We shall see" about himself'.[6] It is not clear whether he spoke to her as well as to Chapman. Nor has Carlyle's letter been found which she sent to Sara Hennell as an autograph, saying, 'He is a naughty fellow to write in the Keepsake and not for us – after I wrote him the most insinuating letter, offering him three glorious subjects.'[7] Perhaps, as in other cases, she had merely drafted a letter for Chapman to copy. Her Coventry friends were sometimes regaled with stories about Carlyle. For example, when he met FitzBall one day, Carlyle asked, 'How is it I never see your name as a dramatic author now?' FitzBall replied, 'Oh' (very much through the nose) 'I'm comfortable now; *my mother's dead.*'[8]

This sort of gossip, comically rendered, probably came to her from George Henry Lewes, with whose life her own was soon to be joined. Born in 1817, he had become one of Carlyle's 'young men' perhaps as early as March 1835, for he told John Fiske that he had gone to Cheyne Row a few days after the burning of the manuscript of *The French Revolution* and 'found Mill on the sofa in paroxyms of weeping and sobbing, while Carlyle was trying to comfort him'.[9] If this account can be accepted, it seems probable that Carlyle introduced Lewes to Leigh Hunt, who lived only a few doors away in Upper Cheyne Row, for in the summer of 1835, when Lewes submitted a story called 'Mary Altonville' to *Leigh Hunt's Journal*, he had no personal acquaintance with Hunt.[10] Their warm friendship grew from a passionate interest in Shelley, whose biography Lewes was determined to write; he sought information from both Hunt and his son Thornton. A highly premature announcement of the book as 'In the Press' appeared four times in the *National Magazine* from January to April 1838.

In their parlour the Carlyles had a 'reminiscent' bust of Shelley by Marianne Hunt,[11] given to them in 1836; but Carlyle considered his poetry 'all a shriek merely',[12] the man 'a poor, thin, spasmodic, hectic, shrill and pallid being', and his revolutionary ardour the ghost of extinct, obsolete Robespierrism.[13] Carlyle's 'universal man', of course, was Goethe, whom he wanted to choose in 1840 for his Hero as Man of Letters. 'But at present', he told the audience, 'such is the general state of knowledge about Goethe, it were worse than useless to attempt speaking of him in this case. . . . Him we must leave to future times.' The man who was to do most to make Goethe known to the English-speaking world was Carlyle's eager disciple George Henry Lewes. Stirred by Carlyle to learn German, Lewes set out for Berlin in July 1838, bearing from its author a presentation copy of *Sartor Resartus* to be delivered to Varnhagen von Ense and a letter of introduction for himself.

Varnhagen, who had corresponded with Carlyle but not yet met him, was the author of a book on Goethe, whom his late wife Rahel had known and adored. He received the young man kindly and introduced him to the best literary circle in Berlin. Lewes worked hard at his German, 'reading *Faust* in the original – no easy task – and translating Goethe's *Torquato Tasso*'. He also worked sporadically at his life of Shelley, finding his old views much changed since he came to Germany and 'feeling the necessity for a deep aesthetical exposition of his poems and philosophy'. At the same time, he wrote, 'I am going regularly through Byron's works for the parallel I intend to draw between him and Shelley, but I get on slowly.' Was he perhaps haunted by Carlyle's stern injunction, 'Close thy *Byron*; open thy *Goethe*'?[14] He asked Hunt to inquire of John Stuart Mill whether an article on Carlyle – 'a general criticism of his whole works, their tendency, influence, force, and weakness, would be acceptable for the London and Westminster? as I have been preparing such a thing.'[15] Nothing came of it, however, Mill having already commissioned John Sterling's article, which appeared in the October 1839 number.

Lewes's interest in Goethe, inspired by Carlyle, grew stronger during his residence of more than a year in Berlin and Strassburg.

After a few months at home, he returned to the Continent in July 1840 and lived for six months in Vienna, where he knew Franz Liszt. The first fruit of his study was a long anonymous article, 'The Character and Works of Göthe', written in February 1842 and published a year later in the *British and Foreign Review*. There Lewes declared that Carlyle's 'fervent and eloquent Essays . . . give no definite image of the man', though, he conceded, 'they are exquisite exhortations to study, rather than information of what the student will find, or how to seek it'.[16] According to Francis Espinasse, who may betray a touch of jealousy, Carlyle thought Lewes's article 'wide of the mark'.[17] It certainly includes much with which Carlyle must have disagreed. To Lewes, Goethe was a man like Shakespeare with no dogmatic philosophy, a Spinozist in individuality, pursuing self-culture without restraint of duty. Despite some youthful exaggeration, later moderated, and with no undue humility, Lewes's eloquent defense was a preliminary sketch for his *Life and Works of Goethe* (1855), a pioneer biography.

While in London in May 1840, between his German visits, Lewes attended Carlyle's lectures *On Heroes and Hero-Worship*. In June, having abandoned all hope of securing through Hunt's intercession the family's consent to a biography, he wrote for the *Westminster Review* a long article on Shelley. In it he quoted from 'The Hero as King':

> Carlyle, speaking of Johnson, said, 'If he had been asked to be Lord Chancellor, he would have felt uneasy at the great weight to be put on his shoulders. What did he care for riding in gilt coaches from Westminster to Whitehall? . . . ' We quote from memory (out of his eloquent Lectures on 'Heroes and Hero-Worship' delivered last May).[18]

In the lecture Carlyle, defending Cromwell from the charge of ambition, wrote that a *great* man would not sell himself to falsehood 'that he might ride in gilt carriages to Whitehall. . . . What could gilt carriages do for this man?' Then, turning to Johnson for comparison, he added: 'Old Samuel Johnson, the greatest soul in England in his day, was not ambitious. "Corsica Boswell" flaunted at public shows with printed ribbons round his hat; but the great old Samuel stayed at home.'[19] Though Carlyle revised his lectures extensively for publication, this variation is probably due to Lewes's faulty memory.

John Stuart Mill, though no longer editor of the *Westminster*, read the manuscript for his 'young friend' Lewes and objected – quite rightly – to its lack of unity:

> I think you should have begun by determining whether you were writing for those who required a *vindication* of Shelley or for those who wanted a *criticism* of his poems or for those who wanted a biographic Carlylian *analysis* of him as a *man*. I doubt if it is possible to combine all these things, but I am sure at all events that the unity necessary in an essay of any kind as a work of art requires at least that one of these should be the predominant purpose & the others only incidental to it.[20]

As eventually published in April 1841 Lewes's article is still open to objection on this score. A more serious fault is the obvious imitation of Carlyle's style. In earlier days Mill himself had undergone the same temptation and had overcome it. A paper of his 'On Genius', published in W. J. Fox's *Monthly Repository* in 1832 under a pseudonym, Lewes had ferreted out, probably tipped off by Fox. Commenting on it in the same letter to Lewes, Mill wrote:

> The 'Genius' paper is no favorite with me, especially in its boyish style. It was written in the height of my Carlylism, a vice of style which I have since carefully striven to correct and as I think you should do – there is too much of it in the Shelley. I think Carlyle's costume should be left to Carlyle, whom alone it becomes and in whom it would soon become unpleasant if it were made common – and I have seen as you must have done, grievous symptoms of its being taken up by the lowest of the low.

This was a timely warning for Lewes, whose early articles frequently imitated Carlyle's worst mannerisms. For example, in defending Goethe against the charge of charlatanism, he wrote sarcastically: 'O ye poor sheep! ye Göthe-humbugged! whither have ye been straying? into what black bogs of murkiest folly have ye been floundering, led by this stolid bell-wether? Think upon your condition!'[21]

That nothing quite so bad survived in his Shelley paper Lewes probably owed to Mill's tactful hint. Yet the influence of Carlyle is apparent throughout the essay, however widely Lewes may differ from him in opinion. Presenting Shelley as one of the 'two most memorable men of this nineteenth century' (the other was Jeremy Bentham!), Lewes asks:

> Where, among his contemporaries, shall we find in so eminent a degree the qualities which Carlyle says constitute the 'original man – the hero'? In commanding intellect, in large-heartedness, but above all, in his heroic preaching and fighting for all that was to him Truth, at grievous personal cost, but with unabated energy, – he stands out as the most memorable man of his day (a day not wanting in heroism or endurance), calling forth our hero-worship. . . . Shelley arose in such an era to proclaim to the world that 'by lies and formulas it could not get on, but must take up some truth and vital energy, if it would live'.[22]

Lewes's heroes were not Carlyle's, and while Carlyle undoubtedly saw the article, it did nothing to soften his unfair opinion of Shelley. Neither did it cool the cordial regard Carlyle and his wife both showed to young Lewes. His amusing stories, told with 'first-rate mimicry', are often recalled in their letters, and though on account of his appearance they referred to him as 'the Ape', Lewes was always welcome at Cheyne Row. Carlyle admitted his diligence in compiling the *Biographical History of Philosophy*, but (according to Espinasse) grumbled at the absurdity of thinking he 'could learn anything about philosophy from that body Lewes'.[23] The biographical element of the book, which was begun in 1837 as a series of lectures at W. J. Fox's Chapel in Finsbury, may suggest the influence of Carlyle. At the end of one chapter Lewes quotes from the tribute to Fichte in Carlyle's essay on the 'State of German Literature'.[24]

As a novelist Lewes pleased neither Thomas nor Jane Carlyle. In 1848 he sent them his *Rose, Blanche, and Violet*, which Jane took with her to Addiscombe on a visit to Lady Harriet Baring. In a letter to Thomas she pronounced it 'execrable'.

> I could not have suspected even the ape of writing anything so silly. Lady H. read it all the way down, and decided it was 'too vulgar to go on with'. I myself should have also laid it aside in the first half volume if I had not felt a pitying interest in the man, that makes me read on in hope of coming to something a little better. Your marginal notes are the only real amusement I have got out of it hitherto.[25]

Espinasse gives a detailed account of Lewes's efforts to discover Carlyle's opinion of the novel.

> Carlyle had read it, but the adventures of Mesdemoiselles Rose, Blanche, and Violet were not, as chronicled by Lewes, of a kind to interest him, yet here was the author bent on discovering his opinion of it! It was amusing, at least to me, to see how Carlyle fenced with the anxious inquirer. The author could extract little more from the reluctant critic than that *Rose, Blanche, and Violet*, showed 'more breadth' than its predecessor, *Ranthorpe*. However, by way of soothing his visitor, Carlyle added that Mrs. Carlyle had taken the book with her to the country, to be read not only by herself, but by 'a very high lady', the Lady Harriet Baring, who became soon afterwards Lady Ashburton. Carlyle commenting in a depreciatory way on the amount of lovemaking in modern novels, Lewes retorted by referring to the amatory episodes in *Wilhelm Meister*. Carlyle rejoined that there was no more of that sort of thing in *Meister* than 'the flirtation which goes on in ordinary life', a very different verdict from Wordsworth's and De Quincey's. 'I would rather have written that book,' Carlyle said, 'than a cartload of others', and he went on to speak of Goethe's 'Olympian silence' and other transcendent qualities. With admirable persistence Lewes took advantage of a pause to ask if some gaming-house scenes in *Rose, Blanche, and Violet* were not to be commended. Instead of answering the question, Carlyle launched into a description of a gaming-house in Paris, to pay a visit of curiosity to which he had been taken, by the late Sir J. Emerson-Tennent, I think, and said that he remembered the faces of the players at the gaming-table so vividly that if he were a painter he could reproduce them even after that long lapse of years. Abandoning his fruitless quest, Lewes spoke of a life of Robespierre, which, as well as his life of Goethe, he had then on the anvil. Seeing that I was surprised at the conjunction of two such tasks, Carlyle said genially: 'Lewes is not afraid of any amount of work.'[26]

Espinasse was then a comparatively new acquaintance of Carlyle, and the edge of ridicule discernible in this account may be attributed to his annoyance at having been interrupted as he was preparing to tell Carlyle about the Chartist gathering that day on Kennington Common. There is no trace of dislike in the letter Jane wrote about him to her cousin Jeannie Welsh:

But what I took up my pen to tell you is that little Lewes – author of Rose Blanche &c., &c. is going to lecture in Liverpool – one of these days and I have given him my card for you – and you *must* try and introduce him to my Uncle; for he is the most amusing little fellow in the whole world – if you only look over his un-paralleled *impudence* which is not impudence at all but man-of-genius-*bonhomie* – either you or Helen saw him here – and his charming little wife. He is [the] best mimic in the world and full of famous stories, and no spleen or envy, or *bad* thing in him, so see that you receive him with open arms in spite of his immense ugliness.[27]

The 'charming little wife', Agnes Jervis, whom Lewes married in 1841, had borne him four sons, the youngest of whom was less than a year old when Mrs Carlyle wrote this description. In addition to doing scores of articles, writing plays, acting and lecturing, Lewes was travelling about the country to gather support for the *Leader*, the radical weekly which he and Thornton Hunt were to edit jointly. Carlyle thought highly of Lewes's part of it and called him 'the Prince of Journalists'.[28] During the few weeks he was away from home at this time Mrs Carlyle's keen eye detected a distinct change. A postscript to a note to John Forster of 20 March 1849 added: 'The Leweses were here last night. "*Great* God"! as *you* say. Poor Lewes looks to me going rapidly to you know whom.'[29] Writing again to Jeannie Welsh, she said:

Little Lewes came the other night with his little wife – speaking gratefully of you all – but it is Julia Paulet who has taken his soul captive ! ! he raves about her 'dark luxurious eyes' and 'smooth firm flesh' – ! his wife asked 'how did he know? had he been feeling it?' In fact his wife seems rather *contemptuous* of his rap-tures about all the women he has fallen in love with on this journey, which is the best way of taking the thing – when one can.

I used to think these Leweses a perfect pair of love-birds always cuddling together on the same perch – to speak figuratively – but the female love-bird appears to have hopped off to some distance and to be now taking a somewhat critical view of her little shaggy mate!

In the most honey-marriages one has only to *wait* – it is all a question of time – sooner or later 'reason resumes its empire' as the phrase is.[30]

In this marriage she had not long to wait. Within a year, on 16 April 1850, soon after the *Leader* began publication, Agnes gave birth to a fifth son, whose father was Lewes's friend and co-editor Thornton Hunt. Unwilling to stigmatise the child as illegitimate, Lewes registered him as his own, giving him, with perhaps a sardonic glance at the bastard in *King Lear*, the name of Edmund. By condoning the adultery, he precluded all possibility of asking for a divorce.

Agnes's relation with Hunt was no passing affair. In October 1851 she bore him a daughter, Rose Agnes, and in October 1853 another daughter, Ethel Isabella Lewes, both within weeks of the birth of two of Hunt's ten children by his own wife. There was a marked contrast between the rosy, blond Lewes boys and the other children, all of whom showed the dark complexion of the Hunts – 'a trace of the African, I believe', Carlyle remarked.[31] He referred to Thornton as a 'little brown-skinned man'.[32] Carlyle had at this time no high opinion of the Hunts, once his feckless neighbours in Cheyne Row. 'They are a generation of fools', he said.[33] But the young George Leweses were different. Late in life he spoke of them to Allingham; he noted that

> Lewes and *his wife* lived in Carlyle's memory in the magic light that surrounded all those who were friends or *friendlies* of the house in Cheyne Row in Mrs. Carlyle's time. 'They used to come down,' he often said, 'of an evening to us through the lanes from Kensington, and were as merry as two birds.'
>
> 'She was a bright creature,' he said one day, 'and far cleverer than – .' Here he suddenly paused and said no more, a most unusual thing with him; but I could guess the course of his thoughts.[34]

They led, of course, to the editor of the *Westminster Review*, 'the strong minded woman' Marian Evans. As soon as it was known that she and Lewes had gone to Germany together, gossips were accusing her of having 'run away' with Agnes's husband. Actually the marriage had collapsed long before Marian ever saw him, and Agnes, who had no intention of giving up Thornton Hunt, expressed the wish that George 'could marry Miss Evans'.[35]

At Weimar, where they were living while Lewes worked at his biography of Goethe, Marian noted in her Journal, 11 October 1854: 'A painful letter from London caused us both a bad night.' It came from Carlyle, who had been driven by the gossip-mongers to enquire about the scandal. In the morning Lewes wrote to him, 'explaining his position'. Neither letter has been found; but on the envelope containing Lewes's (now in the Parrish Collection at Princeton), postmarked 12 October 1854, Carlyle wrote: 'G. H. Lewes and "Strong minded Woman"'. His reply, described by Marian as 'a letter of noble sympathy', is also missing, and we can only infer its contents from the tone of Lewes's answer.

Weimar Thursday night [19 October 1854].

My dear Carlyle

Your letter has been with me half an hour and I have not yet recovered the shock – delightful shock – it gave me. One must have been, like me, long misjudged and harshly judged without power of explanation, to understand the feelings which such a letter creates. My heart yearned towards you as I read it. It has given me new courage. I sat at your feet when my mind was first awakening; I have honoured and loved you ever since both as teacher and friend, and *now* to find that you judge me rightly, and are not estranged by what has estranged so many from me, gives me strength to bear what yet must be borne!

So much in gratitude. Now for justice: On my *word of honor* there is no foundation for the scandal as it runs. My separation was in nowise caused by the lady named, nor by any other lady. It has always been imminent, always *threatened*, but never before carried out, because of those assailing pangs of anticipation which would not let me carry resolution into fact. At various epochs I have explicitly declared that unless a change took place I would not hold out. At last – and this more because some circumstances into which I do [not] wish to enter, happened to occur at a time when I was hypochondriacal and hopeless about myself, fearing lest a chronic disease would disable me from undertaking such responsibilities as those previously borne – at last, I say, the crisis came. But believe me the lady named had not only *nothing* whatever to do with it but was, I solemnly declare, ignorant of my own state of mind on the subject. She knew the previous state of things, as indeed others knew it, but that is all.

Then as to the 'letter to Miss Martineau' – not only is she totally incapable of anything she justly considers so foolish and unworthy; but in fact she has *not* written to Miss Martineau at all – has had no communication with her for twelve months – has sent no message to her, or any one else – in short this letter is a pure, or impure, fabrication – the letter, the purport, the language, all fiction. And I shall feel doubly bound to you if you will, on all occasions, clear the lady from such unworthy aspersions and not allow her to be placed in so totally false a position.

Thus far I give you a solemn denial of the scandal. Where gossip affects a point of honor or principle I feel bound to meet it with denial; on all private matters my only answer is *silence*.

Marshall, who has been absent since my arrival until within the last few days, I find a very agreeable friendly fellow, whom I should have been glad to see earlier. However there has been no end of kindness shown me here, and I have gained such materials for Goethe as could only have been gained *here*. I go to Berlin shortly, and think of wintering there, and quietly finishing my work.

Wilson seems to pine for London, although they do everything they can to make Weimar agreeable to him. Eckermann is very feeble, and his intellect going fast.

With kindest regards to your wife, Believe me, dear Carlyle,

Your very grateful
G. H. Lewes.[36]

At the end of this letter Carlyle has added:

Alas, alas! – I had (at his request) approved unequivocally of parting *such a marriage*; and advised to contradict, if he could, on his word of honour, the bad rumours circulating about a certain 'strong minded woman' and him. He assures me, on his word of honour, the strong minded did not *write* etc.: as well assure me her stockings are both of one colour; that is a very insignificant point! – No answer to this second letter.

Writing to his brother John, Carlyle was more explicit:

Lewes, *Ape* Lewes, or 'hairy Lewes', as we called him, has not only gone to Weimar, but is understood to have a 'strong minded woman' with him there, and has certainly cast away his Wife here, – who indeed deserved it of him, having openly produced those dirty sooty skinned children which have Th[ornto]n Hunt for father, and being ready with a *third*; Lewes to pay the whole account, even the money part of it! – Such are our sublime George-Sand Philosophies teaching by experience. Everlasting peace to them and theirs, – in the Cesspool, which is their home.[37]

If, as this letter suggests, Agnes was pregnant in 1854, the child must have been stillborn, for it was not registered. Carlyle apparently believed that she was then the mother of two, and not three, children by Hunt. Their fourth, Mildred Jane Lewes, was born 21 May 1857, and the liaison continued some years more.

After Lewes returned to London in March 1855, he consulted Carlyle about the *Goethe*, which was ready for the printer in June. Carlyle read some of the first proofs while the book was in the press and wrote Lewes a remarkably interesting letter about it:

Chelsea, 7 August 1855

Dear Lewes, –

I go into Suffolk tomorrow, and am likely to be wandering about for some time; so that I find it will only be a bother to you, and a delay *without* advantage, to shoot those Proofs after me in my erratic course. I found it an amazing thing to read them in the evening, under the cloud of a quiet pipe in the Garden here: I had, as it were, *nothing* to suggest; and felt that my remarks, had they even been of value, came too late.

The Book goes on rapidly (Printer and all), and promises to be a very good bit of Biography; far, far beyond the kind of stuff that usually bears that name in this country and in others. – I desiderate chiefly a little change of *level* now and then; that you could sit upon some height, and shew us rapidly the contours of the region we are got into, from time to time, – well abhorring to be drowned in details as Viehof and Co. are, or to swim about (not quite drowned, but drowning) in endless lakes of small matters which have become 'great' only by being much talked about by fools for the time being.

You missed the *Malefactor's scull* that was on one of the steeples of Frankfort; no great matter. I found out, the other year, *who* the proprietor had been (a foolish *radical* about 1600 or so); but have already almost forgotten again, a proof there was not much for you in the story of him.

Slightly more important for you was another thing I remembered in the reading over of the Proofs, but did not then see how you were to get in: the 'Visitation of Wetzlar', through *Overhauling* (with an eye to repair) of that 'German Court of Chancery', which had been ordered by the Diet, and was just then *beginning*, about the time Goethe went. That was thought a great chime for a young lawyer, – to witness the very *dissection* of Themis. It came as other 'Visitations' had done, to *nothing*. If you make an Appendix, there might be some notice taken of this –, though whither to go for summary information I cannot at this moment direct you. My Pfeffel's Abrégé (in Brit. Mus.) which has an Index, could let it lie altogether! – Best speed to you, dear Lewes.

Yours always truly
T. Carlyle[38]

The Life and Works of Goethe: with Sketches of His Age and Contemporaries, from Published and Unpublished Sources, to give the book its full title, was published 30 October 1855, dedicated in all sincerity to the man who had inspired it: 'To Thomas Carlyle, who first taught England to appreciate Goethe, this work is inscribed, as a memorial of gratitude for intellectual guidance, and of esteem for rare and noble qualities.' Here is Carlyle's acknowledgement:

Chelsea, 3 November 1855

Dear Lewes,

I am sorry to hear you still complain of health; bad health is a very miserable adjunct to one's burden, tho' not an uncommon one to poor wretches of this craft! *Festina lentè*: don't work *too much* (which proves always *too little* by and by): that is the one way of procuring some abatement, if abolition of the misery is not possible.

I know your clean finger in *The Leader* weekly as heretofore; one of the few writing fingers of this epoch which are not dog's paws, or cloven hoofs of mere human swine. Pah! –

Furthermore I got the *Goethe* the other night, almost at the same time with your Note. Every night since, in my reading hours, I am dashing athwart it in every direction; *truanting*; for I won't wait a time to read the work with such deliberation as I well see it deserves. My conviction is, we have here got an excellent Biography, – altogether transcendently so, as Biographies are done in this country. Candid, well-informed, clear, free-flowing, it will certainly throw a large flood of light over Goethe's life, with many German things which multitudes in England have been curious about, to little purpose, for a long while. It ought to have a large circulation, if one can predict or anticipate in regard to such matters. On the whole, I say *Euge*, and that heartily, – tho' dissenting here and there. I ought also to be thankful, and am, for the fine manful words you have seen good to say about my poor self: good words go about too, as well as evil; – and all words go to nothing except they be the copies of things:

> Denn geschwätzig sind die Zeiten,
> Und sie sind auch wieder *stumm*.

Ach Gott ja, most dumb indeed; – and we read with pain in M. Thiers and the like, *femme alors célèbre*, homme alors etc.

I returned from my wanderings, which never went very wide, some three or four weeks ago; and am here in my garret, again, up to the chin in Brandenburg *marine-stores*; uncertain whether I shall not sink dead, and be buried under them, one day; but struggling to hope not.

Once more, *Well-done*, and thanks; and let me see you soon.

Yours always truly
T. Carlyle[39]

To his brother John, Carlyle wrote:

I would at once send you *Lewes's Goethe*, tho' I know not whether so much weight (probably 4 lbs. or so) were worth carrying so far: but Tait has it on loan; . . . so that we must wait till his turn is past. The Book is decidedly good as such Books go, but by no means very interesting if you have a strict taste in Books.[40]

When all the correspondence is collected, it will be possible to determine Carlyle's real opinion of the *Goethe* more positively. Moncure Conway is the source of a story that early in 1878, when Bayard Taylor told Carlyle he was gathering materials for a life, Carlyle said: 'But are there not already Lives of Goethe? There is Lewes's *Life of Goethe*. What fault have you to find with that?' The tone seemed to suggest that Lewes had exhausted the subject. Taylor 'began pointing out errors here and there in the biography', and Carlyle interrupted him 'with a ringing laugh' and cried: 'I couldn't read it through.'[41] No such disparaging remarks are recorded earlier. Carlyle's relations with Lewes after publication of the book were cordial. A letter to Lewes of 7 December 1857, discussing the price offered by Tauchnitz for reprinting the first two volumes of *Frederick the Great* in Germany, ended:

> I have had such a 14 months as was never appointed me before in this world, – sorrow, darkness and disgust, my daily companions; and no outlook visible except getting a detestable business turned off, or else being driven mad by it. – In a three months more, I hope to be at large again, and capable of seeing those I like.[42]

Quoting the first of these sentences in a letter to Sara Hennell, Marian wrote:

> That is his exaggerated way of speaking, and writing is always painful to him; but he has been specially tormented by the short-comings of German commentators and book-makers, on whom he has depended as authorities. Do you know he is 62! I fear this will be his last book.[43]

Her information must have been supplied in part by Lewes, who called occasionally at Cheyne Row, alone or with friends to intro-duce to the Carlyles – Bodenstedt, W. G. Clark and Anthony Trollope, for example. Marian Evans, now living at Richmond and calling herself Mrs Lewes, was not among them. Soon after she and Lewes 'took up with each other', William Allingham reported, Carlyle on one of his daily rides called and 'made her acquaintance. My im-pression is that they met very few times altogether, and that Carlyle went no further than tolerant civility, and even so far against the grain.'[44]

It was probably at Lewes's suggestion that, when *Scenes of Clerical Life* was issued in 1858, reprinted from *Blackwood's*, Mrs Carlyle's name was on the list of nine persons to receive copies of it 'From the Author'. A few days later she sent the unknown George Eliot the following letter:

5 Cheyne Row Chelsea
21st January /58.

Dear Sir,

I have to thank you for a surprise, a pleasure, and a – *consola-tion*(!) all in one Book! and I *do* thank you most sincerely. I cannot divine what inspired the good thought to send *me* your Book; since (if the name on the Title Page be your real name) it could not have been personal regard; there has never been a *George Eliot* among my friends or acquaintance. But neither I am sure could *you* divine the circumstances under which I should read the Book, and the particular benefit it should confer on me! I read it – at least the first volume – during one of the most (physically) wretched nights of my life; sitting up in bed, unable to get a wink of sleep for fever and sore throat; and it helped me through that dreary night, as well – better than the most sympathetic helpful friend watching by my bedside could have done!

You will believe that the book needed to be something more than a 'new novel' for me; that I *could*, at my years, and after so much reading, read it in positive torment, and be beguiled by it of the torment! that it needed to be the one sort of Book, however named, that still takes hold of me, and that grows rarer every year – a *human* book – written out of the heart of a live man, not merely out of the brain of an author – full of tenderness and pathos without a scrap of sentimentality, of sense without dogmatism, of earnestness without twaddle – a book that makes one *feel friends*, at once and for always, with the man or woman who wrote it!

In guessing at why you gave me this good gift, I have thought amongst other things: 'Oh, perhaps it was a delicate way of presenting the *novel* to my Husband, he being head and ears in *History*.' If that was it, I compliment you on your *tact*! for my Husband is much lik[e]lier to read the *Scenes* on *my* responsibility than on a venture of his own – though, as a general rule, never opening a novel, he has engaged to read this one, whenever he has some leisure from his present task.

A severe Influenza, which fell on me the same day I had the windfall of the book, and from which I am but just *beginning* to recover, must excuse the tardiness of my acknowledgements.

I hope to know someday if the person I am addressing bears any resemblance, in external things to the Idea I have conceived of him in my mind – a man of middle age, with a wife from whom he has got those beautiful *feminine* touches in his book, a good many children, and a dog that he has as much fondness for as I have for my little Nero! for the rest, not just a clergyman, but Brother or first cousin to a clergyman! – How ridiculous all this *may* read, beside the reality!

Anyhow, I honestly confess I am very curious about you, and look forward with what Mr. Carlyle would call 'a good, healthy,

genuine desire' to shaking hands with you someday. In the meanwhile I remain your obliged

Jane W. Carlyle.[45]

The delicious irony of Jane's *'feeling friends'* with the 'strong
minded woman' was surely not lost on Marian Evans. Her pseudonym was still intact in February 1859, when a copy of *Adam Bede*
arrived at Cheyne Row, inscribed again by the publisher's clerk:
'Mrs. Thomas Carlyle from the Author'.[46] It brought what she called
in her Journal a 'letter of warm acknowledgement':

5 Cheyne Row Chelsea | 20th February /59.

Dear Sir
     I must again offer you my heartiest thanks. Since I received
your *Scenes of Clerical Life* nothing has fallen from the skies to me
so welcome as *Adam Bede, all to myself,* 'from the author'.
     My Husband had just read an advertisement of it aloud to me,
adding; *'Scenes of Clerical Life? That* was *your* Book wasn't it?' {The
'your' being in the sense not of possession but predilection} 'Yes,'
I had said, 'and I am so glad that he has written another! *Will* he
send me this one, I wonder?' – thereby bringing on myself an
utterly disregarded admonition about 'the tendency of the Female
Mind to run into unreasonable expectations'; when up rattled the
Parcel Delivery cart, and, a startling double-rap having transacted
itself, a Book-parcel was brought me. 'There it is!' I said, with a
little air of injured innocence triumphant! – 'There is *what*, my
Dear?' – 'Why, *Adam Bede* to be sure!' – 'How do you know?' {I
had not yet opened the parcel} 'By *divination.*' – 'Oh! – Well! – I
hope you also *divine* that *Adam Bede* will justify your enthusiasm
now you have got it!' – 'As to *that*' {snappishly} 'I <don't> needn't
have recourse to divination, only to natural logic!' – Now; if it had
turned out *not Adam Bede* after all; where *was* my 'diminished head'
going to have hidden itself? – But Fortune favours the Brave! I
had foretold aright, on both points! The Book was actually *Adam
Bede*, and *Adam Bede* 'justified my enthusiasm'; to say the least!
     Oh yes! It was as good as *going into the country for one's health,*
the reading of that Book was! – Like a visit to Scotland *minus* the
fatigues of the long journey, and the grief of seeing friends grown
old, and Places that knew me knowing me no more! I could fancy

in reading it, to be seeing and hearing once again a crystal-clear, musical, Scotch stream, such as I long to lie down beside and – *cry* at (!) for gladness and sadness; after long stifling sojourn in the South; where there [is] no *water* but what is stagnant or muddy!

In truth, it is a beautiful most *human* Book! Every *Dog* in it, not to say every man woman and child in it, is brought home to one's 'business and bosom', an individual fellow-creature! I found myself in charity with the whole human race when I laid it down – the *canine* race I had *always* appreciated – 'not wisely but too well!' – the *human*, however, – Ach! – *that* has troubled me – as badly at times as 'twenty gallons of milk on one's mind'! For the rest; why you are so good to *me* is still a *mystery*, with every appearance of remaining so! Yet have I lavished more childish conjecture on it than on anything since I *was* a child, and got mistified about – a *door* (!) in our dining-room. What *did* that door open into? Why had I never seen it opened? Standing before it, 'as in presence of the Infinite', I pictured to myself glorious possibilities on the other side, and also horrible ones! I spun long romances about it in my little absurd head! I never *told* how that door had taken hold of me, for I *'thought shame'*; it was a curiosity too sacred for speech! But I lay in wait to catch it open some day; and then I somehow – forgot all about it! – till long after (a year or so) that the recollection of my door-worship occurred to me 'quite promiscuously', and in the same instant, the whole fact as to the door smote me, like a slap on the face! It was a door into – *nothing*! Make-believe! *There* for uniformity! Behind it was bare lath and plaster; behind *that* the Drawingroom with its familiar tables and chairs! Dispelled illusion No. 1! and epitome 'of *much*!' {as Mr. Carlyle might say}

Perhaps *could* I penetrate my little mystery of the present date; I should arrive at the same sort of lath-and-plaster results! and so – I give it up; just 'taking', gratefully and gladly, 'the good the gods {under the name of George Elliot} have provided me'.

Now, Heaven knows if such a long letter to read be not illustrating for *you* also 'the tendency of the female mind to run into unreasonable expectations'! But just consider! Is it possible that, with my opportunities, I should not know perfectly well, what a 'distinguish-author' *does* with letters of compliment *that bore him*; either by their length or their stupidity? He lights his pipe with them or he makes them into spills; or he crushes them into a ball, and pitches them in the fire or waste-paper basket; does anything with them *except read them!* So I needn't take fright about having *bored* you; since, long before it came to that, I should have, or shall have been slit up into spills, or done good service in lighting your pipe! It is lawful for *Clergymen* to smoke, I hope, – for their own sakes? The newspaper critics have decided you are a Clergyman, but I don't believe it the least in the world. You understand the duties and uses of a Clergyman too well, for *being* one! An old Lord, who did not know my Husband, came up to him once at a Public meeting where he had been summoned to give his 'views' {not *having* any} on the 'Distressed Needle Women', and asked; 'pray Sir, may I inquire, are *you* a Stock-Broker?' – 'A Stock-Broker! certainly not!' – 'Humph! Well I thought you *must* be a Stock-Broker! because, Sir, you go to the root of the matter.' – If that be the signal of a Stock-Broker I should say you must certainly be a *Stock-Broker*, and must certainly *not* be a *Clergyman*!

Respectfully and affectionately yours, whatever you be,

Jane W. Carlyle.[47]

In forwarding it to Blackwood George Eliot wrote:

Mrs. Carlyle's ardent letter will interest and amuse you. I reckon it among my best triumphs that she found herself 'in charity with the whole human race' when she laid the book down. I want the philosopher himself to read it because the *pre*-philosophic period – the childhood and poetry of his life – lay among the furrowed fields and pious peasantry. If he *could* be urged to read a novel! I should like, if possible, to give him the same sort of pleasure he has given me in the early chapters of *Sartor*, where he describes little Diogenes eating his porridge on the wall in sight of the sunset, and gaining deep wisdom from the contemplation of the pigs and other 'higher animals' of Entepfuhl.

Your critic was *not* unjustly severe [on] the Mirage Philosophy – and I confess the 'Life of Frederic' was a painful book to me in many respects; and yet I shrink, perhaps superstitiously, from any written or spoken word which is as strong as my inward criticism.

A postscript added:

I have reopened my letter to ask you if you will oblige me by writing a line to Mrs. Carlyle for me. I don't like to leave her second letter (she wrote a very kind one about the C.S.) without any sort of notice. Will you tell her that the sort of effect she declares herself to have felt from 'Adam Bede' is just what I desire to produce – gentle thoughts and happy remembrances; and I thank her heartily for telling me so warmly and generously what she has felt. That is not a pretty message – revise it for me, pray, for I am weary and ailing and thinking of a sister who is slowly dying.[48]

Annie Thackeray, calling on Mrs Carlyle some weeks later, found her

speaking enthusiastically of *Adam Bede*. She has written some of her enthusiasm off to George Eliot and had grateful messages in reply. Mr. Carlyle quite declines reading the book, and when Mrs. Carlyle hoped it might be sent to her, he said, 'What should George Eliot send it to you for?' 'Why shouldn't he, as he sent me his first book?' says she. 'You are just like all weemen,' (Mr. Carlyle always calls them weemen). 'You are always forming unreasonable expectations,' growls he, and at that moment ring at the bell and in comes the maid with a brown paper parcel containing the book![49]

In spite of Carlyle's disclaimer, *Adam Bede* was one of George Eliot's novels that he read. More than twenty years later he told William Allingham: 'I found out in the first two pages that it was a woman's writing – she supposed that in making a door, you last of all put in the *panels*!' William Allingham adds: 'I think this comment (perhaps not well-grounded) was the only one I ever heard him make on George Eliot or her works!'[50] His *ex post facto* opinion should be weighed against Blackwood's account of how his manager George Simpson took a set of the sheets of *Adam Bede* home to his brother, a cabinet-maker in Edinburgh, who read them with great admiration, and maintained that 'the writer must have been bred to the business or at all events passed a great deal of time in the workshop listening to the men'.[51] Carlyle told John Churton Collins that 'the best thing she ever wrote was, in his opinion, her article on Young in the *Westminster Review*. He had, he said, come across *Middlemarch* at a friend's house and 'found it neither amusing nor instructive, but just dull'.[52]

Jane's admiration of the books was quite genuine. Under other circumstances she would probably have enjoyed knowing their 'strong minded' author. But, as Queen Caroline remarked to the Duke of Argyle when Jeanie Deans made her unfortunate allusion to the Seventh Commandment, 'The Scotch are a rigidly moral people'. Thomas Carlyle would never in the Leweses' case overlook the impediment to their union. He would more readily have excused the life of George Sand, about whom (he later confessed to Espinasse) there was 'something Goethian'.[53] Gavan Duffy reports a conversation linking the two Georges:

> Mrs. Carlyle, who was present, said we had small right to throw the first stone at George Sand, though she had been caught in the same predicament as the woman of old, if we considered what sort of literary ladies might be found in London at present. When one was first told that the strong woman of the *Westminster Review* had gone off with a man whom we all knew, it was as startling an announcement as if one heard that a woman of your acquaintance had gone off with the strong man at Astley's; but that the partners in this adventure had set up as moralists was a graver surprise. To renounce George Sand as a teacher of morals was right enough, but it was scarcely consistent with making so much of our own George in that capacity. A marvellous teacher of morals, surely, and still more marvellous in the other character, for which nature had not provided her with the outfit supposed to be essential.
>
> The gallant, I said, was as badly equipped for an Adonis, and conqueror of hearts. Yes, Carlyle replied, he was certainly the ugliest little fellow you could anywhere meet, but he was lively and pleasant. In this final adventure it must be admitted he had escaped from worse, and might even be said to have ranged himself. He had originally married a bright little woman, daughter of Swinfen Jervis, a disreputable Welsh member; but every one knew how that adventure had turned out. Miss Evans advised him to quit a household which had broken bounds in every direction. His proceeding was not to be applauded, but it could scarcely be said that he had gone from bad to worse.[54]

Though he would defend Lewes to this extent, Carlyle would allow no intimacy with George Eliot.

I cannot explain Jane's remarks in a letter to Carlyle of 20 August 1860 about engaging a servant, 'who is really promising (the woman Miss Evans wanted to have)'.[55] During her search Jane had gone twice to Richmond, where the Leweses were then living, but there is no indication that the ladies met. On 26 July 1861, however, going to the Princess's Theatre to see Fechter as Hamlet, Jane wrote: '[I] found myself between Lewes and Miss Evans! – by Destiny and *not* by my own Deserving. At least Destiny in the shape of Frederick Chapman who arranged the thing. Poor Soul! there never was a more absurd miscalculation than *her* constituting herself an improper *woman*. She looks Propriety personified! Oh so *slow!*'[56] To other correspondents – Mrs Oliphant, for example – Jane declared that Miss Evans 'has mistaken her role – that nature intended her to be the properest of women, and that her present equivocal position is the most extraordinary blunder and contradiction possible'.[57] If during the intervals of *Hamlet* Jane Carlyle was able to voice her admiration of those 'most *human* Books', which had made her '*feel friends*, at once and for always' with their author, no record of the conversation has been preserved. It would be strange if the attraction felt for George Eliot by so many intellectual women had failed to touch Jane Carlyle in this accidental encounter. In 1866, hardly a week before she died, Jane wrote to Thomas about Lady Lothian, who wanted her 'to "come some day before luncheon, and then we could go somewhere." To Miss Evans is where we should go still, if you would let us.'[58] I find no reference in the Lewes papers to either Lady Lothian or Mrs Carlyle as visitors, and should be tempted to suspect a different 'Miss Evans' had Carlyle not scornfully glossed the name: 'Famous "George Eliot" (or some such pseudonym)'. A month before his death he said to Browning: 'What a world of pity she should come up to London and fall in with *anti-Christ* Chapman and his set.'[59] Though his hostility to her was unrelenting to the end, George Eliot always spoke charitably of Carlyle. When Madame Bodichon reported one of his outrageous remarks, she wrote: 'That speech of Carlyle's, which sounds so odious, must, I think, have been provoked by something in the *manner* of the statement to which it came as an answer – else it would hurt me very much that he should have uttered it.'[60]

As Carlyle's eightieth birthday approached, a group of his friends proposed a tribute to him. Boehm was commissioned to cut a medallion portrait, which was struck in gold for Carlyle, in bronze for the subscribers. David Masson and John Morley collected 119 signatures of friends and admirers to be appended to an address they had composed. Masson sent two of the programmes to Lewes for signature. 'A most felicitous idea!' he replied. 'Repeats his own tribute to Goethe',[61] alluding to the carved seal that 'Fifteen Eng-

1875

lishmen' – Carlyle among them – had sent to Goethe on *his* eightieth.
Lewes signed one programme and returned it. When Masson in-
quired about George Eliot's, he wrote that she 'was very desirous to
pay her tribute, but did not suggest it lest women should have been
excluded. Herewith her signature!' Then he added a postscript: 'I
find she has written her signature so badly that I will ask you to send
another prospectus on which she may improve!'[62] A few days later
Lewes wrote again:

> Madonna is distressed and 'can't think' what you will think of her
> stupidity and carelessness when you hear that she has blurred
> and spoiled the second programme you sent for signature. En-
> closed is a clean one on a piece of paper. If that won't do, but if it
> must be on the programme, forgive the trouble, and send a third!
> But I suppose this will do as well?[63]

It did. All the signatures were clipped out and mounted in alphabeti-
cal order on a single sheet beneath the engrossed address, which can
be seen at Ecclefechan. 'Shall we present the memorial in person?'
Lewes asked. Perhaps the prospect of seeing his old friend accounts
for his rereading *Heroes and Hero-Worship* at this time; and her sense
of Carlyle's hostile feeling may account for George Eliot's agitation
in signing the memorial. It is unlikely that she would have attended
the presentation in any case. When the birthday came round, there
was snow and fog so intense that they did not even venture out to
the concert.

Carlyle's opinion of George Eliot cropped out when he was collecting and arranging his wife's letters after her death in 1866:

> As to 'talent', epistolary and other, these *Letters*, I perceive, equal
> and surpass whatever of best I know to exist in that kind; for
> 'talent', 'genius', or whatever we may call it, what an evidence, if
> my little woman needed that to me! Not all the *Sands* and *Eliots*
> and babbling *cohue* of 'celebrated scribbling women' that have
> strutted over the world, in my time, could, it seems to me, if all
> boiled down and distilled to essence, make one such woman.[64]

But the object of his scorn still held the generous view of Carlyle
given in her article in the *Leader*:

> When he is saying the very opposite of what we think, he says it
> so finely, with so hearty conviction – he makes the object about

which we differ stand out in such grand relief under the clear light of his strong and honest intellect – he appeals so constantly to our sense of the manly and the truthful – that we are obliged to say 'Hear! hear!' to the writer before we can give the decorous 'Oh! oh!' to his opinions.[65]

Notes

This essay first appeared in *Carlyle and his Contemporaries: Essays in Honor of Charles Richard Sanders*, ed. John Clubbe (Durham, N.C.: Duke University Press, 1976) pp. 181–204.

1. Gordon S. Haight, *George Eliot and John Chapman*, 2nd edn (New Haven, Conn., 1969) pp. 41–2.
2. *The George Eliot Letters*, ed. Gordon S. Haight, 7 vols (New Haven, Conn., and London, 1954–5) vol. I, pp. 122–3.
3. Ibid., vol. I, pp. 252–3.
4. Ibid., vol. I, pp. 372. See also her review of Carlyle's *Sterling* in *Essays of George Eliot*, ed. Thomas Pinney (New York and London, 1963) pp. 46–51.
5. *Leader*, vol. 6 (27 October 1855) p. 1034; reptd in *Essays of George Eliot*, pp. 213–15.
6. *The George Eliot Letters*, vol. I, p. 376.
7. Ibid., vol. I, p. 376.
8. Ibid., vol. II, p. 139.
9. *The Letters of John Fiske*, ed. Ethel Fiske Fisk (New York, 1940) p. 300.
10. George Henry Lewes to Leigh Hunt, 2 October 1835; MS: British Museum, Add. Mss. 29, 755.143.
11. Newman Ivey White, *Shelley*, 2 vols (New York, 1940) vol. II, p. 521; Charles Richard Sanders, *The Correspondence and Friendship of Thomas Carlyle and Leigh Hunt* (Manchester, 1963) p. 44, and 'Carlyle, Poetry, and the Music of Humanity', *Western Humanities Review*, vol. 16 (Winter 1962) p. 63.
12. *William Allingham: A Diary*, ed. H. Allingham and D. Radford (London, 1907) p. 242.
13. Alexander Carlyle (ed.), *Letters of Thomas Carlyle* (London, 1923) p. 292.
14. Thomas Carlyle, *Sartor Resartus*, ed. C. F. Harrold (New York, 1937) p. 192.
15. G. H. Lewes to Leigh Hunt, 15 November 1838; MS: British Museum, Add. Mss. 29, 755.182.
16. [G. H. Lewes], 'The Character and Works of Göthe', *British and Foreign Review*, vol. 14 (March 1843) p. 80.
17. Francis Espinasse, *Literary Recollections and Sketches* (London, 1893) p. 282.
18. *Westminster Review*, vol. 35 (April 1841) pp. 303–4, at p. 317.

19. Thomas Carlyle, 'The Hero as King', in *Works*, ed. H. D. Traill, 30 vols (London, 1896–9) vol. v, pp. 223, 223–4.
20. *The Earlier Letters of John Stuart Mill, 1812–1848*, ed. Francis E. Mineka, 2 vols (Toronto, 1963) vol. ii, p. 449. For Lewes's early collection of Mill's articles, see Geoffrey Tillotson, 'A Mill–Lewes Item', *Mill Newsletter*, vol. 5 (1969) pp. 17–18.
21. [G. H. Lewes], 'The Character and Works of Göthe', *British and Foreign Review*, vol. 14 (March 1843) p. 78.
22. *Westminster Review*, vol. 35 (April 1841) p. 316.
23. Espinasse, *Literary Recollections*, p. 282.
24. G. H. Lewes, *A Biographical History of Philosophy*, 4 vols (London, 1845–6), vol. iv, p. 154, quoting *Edinburgh Review*, vol. 46 (October 1827) p. 344.
25. *Letters and Memorials of Jane Welsh Carlyle*, ed. J. A. Froude, 3 vols (London, 1883) vol. ii, p. 34.
26. Espinasse, *Literary Recollections*, pp. 279–80.
27. [5 February 1849], in *Jane Welsh Carlyle: Letters to Her Family*, ed. Leonard Huxley (London, 1924) pp. 319–20.
28. Espinasse, *Literary Recollections*, p. 282.
29. [20 March 1849]; MS: National Library of Scotland, 604.279.
30. [4 April 1849], *Jane Welsh Carlyle: Letters to Her Family*, p. 329.
31. Thomas Carlyle, *Reminiscences*, ed. C. E. Norton, 2 vols (London and New York, 1887) vol. i, p. 175.
32. *New Letters of Thomas Carlyle*, ed. Alexander Carlyle, 2 vols (London, 1904) vol. ii, p. 93.
33. To John A. Carlyle, 22 June 1840; MS: National Library of Scotland, 523.88.
34. William Allingham, Note on Carlyle and George Eliot; MS: National Library of Scotland, 3823.
35. Gordon S. Haight, *George Eliot: A Biography* (New York and Oxford, 1968) p. 179.
36. *The George Eliot Letters*, vol. ii, pp. 176–8; MS: Princeton.
37. 2 November 1854; MS: National Library of Scotland, 516.86.
38. MS: Fitzwilliam Museum, Cambridge.
39. MS: Yale.
40. *New Letters of Thomas Carlyle*, vol. ii, p. 177.
41. David Alec Wilson, *Carlyle*, 6 vols (London and New York, 1923–34) vol. vi, p. 425.
42. MS: McGill.
43. *The George Eliot Letters*, vol. ii, p. 412; MS: Yale.
44. MS: National Library of Scotland, 3823.
45. *The George Eliot Letters*, vol. ii, pp. 425–6; MS: Frederick W. Hilles.
46. At Yale.
47. *The George Eliot Letters*, vol. iii, pp. 17–19; MS: Yale.
48. Ibid., p. 23; MS: National Library of Scotland.
49. *Letters of Anne Thackeray Ritchie*, ed. Hester Ritchie (London, 1924) p. 110.
50. MS: National Library of Scotland, 3823.
51. *The George Eliot Letters*, vol. iii, p. 23.

52. *Life and Memoirs of John Churton Collins*, ed. L. C. Collins (London, 1912) p. 44.
53. Espinasse, *Literary Recollections*, p. 224.
54. Sir Charles Gavan Duffy, *Conversations with Carlyle* (London, 1892) pp. 222–3.
55. *Letters and Memorials*, vol. III, p. 309.
56. To Alexander Gilchrist, 31 July 1861, in *Anne Gilchrist*, ed. H. H. Gilchrist, 2nd edn (London, 1887) pp. 85–6.
57. *The Autobiography and Letters of Mrs M. O. W. Oliphant*, ed. A. L. Coghill (New York, 1899) p. 180.
58. *Letters and Memorials*, vol. III, p. 329.
59. *Life and Memoirs of John Churton Collins*, p. 47.
60. *The George Eliot Letters*, vol. IV, p. 65.
61. G. H. Lewes to David Masson; MS: National Library of Scotland, 1778.114. For details of the medal, see *New Letters of Thomas Carlyle*, vol. II, p. 119, and Wilson, *Carlyle*, vol. VI, pp. 372–4.
62. MS: National Library of Scotland, 1778.111.
63. MS: National Library of Scotland, 1778.112–113.
64. *Reminiscences*, vol. I, p. 209.
65. *Leader*, vol. 6 (27 October 1855) p. 1035; reptd in *Essays of George Eliot*, p. 214.

8

Dickens and Lewes

No reader of John Forster's *Life* would suspect that Dickens was a good friend of George Henry Lewes for 32 years, almost as long as he knew Forster himself. In the first two volumes of the book Lewes's name is mentioned only twice, once in the cast of a play, and once in a page-long list of 'other acquaintances': 'Mr. George Henry Lewes he had an old and great regard for; among other men of letters should not be forgotten the cordial Thomas Ingoldsby'.[1] J. W. T. Ley, the editor of Forster's *Life of Dickens*, thought that this shabby allusion was inserted to placate Lewes,

> who had certainly been a friend of Dickens, but whose aid had been utterly rejected in the writing of this book. Lewes was certainly offended at Forster's determination to rely wholly upon his own knowledge of Dickens. Wilkie Collins was offended, too, and there were others who, in Dickens's lifetime and afterwards, resented the way in which Forster was apt to arrogate the novelist all to himself. There never was a more jealous friend than Forster. There are no records of the friendship with Lewes. He and Dickens were on excellent terms always, but there were no 'intimacies of friendship'. Lewes's article in the *Fortnightly Review* in 1871 [i.e., 1872] showed that he did not understand Dickens, that he viewed him with eyes that saw only externals. He took part in some of the theatricals.   (p. 544)

Ley's lame and rambling note misrepresents the facts almost as badly as Forster's suppressions. Not the slightest evidence exists to show that Lewes proffered his aid or had it rejected, or that he resented Forster's absurd arrogation of Dickens to himself. Moreover, there are many records of the long friendship which speak for themselves. As for the charge that Lewes did not understand him, I believe that any one who will take the trouble to read his article in the *Fortnightly Review* – one of the first serious studies of Dickens's psychology – will conclude that in some ways he understood him rather better than Forster did.

There are a number of superficial resemblances between Lewes and Dickens. From rather humble and obscure backgrounds, largely self-taught, they became important figures in Victorian literature. Dickens sought work as an actor; Lewes, the son and grandson of actors, had a brief and undistinguished career in the profession and a more successful one as playwright. Both men were unhappily married. Both were mercurial in temperament, witty, energetic, industrious and methodical. But the differences between them were more significant. Dickens was a man of emotion, sentimental throughout; Lewes was a man of intellect, philosophical and scientific. Dickens was a creator, peopling his world with marvellous fecundity; Lewes was a critic, according to Bernard Shaw, 'the most able and brilliant critic between Hazlitt and' – Bernard Shaw.[2]

The contrast struck Lewes at his first meeting with Dickens in 1838, soon after the completion of *Pickwick Papers*:

> Something I had written on that book pleased him, and caused him to ask me to call on him. (It is pleasant for me to remember that I made Thackeray's acquaintance in a similar way.) He was then living in Doughty Street; and those who remember him at that period will understand the somewhat disturbing effect produced on my enthusiasm for the new author by the sight of his bookshelves, on which were ranged nothing but three-volume novels and books of travel, all obviously the presentation copies from authors and publishers, with none of the treasures of the bookstall, each of which has its history, and all giving the collection its individual physiognomy. A man's library expresses much of his hidden life. I did not expect to find a bookworm, nor even a student, in the marvellous 'Boz'; but nevertheless this collection of books was a shock. He shortly came in, and his sunny presence quickly dispelled all misgivings. He was then, as to the last, a delightful companion, full of sagacity as well as animal spirits; but I came away more impressed with the fulness of life and energy than with any sense of distinction.[3]

Lewes was then only twenty, five years younger than Dickens. He had been at schools in London, Jersey, Brittany and Greenwich, worked in a notary's office and a Russia merchant's counting house, and studied medicine for a time before setting out to earn his living by writing. At seventeen he was sending tales and poems to magazine editors, among them Leigh Hunt, whose acquaintance he soon made. Here was a man who had once seen Shelley plain, and young Lewes, who had begun a biography of the poet, urged him to get Mary Shelley to read the manuscript and pumped him for details. Perhaps the life of Shelley was the 'very deep mine' about which Dickens promised to 'take soundings in Counting-House Quarters' for Lewes. His letter in the collection of Colonel Richard Gimbel is published here for the first time with the permission of Mr Henry Charles Dickens.

Doughty Street | Saturday Morning [?June 1838]

My Dear Sir

I write – fortunately for you – short notes, having no time (if I had the inclination) to make them longer.

I will take soundings in Counting-House Quarters and report about that very deep mine to which you devote yourself, in due course.

I don't think I shall be in town again until next Saturday, but between twelve and two on that day I shall be here. I have I am sorry to say several unfixed dinner engagements afoot, but I have at present no reason to fear that any one of them will clash with whatever day may suit Leigh Hunt best. I merely stipulate that you discharge me at an early hour, as I shall go back to Twickenham that night.

With reference to that question of yours concerning Oliver Twist I scarcely know what answer I can give you. I suppose like most authors I look over what I write with exceeding pleasure and think (to use the words of the elder Mr. Weller) 'in my innocence that it's all wery capital'. I thought that passage a good one *when* I wrote it, certainly, and I felt it strongly (as I do almost every word I put on paper) *while* I wrote it, but how it came I can't tell. It came like all my other ideas, such as they are, ready made to the point of the pen – and down it went. Draw your own conclusion and hug the theory closely.

I strongly object to printing anything in italics but a word here and there which requires particular emphasis, and that not often. It is framing and glazing an idea and desiring the ladies and gentlemen to walk up and admire it. The truth is, that I am a very modest man, and furthermore that if readers cannot detect the point of a passage without having their attention called to it by the writer, I would much rather they lost it and looked out for something else.

Faithfully Yours
Charles Dickens.

In the absence of the letter from Lewes which this answers, one can only speculate about the matters discussed here. I have found no account of the meeting it plans. In the autumn of 1838 Lewes went to Germany. When they met again nearly two years later, Dickens was in the full flood of prosperity and fame, living at 1 Devonshire Terrace, Regent's Park. While waiting in the library, Lewes

of course glanced at the books. The well-known paper boards of the three-volume novel no longer vulgarised the place; a goodly array of standard works, well-bound, showed a more respectable and conventional ambition; but there was no physiognomy in the collection. A greater change was visible in Dickens himself. In these two years he had remarkably developed. His conversation turned on graver subjects than theatres and actors, periodicals and London life. His interest in public affairs, especially in social questions, was keener. He still remained completely outside philosophy, science, and the higher literature, and was too unaffected a man to pretend to feel any interest in them. But the vivacity and sagacity which gave a charm to intercourse with him had become weighted with a seriousness which from that time forward became more and more prominent in his conversation and his writings. (p. 152)

The period of greatest intimacy with Lewes was during the private theatricals that Dickens organised for the benefit of Leigh Hunt. 'You know what we are going to do for Leigh Hunt', Dickens wrote on 15 June 1847. 'You have a hearty sympathy for Hunt and are, I am told, an excellent Actor. The characters to let, are, the Host in the Merry Wives of Windsor (a very good part) and old Knowell in Every Man in his Humour. If you will take these characters you will find yourself in excellent good company, and received with open arms.'[4] In 1848 when two performances were given at the Haymarket for the endowment of the Shakespeare House at Stratford-on-Avon (the first of them attended by Queen Victoria and the Prince Consort), Lewes played Sir Hugh Evans in *The Merry Wives of Windsor* and Wellbred in *Every Man in His Humour*. Dickens played Slender and Bobadil, while John Forster was well cast as the jealous husbands, Master Ford and Kitely.[5]

At this time young Lewes's versatile pen was earning him between £300 and £400 a year. In 1846 he published the third and fourth volumes of his *Biographical History of Philosophy* and a book on *The Spanish Drama*; in 1847 and 1848, two novels and dozens of reviews and articles in magazines. About a publisher, probably for his *Life of Maximilien Robespierre*, he consulted Dickens, asking him to propose the book to his printers, Bradbury and Evans. Dickens replied, 17 February 1848:

> Before I hazard a refusal, I think you ought to know this. . . . They do not desire to come into the field as publishers. They think it is likely to hurt their printing business. . . . They are so particular on this head, that in the case of Forster's advertized book on Goldsmith they got Chapman to connect himself with the publishing of it – as I verily believe for no other reason in the world. My impression therefore is, that they would not accept your proposal. But if you still wish it to be made, I will make it, and impress upon them that I do so, confidentially.[6]

Lewes accepted this friendly advice. His *Robespierre* was published in December 1848 by Chapman and Hall, who in 1850 also issued his tragedy *The Noble Heart*.

Another of his books that Dickens read was the novel *Rose, Blanche, and Violet* (1848), a wretched work, which even its author could not reread in later years without 'unpleasant sensations'.[7] Dickens's comment on it, 20 May 1848, is revealing:

> These rehearsals have obliged me to put almost as great a gap between your second and third volumes, as is supposed to occur sometimes, between the second and third act of an Adelphi Melo-Drama. But I read the third yesterday. And I must say to you that it affected me extremely, and manifests I think very great power. It has left the strongest impression on me. The whole history of Chamberlayne and his Wife is admirably done. I had noticed a great many other striking things as I went along, but this swallowed them all up, and left me, last night, in a damned black brooding state . . . which I have not quite come out of this morning. Indeed

I didn't mean to write about it – I take these things so much to heart – but what I *have* written, has leaped out of the inkstand, and it's no use crying 'Back! Back!' to it.[8]

During the publication of *Bleak House* Dickens and Lewes had a prolonged correspondence on the subject of spontaneous combustion,[9] and though they never reached an agreement, their relations remained quite as cordial and friendly as before. After his union with Marian Evans began in 1854 Lewes was away from London a good deal, in Germany writing the first biography of Goethe (1855) and on the coast collecting materials for *Sea-Side Studies* (1858), but constantly encouraging her first efforts at fiction. In January 1858, when *Scenes of Clerical Life* was reprinted from *Blackwood's Magazine*, Dickens was one of those to whom she sent copies. Not even her publisher then knew that the author was Marian Evans, the plain-looking spinster of 33 who had astonished her friends by going openly to live with Lewes. Dickens acknowledged the gift:

> Tavistock House, London, W. C.
> Monday Eighteenth January 1858.

Dear Sir

I have been so strongly affected by the two first tales in the book you have had the kindness to send me through Messrs. Blackwood, that I hope you will excuse my writing to you to express my admiration of their extraordinary merit. The exquisite truth and delicacy, both of the humour and the pathos of those stories, I have never seen the like of; and they have impressed me in a manner that I should find it very difficult to describe to you, if I had the impertinence to try.

In addressing these few words of thankfulness to the creator of the sad fortunes of Mr. Amos Barton, and the sad love-story of Mr. Gilfil, I am (I presume) bound to adopt the name that it pleases that excellent writer to assume. I can suggest no better one; but I should have been strongly disposed, if I had been left to my own devices, to address the said writer as a woman. I have observed what seem to me to be such womanly touches, in those moving fictions, that the assurance on the title-page is insufficient to satisfy me, even now. If they originated with no woman, I believe that no man ever before had the art of making himself, mentally, so like a woman, since the world began.

You will not suppose that I have any vulgar wish to fathom your secret. I mention the point as one of great interest to me – not of mere curiosity. If it should ever suit your convenience and inclination, to shew me the face of the man or woman who has written so charmingly, it will be a very memorable occasion to me. If otherwise, I shall always hold that impalpable personage in loving attachment and respect, and shall yield myself up to all future utterances from the same source, with a perfect confidence in their making me wiser and better.

> Your obliged and faithful Servant, and Admirer,
> Charles Dickens.

George Eliot Esquire.

'There can hardly be any climax of approbation for me after this', George Eliot wrote in sending it to John Blackwood, 'and I am so deeply moved by the finely felt and finely expressed sympathy of the letter, that the iron mask of my incognito seems quite painful in forbidding me to tell Dickens how thoroughly his generous impulse has been appreciated.'[10]

Dickens was one of the seven persons to whom she ordered copies of *Adam Bede* sent in February 1859. This time there was no immediate letter of acknowledgement. But a few weeks later, in April, when he was starting *All the Year Round*, Dickens asked his assistant editor W. H. Wills to send invitations to contribute 'to both the Trollopes, and to George Eliot, care of Blackwood – with a private seal on the latter'.[11] Her reply – if there was one – has not been found, nor has the other one he mentioned in his letter of 10 July 1859:

My Dear Madam,
  I have received your letter here this morning, with the greatest interest and pleasure. It is unnecessary for me to add, that I have received it in confidence. . . .
  This opportunity of writing to you, relieves me from a difficulty in which I have felt myself to be placed ever since you sent me Adam Bede, and for my extrication from which, I have always trusted to the result that has come – for I have always had the vanity to believe that I should one day hear from you as a real individual woman.

I had no means of acknowledging the receipt of that book but through Blackwood, and knowing at that time what changes I was going to make in my publishing arrangements, I had a great delicacy in suggesting to the Scotch-Publishing-Mind through any after-splicing of this and that together, that I had been way-laying you! Confident that you could not doubt my enthusiasm after I had read the book, I therefore resolved not to write to George Elliot, but to wait until I could write to you in person, whoever you might be. . . .

After a long paragraph praising *Adam Bede* Dickens added:

I cannot close this note without touching on two heads. Firstly (Blackwood not now being the medium of communication), if you should ever have the freedom and inclination to be a fellow labourer with me, it would yield me a pleasure that I have never known yet and can never know otherwise; and no channel that even you could command, should be so profitable as to yourself. Secondly, I hope you will let me come to see you when we are all in or near London again, and tell you – as a curiosity – my reasons for the faith that was in me that you were a woman, and for the absolute and never-doubting confidence with which I have waved all men away from Adam Bede, and nailed my colors to the Mast with 'Eve' upon them.

A word of remembrance and regard to Lewes – and of con-gratulation – that I know he will feel and understand as I do. My dear Madam,

Yours faithfully
Charles Dickens.[12]

George Eliot and Lewes were abroad when this gracious letter arrived. On their return Lewes wrote thanking Dickens and inviting him to come see them at Wandsworth. Unwell and working hard at *Tale of Two Cities*, he replied from Gad's Hill, 6 August 1859, that he could not come till he went into winter quarters in London. 'But I will not fail, you may be sure, to propose myself when the opportunity is nearer to my reach, and in the meantime I hope you and George Eliot will hold me in your kind remembrance.'[13] Accordingly he sent word that he would come on 10 November. 'Today we are going to have Charles Dickens to dinner', Lewes wrote to his sons. 'He is an intense admirer of your mother, whom he has has never seen; and we expect a very pleasant dinner, at which two such novelists will gobble and gabble!'[14] Lewes met him at the station. 'He reminded me that it was three and twenty[15] years ago since I first went down to Twickenham to see him, *Eheu! fugaces!* We had a delightful talk about all sorts of things, and I walked part of the way home with him.'

A few days later Dickens wrote to Lewes to ask whether George Eliot would agree to publish her next novel serially in *All the Year Round*, following Wilkie Collins's *The Woman in White*.

The question is, whether it would be consistent with her perfect peace of mind and comfort (I assume her general inclination, from what we said together), to enter into terms for such a story. If yes – in order that the money part of the matter may be (as it should be, of course, and must be) a matter of business and recompense, perfectly apart from me, either as an individual or a writer – my sub Editor and business right hand, Wills, an excellent fellow, shall come to you at any time you may name, and close the matter on any terms perfectly satisfactory to Mrs. Lewes and you. Of course the copyright would remain her own, and the perfect liberty to select her own publisher for the completed story, and to publish it immediately on its completion, would remain her own likewise. An immense new public would probably be opened to her, and I am quite sure that our association would be full of interest and pleasure to me.

Of my personal feeling and wish in the matter, and of the extent to which I have it at heart as an artist, to have such an artist working with me, I have no right to say more in this connexion. I never can overcome the delicacy and difficulty that arise in me, the moment I have to make mention of writing, in any other character than as a writer. Only tell me, therefore, whether you will see Wills, and when?

Now, thank God! I subside into the personage who smoked his cigar in the chair before the fire, last Thursday, and can send my kindest regard and truest sympathy in all things, without a fettered mind.

Faithfully Yours always
Charles Dickens.[16]

George Eliot knew that her novels depend for their effect on an appreciation of form and character that would be dissipated by publication in short weekly episodes. When Dickens made his proposal she was uncertain what Blackwood's attitude would be towards her since the secret of her authorship had leaked out. But 14 December when he offered her £2000 for an edition of 4000 copies of *The Mill on the Floss*, she quickly accepted. She must have reflected that brief weekly instalments would not suit any story that she cared to write. In February 1860 she had Lewes write Dickens that her contribution to *All the Year Round* must be postponed indefinitely.

Tavistock House, Tavistock Square, London, W. C.
Monday Morning Thirteenth February 1860.

My Dear Lewes, –
Your letter has perfectly amazed me. I had not the least idea and I assure you – not the faintest notion – that there was any postponement, far less a postponement sine die. Mrs. Lewes's note merely asked me, in acknowledging the receipt of the Tale of Two Cities, whether something was not sacrificed, through the necessities of such a plan, to terseness and closeness of construction, and proposed that we should speak of that when I next came out to see you. This was its effect, but nothing more believe me. I have no doubt I can lay my hand upon it in the course of today, and you shall both see it.

My sole reason for not having come to see you is the delicacy I have put [felt?] in forcing the matter on Mrs. Lewes's mind, while it was occupied with her book. Both you and she had mentioned her anxious desire to complete it without any distracting reference to her work. Knowing of my own experience how natural and necessary such devotion to one thing is, I resolved (quite against my own wishes) not to come near you, until I could suppose her book to be done. I really put such a strict constraint upon myself in this regard, that on Wills's telling me at the office only a few days ago, that the book was advertized by Blackwood, I replied that this was no evidence of its being finished, and that I would still wait a little longer.

Tomorrow being my day at the office, I will come out to you from there, between half past one and half past three. Meanwhile I only add that I am quite as sure of your good faith as I am of my own. – With kindest regard –

Ever faithfully,
[Charles Dickens][17]

In spite of this editorial disappointment Dickens remained on perfectly friendly terms with the Leweses. When George Eliot's novel appeared she told Blackwood: 'I don't mean to send the "Mill on the Floss" to any one, except to Dickens, who has behaved with a delicate kindness in a recent matter, which I wish to acknowledge.'[18] He in turn sent her an inscribed copy of *The Uncommercial Traveller* in January 1861. One day in 1862 Lewes met him in Regent Street. 'He turned back to walk some way with me, and I turned back again with him. Pleasant talk.'[19] Again, 6 June 1866: 'On my way home met Dickens who walked home with me. Curious stories of dreams, etc.' In his Journal Lewes then recorded in detail Dickens's dream about Miss Napier in the scarlet dress and a number of his impressions during the railway wreck at Staplehurst just a year before. Lewes was one of the stewards at the farewell dinner given for Dickens on 2 November 1867, before he left for America. In the last months of his life Dickens came several times to the Priory. Lunching with the Leweses on 6 March 1870, he told them a fine story of Lincoln's dream which recurred the night before he was shot, and a curious psychological experience of his own in the publication of a ghost story. They thought he looked dreadfully shattered that day; 'it is probable', George Eliot wrote, 13 June 1870, 'that he never recovered from the effect of the terrible railway accident'. A few days before the news of his death came she was reading the third number of *Edwin Drood* aloud to Lewes.

When the first two volumes of Forster's *Life of Dickens* appeared, Chapman and Hall asked Lewes to write an article on it for the *Fortnightly Review*. In a letter to Sara Hennell, 15 December 1871, George Eliot pronounced the book 'ill-organized and stuffed with criticism and other matter which would be better in limbo; but the information about his boyish experience and the letters from America, which show his rapid development during his first travels there, make it worth reading'. Since 1868 Lewes had written no reviews, devoting all his time to philosophical and psychological studies for his *Problems of Life and Mind*, the first volume of which appeared in 1873. But he accepted this opportunity to discuss the psychological aspects of Dickens's imagination, which interested him very much and which Forster's account ignored.

Beginning with some general remarks on criticism, which tends to 'pronounce absolute verdicts', to speak for all when giving individual impressions, Lewes says that in Dickens's case there probably never was a writer of so vast a popularity whose genius was so little *appreciated* by the critics. . . . Fastidious readers were loath to admit that a writer could be justly called great whose defects were so glaring. . . . It was not by their defects that these works were carried over Europe and America. . . . It is clear, therefore, that Dickens had powers which enabled him to triumph in spite of the weaknesses which clogged them; and it is worth inquiring what those powers were, and their relations to his undeniable defects.[20]

The primary cause of his success was 'his overflowing fun'. But great as he is in fun,

so great that Fielding and Smollett are small in comparison, he would have been only a passing amusement for the world had he not been gifted with an imagination of marvellous vividness, and an emotional, sympathetic nature capable of furnishing that imagination with elements of universal power. . . . He was a seer of visions; and his visions were of objects at once familiar and potent. Psychologists will understand both the extent and the limitation of the remark, when I say that in no other perfectly sane mind (Blake, I believe, was not perfectly sane) have I observed vividness of imagination approaching so closely to hallucination. Many who are not psychologists may have had some experience in themselves, or in others, of that abnormal condition in which a man hears voices, and sees objects, with the distinctness of direct perception, although silence and darkness are without him; these *revived* impressions, revived by an internal cause, have precisely the same force and clearness which the impressions originally had when produced by an external cause. In the same degree of vividness are the images *constructed* by his mind in explanation of the voices heard or objects seen.   (p. 144)

The difference between hallucination in the insane and in the sane is 'the coercion of the image in *suppressing comparison* and all control of experience'. Though Lewes declared that 'I have never observed any trace of the insane temperament in Dickens's works, or life, they being indeed singularly free even from the eccentricities which often accompany exceptional powers' (p. 145), he believed that considerable light was shed upon the novels by the action of the imagination in hallucination.

To him also *revived* images have the vividness of sensations; to
him also *created* images have the coercive force of realities, excluding all control, all contradiction. What seems preposterous,
impossible to us, seemed to him simple fact of observation. . . . He,
seeing it thus vividly, made us also see it; and believing in its
reality however fantastic, he communicated something of his belief
to us.　(p. 145)

Turning to Dickens's characters Lewes adds:

This glorious energy of imagination . . . made his creations universally intelligible, no matter how fantastic and unreal. His types
established themselves in the public mind like personal experiences. Their falsity was unnoticed in the blaze of their illumination
. . . . Unreal and impossible as these types were, speaking a
language never heard in life, moving like pieces of simple mechanism always in one way . . . these unreal figures affected the
uncritical reader with the force of reality. . . . Give a child a
wooden horse, with hair for mane and tail, and wafer-spots for
colouring, he will never be disturbed by the fact that this horse
does not move its legs, but runs on wheels – the general suggestion suffices for his belief.　　　　. . . It may be said of Dickens's
human figures that they too are wooden, and run on wheels; but
these are details which scarcely disturb the belief of admirers. Just
as the wooden horse is brought within the range of the child's
emotions, . . . so Dickens's figures are brought within the range of
the reader's interests, and receive from these interests a sudden
illumination, when they are the puppets of a drama every incident of which appeals to the sympathies.　(p. 146)

The adverse comments of critics Lewes tried to explain by a 'bias
of opposition', which makes them undervalue an author's great
qualities in irritation at his little faults, and a 'bias of technical estimate', which makes them deny the importance of subject and find
the supreme importance in technique, 'the pleasure derived from the
perception of difficulty overcome'. Dickens's art laid hold on readers
of every class. Only the cultivated, Lewes continued,

paused to consider the pervading commonness of the works, and
remarked that they are wholly without glimpses of a nobler life;
and that the writer presents an almost unique example of a mind

of singular force in wnich, so to speak, sensations never passed into ideas. Dickens sees and feels, but the logic of feeling seems the only logic he can manage. Thought is strangely absent from his works. . . . one sees no indication of the past life of humanity having ever occupied him; keenly as he observes the objects before him, he never connects his observations into a general expression, never seems interested in general relations of things. Compared with that of Fielding or Thackeray, his was merely an *animal* intelligence, *i.e.*, restricted to perceptions. On this ground his early education was more fruitful and less injurious than it would have been to a nature constructed on a more reflective and intellectual type. It furnished him with rare and valuable experience, early developed his sympathies with the lowly and struggling, and did not starve any intellectual ambition. He never was and never would have been a student.   (p. 151)

It is easy to see why this severe but fundamentally sound criticism was anathema to the idolatrous Forster. In the third volume of the *Life* he inserted an angry and violent attack on Lewes: 'the trick of studied depreciation was never carried so far or made so odious as in this case, by intolerable assumptions of an indulgent superiority; and to repel it in such a form once for all is due to Dickens's memory' (ed. Ley, p. 716). Forster's account of the article provides an excellent example of the 'bias of opposition'. It is not enough that Lewes has placed Dickens above Fielding and Smollett for 'fun': Forster insists that 'humour he does not concede to him anywhere'. But the bitterest personal invective is turned upon Lewes's suggestion of the resemblance between vivid imagination and hallucination and his opinion that Dickens's characters are 'wooden, and run on wheels'.

Risum teneatis? But the smile is grim that rises to the face of one to whom the relations of the writer and his critic, while both writer and critic lived, are known; and who sees the drift of now scattering such rubbish as this over an established fame. . . . Since Trinculo and Caliban were under one cloak, there has surely been no such delicate monster with two voices. . . . One other of the foul speeches I may not overlook, since it contains what is alleged to be a personal revelation of Dickens made to the critic himself. . . . To establish the hallucinative theory, he is said on one occasion to have declared to the critic that every word uttered by his characters was distinctly *heard* by him before it was written down. Such an averment, not credible for a moment as thus made, indeed simply not true to the extent described, may yet be accepted in the limited and quite different sense which a passage in one of Dickens's letters [to Forster, of course] gives to it.   (pp. 718–20)

Forster then quotes Dickens's remark that he doesn't invent his scene, *'but see it*, and write it down'. How this slight variation can justify the vulgar charge of untruth against Lewes's statement that Dickens said he *heard* his characters speak could be explained only by a psychological study of the twisted mind of Forster himself. Ley's note (p. 680) on the part Forster played in the separation between Mr and Mrs Dickens, though somewhat altered by subsequent revelations about Ellen Ternan, shows that his jealousy extended even to his hero's wife.

Almost the only person it did not include was Dickens's sister-in-law, Mary Hogarth, who had died soon after Forster was introduced to her. Edgar Johnson suggests that Dickens's devotion to her also had its share in the rupture of his marriage.[21] The intense, idealised emotion with which he surrounded her memory dazzled the world in Little Nell; it shines for the modern biographer with quite a different light from the pure radiance it had for Forster. Lewes was the first critic to put his finger on this strange part of Dickens's story. After quoting the well-known passage in which Dickens describes his desire to be buried next to Mary ('I cannot bear the thought of being excluded from her dust'), Lewes tells something that Forster had omitted:

Several years afterwards, in the course of a quiet chat over a cigar, we got on a subject which always interested him, and on which he had stored many striking anecdotes – dreams. He then narrated, in his quietest and most impressive manner, that after Mary's death her image not only haunted him by day, but for twelve months visited his dreams every night. At first he had refrained from mentioning it to his wife; and after deferring this some time, felt unable to mention it to her. He had occasion to go to Liverpool, and as he went to bed that night, there was a strong hope that the change of bed might break the spell of his dreams. It was not so however. That night as usual the old dream was dreamt. He resolved to unburthen his mind to his wife, and wrote that very morning a full account of his strange experience. From that time he ceased to dream of her. I forget whether he said he had never dreamt of her since; but I am certain of the fact that the spell had been broken then and there.   (pp. 153–4)

The Freudian implications, now so obvious, were even then apparent to Lewes, a pioneer in the study of the unconscious. But Forster had to have the last word. In Volume III, without mentioning Lewes's anticipation in the *Fortnightly* article, he referred to this dream, which, though it 'would leave him for a time, unfailingly came back. . . . whatever was worthiest in him found in this an ark of safety; and it was the nobler part of his being which had thus become also the essential' (ed. Ley, p. 842).

None of Lewes's friends was surprised at Forster's virulence, for he was notoriously quarrelsome. 'It looks like an outbreak of bad health and worse temper', wrote John Blackwood to George Eliot, 9 March 1874. Lewes, however, was deeply disturbed by the vicious attack, not for its dissent from his criticism, but 'because it seemed to indicate unfairness towards a fellow-author who was dead'.[22] He discussed the matter fully with Trollope, 9 February 1874, and gave him a draft of his letter to Forster to correct after reading the article and the attack. Trollope returned it the next day with a few suggested modifications, and Lewes rewrote it and sent it off. Neither the letter nor any reply has been found.

Today the personal animosities are dead and the facts can be judged coolly. Forster's book seems more than ever what Lewes is alleged to have called it: a 'Life of John Forster with notices of Dickens'.[23] Though Lewes's opinions were certainly coloured by his admiration of a very different kind of novel, few modern critics will disagree with the sentences that end his article on Dickens:

We do not turn over the pages in search of thought, delicate psychological observation, grace of style, charm of composition; but we enjoy them like children at play, laughing and crying at the images which pass before us. And this illustration suggests the explanation of how learned and thoughtful men can have been almost as much delighted with the works as ignorant and juvenile readers; how Lord Jeffrey could have been so affected by the presentation of Little Nell, which most critical readers pronounce maudlin and unreal.   (p. 154)

Notes

This essay first appeared in *PMLA*, vol. 71 (March 1956) pp. 166–79.

1. *The Life of Charles Dickens*, ed. J. W. T. Ley (London, [1928]) pp. 456, 531.
2. *The Works of Bernard Shaw*, 33 vols (London, 1930–8) vol. xxv, p. 163.
3. G. H. Lewes, 'Dickens in Relation to Criticism', *Fortnightly Review*, vol. xvii (February 1872) p. 152.
4. Sotheby and Co. catalogue, 27 June 1923, item 610.
5. From the playbills in Colonel Richard Gimbel's collection.
6. *The Letters of Charles Dickens*, ed. Walter Dexter, 3 vols (London, 1938) vol. ii, p. 72.
7. Lewes's Diary, 6 December 1875 (Yale).
8. *The Letters of Charles Dickens*, vol. ii, p. 90.
9. See Chapter 9 in the present volume.
10. *The George Eliot Letters*, ed. Gordon S. Haight, 7 vols (New Haven, Conn., and London, 1954–5) vol. ii, pp. 423–4.
11. *The Letters of Charles Dickens*, vol. iii, p. 100.
12. *The George Eliot Letters*, vol. iii, pp. 114–15.
13. *The Letters of Charles Dickens*, vol. iii, p. 115.
14. *The George Eliot Letters*, vol. iii, p. 195.
15. Actually 21 years. Dickens rented the cottage at Twickenham during June and July 1838. This is quoted from Lewes's Journal, 10 November 1859 (Yale).
16. *The George Eliot Letters*, vol. iii, pp. 203–4.
17. *The Letters of Charles Dickens*, vol. iii, pp. 150–1.
18. *The George Eliot Letters*, vol. iii, p. 279.
19. Lewes's Journal, 27 February 1862 (Yale).
20. *Fortnightly Review*, vol. xvii (February 1872) p. 143.
21. Edgar Johnson, *Charles Dickens: His Tragedy and Triumph*, 2 vols (New York, 1952) vol. i, p. 204.
22. Anthony Trollope, 'George Henry Lewes', *Fortnightly Review*, vol. xxxi (January 1879) p. 23.
23. The only source I know of this remark is Ley's note, p. 544. In his *Fortnightly* article Lewes was careful to say little about the *Life*; but he wrote to Blackwood on 25 November 1872 that he thought Forster's book 'a lasting injury to his friend, whom it presents in a constant state of *rouge* and footlights'.

9

Dickens and Lewes on
Spontaneous Combustion

At the end of Part X of *Bleak House*, published in December 1852, Dickens described the death of Krook by spontaneous combustion (ch. 32). He had been preparing for the scene from Krook's first appearance with his fierce cat Lady Jane in the rag and bottle warehouse by the wall of Lincoln's Inn. 'He was short, cadaverous, and withered; with his head sunk sideways between his shoulders, and the breath issuing in visible smoke from his mouth, as if he were on fire within. His throat, chin, and eyebrows were so frosted with white hairs, and so gnarled with veins and puckered skin, that he looked from his breast upward, like some old root in a fall of snow' (ch. 5). The discovery of his 'remains' like 'the cinder of a small charred and broken log of wood sprinkled with white ashes, or is it coal?' provides one of the most gruesome effects in this remarkable novel.

Among the readers of Part X was Dickens's old friend George Henry Lewes, now at the height of his enthusiasm for Auguste Comte, whose work he had been discussing in a series of papers in the *Leader*, reprinted in 1853 as *Comte's Philosophy of the Sciences*. Lewes made it his business to attack any superstition that raised its head. Krook's death was too good to pass up. In his 'literature' column, 11 December 1852 (p. 1189), he objected to the episode as overstepping the limits of fiction and giving currency to a vulgar error. Granting that as a novelist he was not to be called to the bar of science, Lewes doubted whether Dickens could find an organic chemist of any authority to countenance his explanation: 'he has doubtless picked up the idea among the curiosities of his reading. . . . Captain Marryat, it may be remembered, employed the same equivocal incident in *Jacob Faithful*.'

Dickens did not ignore the challenge. In the January number, Part XI, which opens with the inquest on Krook (ch. 33), he inserted a paragraph citing his authorities:

Out of the court, and a long way out of it, there is considerable excitement too; for men of science and philosophy come to look, and carriages set down doctors at the corner who arrive with the same intent, and there is more learned talk about inflammable gases and phosphuretted hydrogen than the court has ever imagined. Some of these authorities (of course the wisest) hold with indignation that the deceased had no business to die in the alleged manner; and being reminded by other authorities of a certain inquiry into the evidence for such deaths, reprinted in the sixth volume of the Philosophical Transactions; and also of a book not quite unknown, on English Medical Jurisprudence; and likewise of the Italian case of the Countess Cornelia Baudi as set forth in detail by one Bianchini, prebendary of Verona, who wrote a scholarly work or so, and was occasionally heard of in his time as having gleams of reason in him; and also of the testimony of Messrs. Fodéré and Mere [i.e., Marc], two pestilent Frenchmen who *would* investigate the subject; and further, of the corroborative testimony of Monsieur Le Cat, a rather celebrated French surgeon once upon a time, who had the unpoliteness to live in a house where such a case occurred, and even to write an account of it; – still they regard the late Mr. Krook's obstinacy, in going out the world by any such by-way, as wholly unjustifiable and personally offensive.

This brought a quick response from Lewes in the *Leader*.[1] After remarking that the unscientific mind is more impressed by personal or historical than by scientific evidence, he told of a gentleman who refused to doubt the fact of spontaneous combustion because he had read a circumstantial account of a case in the *Chelmsford Chronicle*. Dickens had referred to five (actually six) authorities, and Lewes announced his intention of examining them and reporting in due course.

No one has ever accused Lewes of lacking humour. In this case his zeal for scientific truth was reinforced by a journalist's understandable respect for timely copy. Three weeks later in the *Leader*, he addressed the first of two open and signed letters to Dickens:

My dear Dickens, –
What you write is read wherever the English language is read. This magnificent popularity carries with it a serious responsibility. A vulgar error countenanced by you becomes, thereby,

formidable. Therefore am I, in common with many of your admirers, grieved to see that an error exploded from science, but one
peculiarly adapted to the avid credulity of unscientific minds, has
been seriously taken up by you, and sent all over the world with
your imprimatur – an act which will tend to perpetuate the error
in spite of the labours of a thousand philosophers. No journal but
the *Leader* has taken up this matter; but I would fain hope that if
the case can be clearly stated, and the error shown, on all sides, to
be an error, the press of England will lend its aid towards the
disabusing of the public mind, and that you yourself will make
some qualifying statement in your Preface.[2]

Against the possibility of death by spontaneous combustion Lewes
then proceeds to range the testimony of Liebig, Bischoff, Regnault,
Graham, Hofmann and Richard Owen. 'I only name those whom I
know to have pronounced unequivocally on this point, but I believe
you will find no one eminent organic chemist of our day who credits
Spontaneous Combustion.' The cases Dickens had cited in his January number receive the cool evaluation they deserve:

Humorous, but not convincing! The authority of the *Philosophical
Transactions* of 1750 can be brought into no chemical court of 1853;
Beck's *Medical Jurisprudence*, though an excellent work, is only a
work of erudition, not of scientific authority; the same of Fodéré's
Médecine Légale; the prebendary of Verona may have been a first-
rate scholar, but you will not ask any one to accept his authority
in chemistry. . . . Then, as to Le Cat, the fact of his 'having lived in
the house where such a case occurred' is evidence only to the fact
of combustion, not at all to the fact of the combustion having been
spontaneous.

Next Lewes quotes Liebig's observations in the *Letters on Chemistry* that no one was ever present during the combustion or ascer-
tained exactly what preceded it. The accounts usually state that the
body entirely disappears, leaving only a dark greasy stain on the
floor and some remains of bones. But in fire, says Liebig, the smallest
bone becomes white and retains two thirds of its weight and usually
its original shape. He also points out that the accounts often omit
vital facts such as the presence in the room of a lamp filled with oil.
Perhaps the most lurid of the fifty cases he had studied was that
reported in 1749 by a priest named Boineau of

a woman of eighty, who drank nothing else than brandy. She began to burn, sitting on a chair, and burned, although water was poured upon her, till all the flesh was consumed. The skeleton alone remained, sitting in the chair. . . . The narrator was not present, and did not see the flame; and the story plainly indicates a good intention on his part, – that of inoculating his flock with a wholesome terror for brandy-drinking.

'Let us not deceive ourselves respecting the value of reported cases', Lewes concludes. 'You, Dickens, would not believe a whole neighourhood of respectable witnesses who should declare that the lamppost has been converted, by a flash of lightning, into an elm tree.'

In the second letter, published 12 February 1853,[3] Lewes carefully reviewed the scientific facts: that a body weighing 120 pounds contains about 90 pounds of water and can no more burn than gunpowder mixed with three times its own weight of water; that the tissues cannot be saturated with alcohol; that phosphuretted hydrogen is not formed in the body, living or dead. Again he urged Dickens to 'make some qualifying statement in the preface to *Bleak House* so as to prevent the incident of Krook's death from promulgating an error'. Even if investigation should fail to shake his faith in spontaneous combustion, he might say

that although you believe in the phenomenon, it is a belief rejected by the highest scientific authorities of the day. . . . Your genius has moved with beneficent power in so many other directions than that of Physiology, it would cost you nothing to avow a mistake, even were you not countenanced by a host of very respectable authorities, as is the case in this mistaken hypothesis of Spontaneous Combustion.   (p. 163)

Dickens could hardly remain unmoved under this barrage. On 7 February 1853, two days after Lewes's first letter appeared, he wrote to his friend Dr John Elliotson, thanking him for the loan of his

remarkable and learned Lecture on Spontaneous Combustion; and I am not a little pleased to find myself fortified by such high authority. Before writing that chapter of Bleak House, I had looked up all the more famous cases you quote (as I dare say you divined in reading the description); but three or four of those you incidentally mention – two of them in 1820 – are new to me – and your explanation is so beautifully clear, that I could particularly desire to repeat it several times before I come to the last No. and the Preface.

May I keep it carefully by me until the summer? I can warrant myself most reliable in all matters connected with the preservation of papers, and should have it here under my hand at any time. Or shall I return it to you, first copying it? – which I do not like to do without your permission.

It is inconceivable to me how people can reject such evidence, supported by so much familiar knowledge, and such reasonable analogy. But I suppose the long and short of it is that they don't know, and don't want to know, anything about the matter.[4]

Elliotson was not the soundest guide for Dickens in this affair. Thoroughly educated at Edinburgh (where he got his MD at nineteen) and at Cambridge, he served on the staff of St Thomas' Hospital for seventeen years and then from 1832–8 was professor of the practice of medicine at University College, London. He had long been a leading exponent of phrenology before he became convinced in 1837 of the power of mesmerism to cure all sorts of diseases from headache to 'true cancer'. His fanatical advocacy of the new cult led him to resign his professorship, withdraw from University College Hospital, which he had done so much to establish, and set up the Mesmeric Infirmary. Though his lecture on spontaneous combustion has not been published, its tone may be inferred from the credulity he shows in other works. Presumably he allowed Dickens to keep the manuscript from which the ammunition for his reply to Lewes was extracted. With the permission of Mr Henry Charles Dickens this letter in the collection of Mrs Carrington Ouvry is here published for the first time:

Private

TAVISTOCK HOUSE
Twenty Fifth February 1853.

My Dear Lewes, –
    Liebig is a great man, deserving of all possible respect, and receiving no greater deference from any one than from me. But I cannot set his opinion – his mere opinion and argument – against full scientific evidence of a fact. That evidence appears to me to

exist, on the subject of what is called (rightly or wrongly) spontaneous combustion. If I take anything on evidence, I must take
that. I have the greatest regard for, and admiration of, Owen. But
if I had such evidence of the existence of a Sea Serpent as I have of
cases similar to Krook's I could not for a moment set even his
ingenious argument against such human experience.

In the beginning you rather hastily (and not quite, I think in all
good humour, with that consideration which your knowledge of
me might have justified) assumed that I knew nothing at all about
the question – had no kind of sense of my responsibility – and had
taken no trouble to discriminate between truth and falsehood.
Now the object of my note is simply to assure you that when I
thought of the incident – which came into my mind, as having
that analogy in it which is suggested at the end of the chapter – I
looked into a number of books with great care, expressly to learn
what the truth was. I examined the subject as a Judge might have
done. And without laying down any law upon the case, I placed
the evidence impartially before myself, the way as I will place it
before you.

Into the argument it appears to me quite unnecessary, with
such evidence, to enter. No one can suppose that such a death
comes of any normal or natural condition of the body. No one can
know what astonishing change has taken place *in* the body when
it arrives at that pass; because the body is in the main destroyed.
The difficulty of consuming a human body by ordinary fire (which
is enormous) exaggerates beyond all bounds the impossibility of
accounting for the deaths of this catalogue of people by any
ordinary means. I know very well that phosphuretted hydrogen
gas will burn when it is almost surrounded by water. [About 20
words deleted.] I also know that this gas is not usually formed in
human beings, and I likewise know that of every human being so
many pounds of water form a component part. But I know that
before such a death can take place, there must be a stupendous
disturbance of the usual functions of the body; and to tell me that
if the gas were not there, and the water were all there, or other
such proportions and balances were preserved, the body could
not be consumed, is merely to tell me in other words that if I be
always quite well, I shall never die; or that if I retain the sight of
both eyes, I cannot possibly be blind.

The question is a question of evidence. Have people been found
almost consumed, when there were no external agencies by which
they could have been reduced to that state? If so, have there

usually (not without exception, but usually) been pervading circumstances of age, sex, or previous habits, or all three, suggesting the presence of pretty uniform conditions, essential to the extraordinary law (extraordinary that is to say, within our small experience) governing such cases?

Refer to an article by Pierre Aime Lair in the Journal de Physique, or to the sixth volume of the Philosophical Transactions where it is presented in another article by Alexander Tilloch. You will there find a number of cases – all of women in the decline of life. Refer to the Annual Register for 1773 [i.e. 1775] for the case of Mary Clues – a woman of fifty, and a drunkard. To the Transactions of the Royal Society of London for the case of Grace Pitt – a woman of sixty: not stated to be a drunkard, but not likely to have been a lady of very temperate habits, as she got out of bed every night to smoke a pipe, and had drunk an immense quantity of spirits within a few hours of her death. Refer to Le Cat for the case of Madame Millet who got drunk every day. He lived in the house, and minutely states the case. And besides his being a man of very high scientific and medical reputation, there was a certain M. Chretien, a surgeon, *who examined what remained of the body on the spot where it was consumed*, and gave his evidence in detail before the Tribunal of Justice which found the woman's husband guilty of her murder; though a High Court of Appeal, expressly on the ground that it was a case of spontaneous combustion and on the irresistible strength of the evidence, acquitted him. Refer to the Life of Bianchini, prebendary of Verona, to observe that the overpowering evidence of the death by these means of the Contessa Baudi (a most exact and minute account of the smallest particulars of which case he drew up with judicial precision and formality) quite devoted him to the theme afterwards: so important did it appear to him in Medical Jurisprudence, and so strong was his apprehension that its not being credited might lead to the conviction of innocent persons. This old lady was not a drunkard, but had been in the habit of bathing in great quantities of camphor. Refer to the Journal de Medicine Vol. 21X, for the case of a woman at Aix (a little drunken old woman) also minutely reported by M. Rocas, a surgeon who saw the cindery body and the room before they were disturbed. Dr. McCormac of Belfast (formerly a student at the Hotel Dieu in Paris) wrote to me a few days since, 'Dupuytren, whose experience in burns was immense, was wont indeed, to consider the burns from human combustion, by some termed spontaneous, as a sixth form of burns.'

I would refer you to more cases, but these are enough. And throughout them there is apparent, not only the same general set of circumstances before death, but the same general appearances afterwards. Opinions on the subject, supporting me, and opinions of great practical men, I could give you by the score. But I lay them all aside, even those of the best lecturers and writers on Medical Jurisprudence (though those I might fairly impress, as being founded on the evidence); but the evidence is enough for me: and so far from making any qualifying statement in the Preface to Bleak House I can only say that I have read your ingenious letters with much pleasure – that I champion no hypothetical explanation of the fact – but that I take the fact upon the testimony, which I considered quite impartially and with no preconceived opinion.

Ever my Dear Lewes,
Faithfully yours,
Charles Dickens

G. H. Lewes Esquire.

Lewes's reply to this strange defence has not been found. It is clear that he was most concerned over Dickens's ambiguous remark that he had 'rather hastily (and not quite, I think in all good humour, with that consideration which your knowledge of me might have justified) assumed that I knew nothing at all about the question'. But a second letter two days later assured him that Dickens had not been hurt.

TAVISTOCK HOUSE
Sunday Morning, Twenty-Seventh February 1853

My Dear Lewes, –
   I cannot help laughing, – though I am really vexed – at a preposterous mistake which my hand-writing must have occasioned. When I have been long at work on my own manuscript, I write so illegibly and strike out so remorselessly, that at such times my hand (as I well know) is anything but a plain one. Look back to my note and I think you will certainly find that there is no such word as 'not', before 'in all good humour'. There most positively and unquestionably was no such word in my mind, and I cannot believe that it has got in the note without my ob-

servation. There may be a 'but', or there may be an erasure; I cannot sufficiently remember the context, to suggest what the marvellous sign may be – but this Deponent maketh oath and saith it is *not* 'Not'. The meaning is, that *I* (the undersigned) *in all good humor* make that observation. I am as thoroughly persuaded of your good humor in the matter as I am of my own, and I am at once amazed and concerned to find how easily a meaning becomes changed.

I am very unwilling to request that you will not publish my note, because my old regard for you and our old association take it out of the category of ordinary communications. But my objection originates in my own knowledge of the amazing correspondence of which I am the daily victim, and of the attempts that would certainly be made (if I departed in this instance from my invariable rule) by the smaller fry, to draw me into other explanations and statements – and if I wouldn't be drawn, to assume that I allowed judgment to go by default, because when Mr. Lewes &c &c Mr. Dickens not only &c &c but actually &c &c &c.

If you would like, in any article of your own, to set forth this objection, and the reasonable necessity of it; and so refer to a private note you had received from me under the exceptional circumstances of our being old friends; and in that manner to quote its contents; I don't know that I should have the resolution still to ask you not to do so. But although no one save yourself can imagine the full extent of the grounds I have for never stepping out of my picture-frame to address the spectators, I know your sense and candor will give me credit for there being very strong interest when I assure you that I would infinitely rather be unheard in this regard.

Set me right about that NOT, with yourself, whatever you do.

> Ever my Dear Lewes,
> Faithfully yours,
> [Charles Dickens.][5]

For six weeks the *Leader* was silent about the controversy. Then Lewes published the letters his articles had evoked:[6]

In a private note, Charles Dickens, while expressing the utmost deference to the authority of Liebig and Owen, maintains his original position, because he thinks it justified by the evidence. 'If I take anything on evidence, I must take that', he says. And he enumerates the sources whence that evidence is drawn. The point of interest in his note, is an emphatic protest against my too hasty assumption, that, in adopting the notion of Spontaneous Combustion, he had not taken the trouble of investigating the subject; he assures me, on the contrary, that he 'looked into a number of books, with great care, expressly to learn what the truth was. I examined the subject as a judge might have done, and without laying down any law upon the case.'

The other letters were a long and rambling one signed 'Ignis', explaining the phenomenon by the 'vital force' acting like electricity on the water in the body; an even longer one from Lewes's friend George Redford, arguing less for spontaneous combustion than for an open mind, even about chemistry; and two bigoted letters from the Dr McCormac of Belfast whom Dickens had mentioned, citing the old cases in refutation of modern science.

In September, when *Bleak House* was reissued in one volume, the preface contained a paragraph on the subject:

> The possibility of what is called Spontaneous Combustion has been denied since the death of Mr. Krook; and my good friend Mr. Lewes (quite mistaken, as he soon found, in supposing the thing to have been abandoned by all authorities) published some ingenious letters to me at the time when that event was chronicled, arguing that Spontaneous Combustion could not possibly be. I have no need to observe that I do not wilfully or negligently mislead my readers, and that before I wrote that description I took pains to investigate the subject.

After citing again the cases of Bianchini and Le Cat Dickens continues:

> I do not think it necessary to add to these notable facts, and that general reference to the authorities which will be found at page 329, the recorded opinions and experiences of distinguished medical professors, French, English, and Scotch, in more modern days; contenting myself with observing, that I shall not abandon the facts until there shall have been a considerable Spontaneous Combustion of the testimony on which human occurrences are usually received.

> In Bleak House, I have purposely dwelt upon the romantic side
> of familiar things.

Lewes's position was naturally unchanged. In the *Leader*, 3 September 1853, he wrote:

> This month the tangled threads of narrative in *Bleak House* are
> finally unwound, and readers have no more 'new numbers' to
> look forward to. In his Preface, Dickens emphatically declares
> that everything set forth in *Bleak House* concerning the Court of
> Chancery is substantially true, and within the truth. He also *partly*
> complies with the wish expressed in this Journal, that he would
> make some qualifying statement respecting Spontaneous Com-
> bustion; but we regret to add that he has not made that statement
> with the fulness and impartiality demanded by the case, even
> although his own private conviction remain perfectly unshaken.
> It is unpleasant to be forced to recur to this subject, the more so
> because our protest must necessarily be so ludicrously dispro-
> portionate to the effect of his assertion, carried as it will be all over
> Europe. We should not, however, be true to our office, if we
> allowed the assertion to pass without rectification.[7]

He then recapitulates the scientific argument. Dickens has 'forgotten, or disregarded' his appeal to state in the preface that, though he
believes in spontaneous combustion, the scientists of the day reject
it. While 'he was at liberty to cite all the authorities in his favour, he
was *not* at liberty to disregard and pass over in silence the names of
Liebig, Bischoff, Regnault, Graham, Hofmann, and Owen; and against
that omission we protest'.[8]

The petulant note heard in this correspondence is not characteristic of Lewes. It is probably attributable to the ill health and painful
domestic difficulties he faced at this time. Having known Dickens
for fifteen years, he realised that no weight of evidence was likely to
convert him. Dickens's notions of physiology were always vague
and naïve. In the mob scene in *Barnaby Rudge* (1841) he had described the lead running off a burning roof on to a drunken man
below, 'streaming down in a shower of liquid fire, white hot, melting
his head like wax' (ch. 55). This discussion of spontaneous combustion gives a striking example of the intellectual limitations that made
him indifferent or hostile to the scientific developments of his age.
There is scarcely a trace in his novels of the new theories that revo-

lutionised man's view of himself and his universe in the nineteenth century. But as George Gissing says, 'Nature made him the mouth-piece of his kind, in all that relates to simple emotions and homely thoughts. Who can more rightly be called an artist . . .?'[9]

Notes

This essay first appeared in *Nineteenth-Century Fiction*, vol. 10 (June 1955) pp. 53–63.

1. *Leader*, 15 January 1853, p. 64.
2. Ibid., 5 February 1853, pp. 137–8.
3. Ibid., 12 February 1853, pp. 161–3.
4. *The Letters of Charles Dickens*, ed. Walter Dexter, 3 vols (London, 1938) vol. II, pp. 446–7.
5. Ibid., pp. 448–9.
6. *Leader*, 26 March 1853, pp. 303–6.
7. Ibid., 3 September 1853, p. 858.
8. Lewes summed up the whole subject again in 'Spontaneous Combustion', *Blackwood's Magazine*, vol. LXXXIX (April 1861) pp. 385–402, without alluding to *Bleak House* or his correspondence with Dickens.
9. George Gissing, *Charles Dickens* (London, 1898) p. 83.

10

George Meredith and the *Westminster Review*

I

The biographies of Meredith are almost blank for the years 1857 and 1858, when the collapse of his marriage gave him more than the usual reasons for reticence. Though he must have earned a living somehow, his *Poems* (1851), *The Shaving of Shagpat* (1856) and *Farina* (1857) could hardly have supported him. Late in life, when John Lane asked whether he had been 'responsible for any anonymous or pseudonymous volume or contributions to periodical literature', Meredith replied: 'Nothing anonymous, except political leaders & short essays, chiefly to the *Pall Mall Gazette* under F. Greenwood. Let them lie.'[1] However, it is now known that from April 1857 until January 1858 Meredith wrote the Belles Lettres and Art section of the *Westminster Review*. In the Parrish Collection at Princeton there is a receipt given to the editor John Chapman for £12.12s., 'being payment for an Article forming Section 4 of the Contemporary Literature published in the Westminster Review for April 1857', signed George Meredith; a similar receipt for October 1857 is owned by Professor R. L. Purdy of Yale. From internal evidence it is clear that Meredith also wrote the articles for July 1857 and January 1858. Altogether nearly 40,000 words are now added to the canon of his works.

His predecessor in the Belles Lettres section was George Eliot, who wrote it from July 1855 to January 1857, when her career as a novelist began with *Scenes of Clerical Life*. Her reviews are better balanced than Meredith's, more intellectual in tone, and written more carefully. Meredith seems more intent on being amusing, obviously enjoying his brilliant ridicule of inferior books. Two of the eighteen pages of his article for April 1857 are wasted on a new edition of John Abraham Heraud's *The Judgment of the Flood*, first published in 1834, of which nothing good could be said. Nor can he find much to praise in John Stuart Blackie's *Lays and Legends of Ancient Greece*. A Meredithian phrase is kindled by Blackie's accenting *Marathon* on the last syllable; after quoting Byron's line, Meredith remarks that

> when the last line is a foot shorter than its predecessor, to end it with a word of three syllables is to turn Pegasus afield with a heavy drag on his fetlock, and stressing the last syllable makes the good horse too conscious of a tether.   (vol. LXVII, p. 606)

Meredith's schooldays at Neuwied are recalled by Blackie's 'Farewell to the Rhine', which 'gives us that strange *Sehnsucht nach dem Rhein* known to those who have a deeper than steamboat acquaintance with the noble old river' (p. 606). Two other volumes of poetry are noticed briefly: Feltham Burghley's *Sir Edwin Gilderoy* Meredith describes as 'a sorry figure of a ballad-knight, fitter to ride from the Mansion-house to Westminster than from Eltham to Normandy; . . . Eltham gave him birth, and Limbo claims him for her own' (p. 606). The Rev. M. Vicary's *Pencillings in Poetry* evinces no power, original or imitative; 'we are astonished that he should have allowed phrases to stand which read like the cutting of cork to our ears, and are altogether unendurable' (p. 607).

Charles Kingsley's *Two Years Ago*, the best novel that fell in this quarter, deserves the strokes Meredith administers. The plot hangs on a belt worn by the hero Tom Thurnall, 'a modern Amyas Leigh, adventurous, muscular, and Saxon'.

> Tom is a shrewd fellow, and to say he has seen the world is small commendation for a man who has been several times shot through the body, once hanged, and almost roasted for a cannibal feast. . . . Tom, brought to the sense above senses by captivity in the prison of an ex-machina Khan, ceases to be an infidel. . . . Mr Kingsley has hit upon the right sort of lesson for a nature like Tom's – incarceration. But it will be seen that he has a purpose, and has consequently given us melodrama instead of life. The characters are in a state of hopeless subjection to purpose. . . . Mr Kingsley wanted to show the godlessness of a life surrendered entirely to dreams and desire for glory as opposed to what he (and we) must love best – a plain, practical Englishman, doing his work, respecting his dinner, and honestly seeking to better himself and all men. The consequence of laying down this plan is, that

[in Elsley Vavasour] we have a figure stuffed with reeking straw, and Mr Kingsley has just as much fellow-feeling for him as we have. Were his creation in the least human, Mr Kingsley is the man to give him a trifle of sympathy; but Elsley is not. He is a chip of purpose, born two years ago to play the fool with a sweet little woman, blight her and everybody dependent on him, stumble up mountains at midnight, fire a frantic pistol at his supposed rival, drink laudanum, die, and point a spasmodic moral. No wonder Mr Kingsley is constantly pummelling him. Compassion for this puny Frankenstein is out of the question.   (pp. 609-10)

It is of course in Kingsley's favour that 'he sketches women with the reverence of a true artist. Valencia is pure flesh and blood.' But Meredith objects to having her

coupled with a weak-chested curate. She will be just as faithful and deep-hearted to the death as Lucia, we know; still, it is not a fair conjunction. The love-making is done in very pretty fashion, however, and as there is no one else in the book on whom to bestow her, we must accept the decree, and bless the fortunate curate.   (p. 610)

Meredith complains of the sense of haste in the book, the violent changes in scene; it seems to have been hurriedly thrown off, and 'in both dialogue and description Mr Kingsley has used very broad brushes'.

It is when Mr Kingsley speaks in person that we are most content. The bold and beautiful manliness of his remarks on marriage, and love in marriage, will be appreciated. In fact, if we regard this novel as a hearty sermon, with illustrations, dramatic and pictorial, we shall better estimate its character, and learn to accept it as the fresh outpouring of a mind constitutionally noble. The novel is only not artistic, because Mr Kingsley is always in the pulpit.   (p. 611)

Though Meredith dislikes the London society described in E. M. Whitty's *Friends of Bohemia*, he admits that 'those who have a taste for Thackeray, will at least endure Mr Whitty'.

We have hitherto resolutely shut our eyes – or, at least our circulating libraries – to it. After living the life of princes or beggars (for there is no middle class), in this fascinating foul country, and eating of the hog dressed whole, we pretend not to know that it exists.   (p. 612)

The true artist and the best satirist, declares Meredith, 'can portray the world with colours blushing through its brazen face – not painted on'. Whitty's satire strikes. But,

> Ideas do not seem to form a residuum in his mind for judgment to sit on, and hatch putative wisdom (pass the metaphor); on the contrary, they fret for immediate expression and a stout foe. . . . No amount of poetry, or descriptive genius, could surpass in depth of gloom and pathetic horror some of the things here said. It is terrible plain prose. Mr Whitty's book is not infant's food. You are offered strong meat and sharp tonic.   (pp. 612–13)

Of sentimental novels, most of them by women, Meredith says a good deal that illuminates his own theory of fiction.

> It is a rare case when the rage for the autobiographical form of authorship, communicated among lady novelists by the success of 'Jane Eyre', does not present us with at least one quarterly example of its continued prevalence; and, we suppose we must imply, the undiminished appetite of the public for gimcrack reminiscence and pincushion history. . . . Many hundreds of villages in the United Kingdom have their tens and twenties of ladies ready and willing to recite all, and more than all, that they have felt and undergone, for the benefit of what men and maidens may choose to listen thereto. They esteem it a delightful labour. Human nature loves to talk of itself. Will the public give ear? Their task is so easy, their stories so flowing, and their capacity for selection so unrestrained, that no more flourishing profession could be indicated. With ourselves for our theme, fiction never fails us. Nevertheless, these ladies tell marvellous little story, and necessarily obtrude their own full lengths on the picture a great deal too much. We must accept them as the heroines of their own romance. They may affect to give you portraits of sweet women; but it is as impossible, as it would be ungallant, to forget the fair speaker. Has she not already coloured heaven and earth for you from her special impressions? You see nothing but through her perceptives. Well you know the secret something she nurses within her sensitive bosom, and beautifully she contrives that your sym-

Contemporaries

pathies shall be constantly alive to it! You may like other ladies
better, but you are bound to prefer her claim on the hero, and
second it by all the ardent vows of a zealous novel-reader. There
is no escape. She snares you first by an excessive humility; then
you grow morbid with her; finally maudlin.   (pp. 613–14)

After a devastating summary of *Florence Templar* he adds:

We are sorry to speak slightingly of this quiet and unpretending
work, but it is one of a bad class. Jane Eyre and Villette can only
be done once. The autobiographer should both be something, and
have something to say. We are offered instead shadows and tittle-
tattle. If ladies still persist in adhering to this, which seems the
easiest, but is really the most difficult, form of pure fiction, we beg
them to throw over and mentally annihilate Miss Brontë's too-
fascinating works, and turning to the one great masterpiece we
possess, take a course of 'Robinson Crusoe'.   (pp. 614–15)

Hereditary insanity, the theme of Mary C. Hume's *The Wedding
Guests*, Meredith pronounces

unpleasant to us personally. A very little jars on the delicate
nerves of fiction; . . . it never can be satisfactorily handled in a
novel, and does but make that dainty dish one of troubled waters.
. . . Sick as we are of 'purpose' in novels, we do not ask for nothing
but pleasure. If life in the present is to be portrayed, some hard
things must needs obtrude. The province of Art is to subordinate
and soften them down. There are few subjects not legitimate to
the novelist, but as we are happily constituted to shun and detest
the sight of evil, it should be the novelist's care not to give what is
painful undue prominence, and especially not to strike a doubtful
chord in the mind. We look on life apprehending the bad and
searching for the good. In the picture of life, this search should be
assisted without compromising truth, and to do this, and not
throw dust in our eyes, is to be a great and worthy artist.   (p. 615)

Meredith complains of the 'very feminine style' of the novel, heavily
burdened with dialogue. 'Miss Hume's conversation is easy, but
altogether wants salt and flavour. After a satisfactory construction of
plot, when to dramatize and when to narrate, is the novelist's lesson'
(pp. 615–16).

Lady Rachel Butler's Highland story, *Jessie Cameron*, wins brief if mild approval for its 'deep feeling, void of sentimentality'. As a 'simple story simply told' it 'weighs more than a pile of fashionable novels in the critical scale' (p. 618). But in Alfred Elwes's *Giulio Branchi*, laid in the robber-haunted mountains and forests of Sardinia, Meredith observes, 'Fra Diavolo is himself again. Those gentlemen who are tired of civilization had better go to Sardinia' (p. 616). The account of this cloak-and-dagger romance is written with all the gusto of *Punch's Prize Novels* and at greater length than the *Westminster* should have given such a book. Meredith's objections to the feeble clichés describing Giulio's amour with the Marchesa are interesting for their reflection on his own novels:

> Eyes are 'moistened with sympathetic emotions'; young lips are 'ruddy with saucy health', and drawn to each other by 'irresistible magnetism'; 'place, time (midnight and a boudoir), ardent feeling, delicious atmosphere, and the witchery of the hour', are invoked. This is not describing, but blurring. If the writer wished to drop a veil on such scenes – and we have no objection whatever, – it is possible for the most passionate love to be delicate without endangering apprehension, – always sufficiently alive when not misled; and the more deeply passionate, the more tenderly delicate it will present itself to us. . . . Assuredly, any example is preferable to that of the French school in these cases; but when they are touched on – if we must have them – there is a vice in conventionalism only just better than rank licence. (p. 617)

Comment on contemporary art had first been added to the Belles Lettres section of the *Westminster Review* in April 1856, when George Eliot reviewed Volume III of Ruskin's *Modern Painters*. Critics have not yet fully realised the importance of Ruskin's influence on the nineteenth-century novel. George Eliot wrote:

> The truth of infinite value that he teaches is *realism* – the doctrine that all truth and beauty are to be attained by a humble and faithful study of nature, and not by substituting vague forms, bred by imagination on the mists of feeling, in place of definite, substantial reality. (vol. LXV, p. 626)

This is the Pre-Raphaelite idea, which Ruskin recognised in Holman Hunt and Millais. Meredith in attacking Edward Young's *Pre-*

Raffaellitism leans towards Ruskin's view. The danger of idealism to art is

> that it weans the mind from the significant humanity of things. And therefore is idealism, as a school, false – a mere copying of phantoms. But the tendency of art is to excellence, and that of the spirit to idealism. It will not for ever walk earth and pore on nature. It has the quality of flame once kindled. Consequently, the idealists represent a principle, and a high truth. Small realists may live, small idealists never. The substantial has a shadow, the insubstantial none. The greatest idealists sprang from a school of hard realism. To imitate them is to paint on air without the brush of light. Realism, then, is the only basis of art. Its sins are naturally the reverse to those of idealism. The latter demands mastery; the former taste. Lacking taste, the artist falls into the foulness of an Orcagna; and not possessing mastery, he is hopelessly lost in the puerilities of the Raphaelites. We believe that pre-Raphaellitism will lead to a good and great English School of Art, and that it is our sole chance.   (vol. LXVII, p. 608)

Meredith's closest connexion with the movement at this time was through his friend Henry Wallis, for whose *Chatterton* he is said to have been the model. He is clearly offended by Young's sneering dismissal of the picture as 'a pair of puce breeches'.

> If Mr Young can see nothing in 'Chatterton' but a pair of puce breeches, he is betrayed by his eye for colour, or by his antagonism to Mr Ruskin, or by some haunting sense of the general importance of those indispensables. It is hard to say which. The colour is wonderful, but the chief merit of 'Chatterton' is its subordination of parts to expression of the sentiment. It is a picture that requires no defence.   (p. 608)

This warm tribute to Wallis, whose liaison with Mrs Meredith was soon to bring their marriage to a tragic end, is of great biographical interest. No trace of resentment towards Wallis is visible even so late as July 1857, when in reviewing Ruskin's notes on the Royal Academy Meredith goes out of his way to remark that

> Mr Ruskin might have drawn attention to the head of 'Montaigne' (Wallis), masterly in conception and execution, and altogether a most enjoyable picture – one that they who love the old wise

Gascon are not likely to forget. He has rightly complained of the way it is hung, which throws a meritorious work into false light. (vol. LXVIII, p. 304)

When this number of the *Westminster* appeared, Mrs Meredith was off in Wales, probably with Wallis, by whom she had a son born 18 April 1858.[2]

II

The Belles Lettres article for July 1857 follows in general the same pattern, with Meredith happily exercising his wit on wretched poems and novels that scarcely deserve mention. It opens with two pages on the fourth edition of the poetical works of John Edmund Reade.

Not Wordsworth among poets, not Mahomet among prophets, had a greater fund of the buoyant confidence that whispers future triumph during present defeat, than Mr Reade: and in him it is the more marvellous, as it must exist without external support – in complete isolation. . . . It would be better, perhaps, to pass the volumes over in silence and leave time to do its certain work, but that, although the safer process, implies a contempt we do not feel for Mr Reade's powers and accomplishments. (vol. LXVIII, p. 296)

Reade's early imitations of Byron were notorious and not worth notice; but his later poems deliberately copying Wordsworth and Tennyson aroused Meredith's wrath.

A young poet may be allowed to copy the style of the great masters of his art: nay, he will attain strength and boldness from the devotion – they are the ladders that uplift him to the empyrean of his free powers: but we insist on the conception being his own – he may work at another man's mill, but he must bring his own grist. Mr Reade is not a young poet. (p. 297)

Quoting 'Life and Death in Eden', which is almost a paraphrase of Tennyson's 'Love and Death', Meredith says:

In a younger man we should have said that the way the tone and thought of him who makes metaphysics beautiful to us is here caught, might be a sign of promising ability; but the very cleverness is condemnation to a writer of established years. In the mechanism of his art – as the above extract shows – Mr Reade is sufficiently capable. To take him from his books, he has a cultured mind, a gentle heart, a trained intellect, right feelings: with such a combination of gifts, one who has lived long enough to publish four editions should bear with equanimity to be told that he is not a poet.   (p. 297)

Another work that might better have been ignored is *The Last Judgment, a Poem in Twelve Books*. 'What have we done', Meredith writes, 'to deserve three hundred and thirty-five pages of closely-printed rhymed heroics on the final argument of Providence with man?' The author was anonymous.

> We should presume him to be a disciple of Mr Spurgeon: and if that great orator were some day to leave his hungry flock in the lurch, and put on singing-robes, he could hardly scatter damnation around him with a more dulcet indifference.   (p. 298)

Though there is no receipt for the July 1857 article, Meredith's style is unmistakable. One or two allusions confirm his authorship. In the notice of Robert Bell's *Ancient Poems, Ballads, and Songs* he quotes the text of 'Old Adam' as a 'gentleman of our acquaintance heard it in his youth sung by an old crone down the streets of Chertsey'. The gentleman is doubtless Meredith's father-in-law, Thomas Love Peacock, whose childhood was spent at Chertsey. One recognises Meredith too in the comparison of Chapman's Homer to 'the continuous rushing in of long-ridged waves to land under a strong south-wester' (p. 300). In an article on Homer in the *Fortnightly Review*, reprinted in the Memorial edition, Meredith uses the same image for Chapman's lines: 'getting the swell and rush, and the emphatic pause here and there – the seventh wave, as one may say'.[3]

Two American books occasion the most interesting reviews in July 1857. Delia Bacon's *Philosophy of the Plays of Shakespere Unfolded* suffers, Meredith declares, from the obscurity of her style.

> Hyphens, brackets, involutions of all kinds abound, and bewilder the traveller from paragraph to paragraph, while the more to perplex and confound him in his darkness, strange italics are perpetually being bawled in his ear; and around him unexpected, inexplicable capitals go off with a bang. It is a perfect study of

emphasis; but we cannot think the lady to have always dashed her pen under the right word. We rarely get a clue to her mystic meanings. As sometimes in society one comes across people who accompany the commonest remarks with glances of intense abstract signification, so Miss Bacon will italicize prepositions, conjunctions, and articles, until these appear to contain the very marrow of her ideas. Now and then she reminds us of Miss Toppit, in 'Martin Chuzzlewit',

whose wonderful speech beginning 'Mind and matter slide swift into the vortex of immensity' Meredith here quotes in full. He then summarises the argument that 'Jester Will' Shakespeare was used by Bacon and Raleigh as their instrument in a plot to undermine the despotism of the Crown:

> The idea of so lofty and subtle a conspiracy as this she attributes to the great men of Elizabeth's age, is creditable to Miss Bacon's imagination. We have thought highly of them, but not so highly as that. When she furnishes us with facts we shall be happy to answer them. Mr Hawthorne's preface is extremely eulogistic of the lady, as was Elijah Pogram's speech to Mrs Hominy. We cannot see that he exactly subscribes to her doctrine; but he does enough to blind the general reader, if the book should command such an individual. Meantime, as there is an English claimant [W. H. Smith] to the distinguished honour of disputing the paternity of the Shakespeare plays, and as Miss Bacon is proud of her discovery, we may as well help the announcement of its being incontrovertibly her own.   (p. 303)

The other American book Meredith reviews is Herman Melville's *The Confidence Man*, and this sympathetic account adds new evidence that Melville was not ignored by his British contemporaries.

> Perhaps the moral is the gullibility of the great Republic, when taken on its own tack. At all events, it is a wide enough moral to have numerous applications, and sends minor shafts to right and left. Several capital anecdotes are told, and well told; but we are conscious of a certain hardness in the book, from the absence of humour, where so much humanity is shuffled into close neighbourhood. And with the absence of humour, too, there is an absence of kindliness. The view of human nature is severe and sombre – at least, that is the impression left on our mind. It wants

relief, and is written too much in the spirit of Timon; who, indeed, saw life as it is, but first wasted his money, and then shut his heart, so that for him there was nothing save naked rock, without moss and flower. A moneyless man and a heartless man are not good exponents of our state. Mr Melville has delineated with passable correctness, but he has forgotten to infuse the colours that exist in nature. The fault may lie in the uniqueness of the construction. Spread over a larger canvas, and taking in more of the innumerable sides of humanity, the picture might have been as accurate, the satire as sharp, and the author would not have laid himself open to the charge of harshness. Few Americans write so powerfully as Mr Melville, or in better English, and we shall look forward with pleasure to his promised continuation of the masquerade. The first part is a remarkable work, and will add to his reputation.   (p. 311)

Some of the notices of trashy novels that make up the rest of the July Belles Lettres section are noteworthy for the light they throw on Meredith's view of the art of fiction. *The Roua Pass* was by 'Erick MacKenzie', whom Meredith easily guesses to be a woman. 'The prominent male characters are undeniably women's men; that is, they are a woman's idea of what men are, mixed up with certain salient manly characteristics, which may have been conceived from observation, and are possible to us' (p. 305). The point is illustrated amusingly. In spite of its absurdities Meredith pronounces *The Roua Pass* 'a good novel – the best of the season'.

> The authoress, an idealist in treatment, and one by instinct, has a close acquaintance with the peculiar life she depicts, and loves nature warmly. Exquisite bits of Highland scenery abound, and there are sweet as well as amusing social interludes. Our highest admiration must be reserved for the style. It is not new for a woman to write powerfully; but, in general, when they are powerful, they are, or have been, morbid. They have a French love of detail, – part due to themselves, part to the study of Balzac, and this is brought to bear indiscriminately upon character and localities. The authoress of the 'Roua Pass' is averse to dissection. Her mind is healthy and active. Her pen flows on with delightful ease, and we hope not to seem ungallant in terming it masculine freedom.   (pp. 305–6)

It is easy to see why George Eliot chose a masculine pseudonym.

Meredith deals more sternly with *Below the Surface*, an anonymous novel, which, if it had been called *Life in the Shires*, 'would have fulfilled its aim, and have caused no disappointment'. The author's

knowledge of the *bourgeoisie* seems to be derived from Bulwer, and the chapter describing the funeral of Mr Usherwood is worthy of that novelist's pen – which is not high praise. The story is made to hinge on the loss of a child, and on the connubial difficulties of a couple that must ultimately come together again as they do so often in novels, so seldom in life. The novel is, in point of story, sufficiently amusing, and jogs on comfortably to the end; doubtless, however, story was a secondary consideration with one who was planning a social satire, and had set himself to demolish workhouses and lunatic asylums. But why relinquish the pamphlet, the ancient, approved, and honourable weapon of controversy, in order to over-freight fiction with a load that sinks it? Here is another novel of 'purpose', well intended, well written, but failing in both ways – the fiction is burdened by the fact, and the fact rendered dubious and weak by the fiction. We shall begin at last to feel like those unhappy boys who have had much medicine administered to them in sugar – shy of the adored sweets. Surely, the public must be in an unwholesome condition, if this is the only means to move them. It is manifestly unfair; the statement cannot but be one-sided. We have a race of writers now who imagine they would be disgraced by simply telling a story. They deliberately look out for some political or social object to annihilate, that will at the same time dignify the events they are condescending to relate; and also – last, not least – secure to them a large and zealous sect as readers. One or two may have higher motives; the author of 'Never too Late to Mend' was certainly in earnest, and so is the author of 'Below the Surface', whom we thank for a pleasant book, and respect as a brave, high-minded man, hoping to meet him again on his old ground (if rumour is right in ascribing the novel to Sir Arthur Hallam Elton); for here his ability and courage are all but wasted, and fruitless. It is not every knight can take the minstrel's seat; even when this is done, the knightly aim and the bardic faculty are rarely found in harmonious union, save when fired by the immediate calls of country; and there is no longer a distinction between patriots. Let writers with a purpose not forget that when they make use of fiction to develope their views, these, not to appear contemptible, require the display of narrative and dramatic power; and even when possessed of such aids, they are but cunning advocates hoodwinking the jury in a larger and more licensed court. (pp. 306–7)

III

Meredith's authorship of the Belles Lettres and Art section of the *Westminster Review* for October 1857 is established by his receipt (now owned by Professor R. L. Purdy) acknowledging John Chapman's payment of £12.12s. for the article. He begins with a long notice of Alexander Smith's *City Poems*. Smith, he says, like the author of *Festus* (P. J. Bailey), was one of the few poets who woke to find themselves famous. 'We trust that he is not, in imitation of his rival, going to treat us to a series of disappointments.' Though *The Life Drama* 'was remarkable as the work of a very young man in a season of poetic dearth', the new poems are not up to the mark. Their style recalls Smith's earlier work, and he 'has not got a whit nearer to real life'. He 'talks and talks: he is more and more Alexander Smith, and proportionately less the poet we hoped he would be'. He

> is not creative, and we cannot say that he is even original. The spirit and tone of Tennyson are reproduced in the 'City Poems'; it is impossible to forget the Laureate while we read them. His characters are the merest abstractions – pegs for the hanging of poetic bravery on; and so long-winded are the reflective parts, the digressions so random, that all story is lost in them. . . . We are to presume, doubtless, that Charles, James, Max, John, and Harry, are a group of spasmodic poets disguised under Christian-names. At least their hostility to our class, contempt for cotton, and general preference of soliloquy to dialogue, may warrant the supposition. For the rest, they speak more sensibly than the race usually does. (vol. LXVIII, p. 586)

Echoes of Tennyson, real or imaginary, always stir Meredith's rage.[4] He quotes the following stanza from 'The Night before the Wedding':

> The country ways are full of mire,
> The boughs toss in the fading light,
> The winds blow out the sunset's fire,
> And sudden droppeth down the night.
> I sit in this familiar room,
> Where mud-splashed hunting squires resort;
> My sole companion in the gloom
> This slowing dying pint of port.

We can pardon such epithets as the 'dying day', and many of the kind made popular by Shelley; but if this grandiloquence applies to the daily ebbing of our decanters, it may extend to our legs of mutton, and will have a range of infinite bathos. We are not of those who accuse Mr Smith of plagiarism, nor hold the accusation good. . . . But let whoever will, read the above stanza, and say if it be not an almost servile echo of Tennyson! The treatment, the tone, the very rhymes, are his. Mr Smith should have been careful, where so much was expected of him, not to publish these reproductions of a master, involuntary though they may be. There is surely such a thing as a poetic conscience, to warn young votaries of the Muse when they are appropriating property not their own? At all events, there are laws to restrain the practice.   (pp. 587–8)

Meredith's charge cannot be well sustained in the case of the rhymes; *light–night, gloom–room* are too common to belong to anyone, and Tennyson nowhere rhymes *mire* with *fire*. Though the *resort–port* rhyme recurs several times in 'Will Waterproof's Monologue', the rhythm, stanza form and whole tone of the poem differ from Smith's. Apart from this imagined fault Meredith finds considerable charm in Smith's verse.

He is not, we are glad to see, corrupted by the noxious applause of many of the critics who first welcomed him: he has written right on the best that was in him. Public taste has much advanced since we had the 'Life Drama', thanks to the intolerable outrages on English common sense and language of which the spasmodic poets became latterly guilty. That it does not condemn and reject the 'City Poems', but accepts them, however disappointing, as a proof of sensible progress in Art, must satisfy Mr Smith that he is in the right track, and be the present reward for his efforts.   (p. 589)

The Pre-Raphaelites reappear in Meredith's account of the illustrated edition of Tennyson's poems, the failure of which he regards
as less the artists' fault than a proof of Tennyson's powers. 'It was an
easy task to illustrate Byron and Moore', says Meredith; but the
peculiarity of Tennyson is that

> he never draws a picture without dipping it in a thought, or
> suffusing it with a profound sensation. . .; his spell is on us, and it
> is vain for Art to attempt to rival these vivid impressions. The
> wonder is that Messrs Millais, Hunt, and Rosetti [*sic*] have not failed
> more signally and shocked our prejudiced views altogether.
> (p. 591)

Meredith finds Holman Hunt's *Godiva* chastely conceived; his *Lady
of Shalott* misses 'the sweet and dim romance of the poem'; but his
two *Oriana* drawings are the best of the illustrations.

> Rosetti's [*sic*] drawings are intensely mediaeval and mystic;
> but this artist has the sense of beauty so deeply seated, that we
> admire even when we do not always understand him. The weeping
> queens watching King Arthur in the vale of Avelon [*sic*] are lovely
> and queen-like women; so is the face of the Lady of Shalott, who
> has sung her last song: the attitude of Lancelot also is profoundly
> tender, and the drawing is crowded with suggestive accessories.
> Rosetti improves on Tennyson too much; but if we forget the
> poetry his drawings affect to illustrate, and take them for what
> they are, we shall find that each one is a poem in itself, and
> despite the quaintness and excessive richness, a poem that we
> may cherish and enjoy, or we are beneath the artist's level. The
> fervid devotion of 'Mariana in the South', kissing the Saviour's
> feet, and the ecstasy of the rapt St Cecilia under the Angel's salute,
> are due to a man of genius who may be too much given to
> symbolic elaborations, but who comprehends beauty with his
> whole soul, and can represent the highest and the noblest forms of
> grace. True feminine visages are the key-notes to the pictures, and
> if we fix our attention on them, we shall no longer feel offended
> by the pedantic fulness of detail. And yet we hardly like to
> object to that which furnishes so wonderful a mediaeval study.
> (pp. 591–2)

Millais's drawings Meredith finds unequal, some being
nearly perfect, others 'below criticism and contempt', and he

particularly objects to Millais's conception of Cleopatra:

> The 'queen with swarthy cheeks and bold black eyes' was not
> negrine. She had no cause to be even olive-tawny. Cleopatra was
> a daughter of Ptolemy, a Greek; and the Egyptian climate would
> never have burnt and burnished her white blood to anything like
> the extent insisted upon by the artist. Indeed, custom would have
> soon 'staled her infinite variety' had she been a nigger. She is
> absolutely made to point with a black finger to a black breast,
> which no sensible aspick would touch. The poet has not altogether
> insulted her memory and the taste of Roman generals by giving
> her 'swarthy cheeks', though it may be questioned how far that
> may be admissible; but the artist does nothing but outrage to the
> shade of Mark Antony. Mr Millais has, moreover, made her ex-
> pose her teeth – doubtless to get a little light into his drawing; but
> it wears the aspect of a curious case of insistence, as if the glorious
> beauty must not only be black like Dinah, but grin in sisterhood.
> Historic and intuitive evidence, Mr Millais, tells us that the Ser-
> pent of old Nile was fair. The most destructive women are always
> fair.   (p. 592)

Ruskin's *Elements of Drawing* is reviewed at some length.

> A better instructor could not be placed in the hands of the
> young beginner of Art. . . . The eloquence of the writing will be a
> spur to his energies; and its extreme lucidity will leave him nothing
> to desire in the way of explanation of particulars. Accompanied
> by this book, the student has a friend in his wanderings over hill
> and dale in the depth of country peace, and in the heart of beauty;
> a friend gentle, wise, and most inspiriting. The dogmas here are
> many, but they do not bite young people. Mr Ruskin's dogmatism
> is the direct one-view of a profound conviction founded on rev-
> erent study, and the act of seeing and thinking for himself. We no
> more object to his expressing himself in dogmas than to his having
> an opinion. There are two or three touches of sarcasm to relieve
> the dryness of instruction, of a kind to make little ladies giggle
> and grave women look fond.   (pp. 593–4)

Meredith quite properly objects to the Appendix, in which Ruskin,
suggesting 'Things to be Studied', recommends of modern poets
only 'Scott, Wordsworth, Keats, Crabbe, Tennyson, the two
Brownings, Lowell, Longfellow, and Coventry Patmore'.

Mr Ruskin has no right to dogmatize on poetry and poets. He recommends Lowell, Longfellow, and Coventry Patmore to young people, excluding Coleridge as 'sickly and useless', and Shelley as 'shallow and verbose'. Shelley has faults, and so has Coleridge; but this off-hand dictum is an impertinence – nothing less. Besides, there are nobler poets than the above three for the young to read. We do not think there was need for a caution against fiction and the drama. Shakespeare *is* the drama in England, and surely he may be read by the young? We fancy it is for a very feminine order of mind that Coventry Patmore is made to supersede Shakespeare. (p. 594)

Trollope's *Barchester Towers* Meredith pronounces

decidedly the cleverest novel of the season, and one of the most masculine delineations of modern life in a special class of society that we have seen for many a day. . . . Mr Trollope has satisfactorily solved a problem in this production. He has, without resorting to politics, or setting out as a social reformer, given us a novel that men can enjoy, and a satire so cleverly interwoven with the story, that every incident and development renders it more pointed and telling. . . . In general our modern prose satirists spread their canvas for a common tale, out of which they start when the occasion suits, to harangue, exhort, and scold the world in person. Mr Trollope entrusts all this to the individuals of his story. The plot is as simple as the siege of Troy. We are sure that Mr Slope cannot succeed, or that if he is allowed to, another three volumes will confound him. We are equally convinced that the Widow Bold will never surrender to him, or that if she should, he will have to repent it equally. Nevertheless, our appetite for the closing chapters does not languish. . . . Mr Slope is possessed of extraordinary powers. He cannot move without inspiring nausea even in the female bosom (for it is notorious how much the sex can bear); yet he contrives to make men jealous of him. We have all of us met somebody like Mr Slope, and wished that, if he indeed could lay claim to the odour of sanctity, it were pleasanter to the poor human sense of smell . . . .
Mr Trollope seems wanting in certain of the higher elements that make a great novelist. He does not exhibit much sway over the emotional part of our nature: though fairer readers may think that the pretty passages between Eleanor and her baby-boy show

a capacity for melting woman's heart, at least. He is also a little too sketchy; the scenes are efficient in repose and richness: but let us cut short our complaints, thankful that we have a caustic and vigorous writer, who can draw men and women, and tell a story that men and women can read.   (pp. 595–6)

In contrast to *Barchester Towers* Meredith places Mrs Oliphant's *The Athelings*, which he finds 'in construction and execution altogether feminine'.

Now, Mr Trollope has a distinct intrigue on foot, which the reader never loses sight of, and the characters successively help to unfold it; but the authoress of the 'Athelings' has nothing of the sort, and we have to look through her three volumes again and again to discover how it is she can possibly have contrived to spin out dreary conversation to such an extent as to fill them, and preserve a vestige of interest. The secret is that the novel is addressed to the British Home, and it seems that we may prose everlastingly to the republic of the fireside. . . . The Authoress is clever: she can describe society: . . . Her main fault has killed the most charmingly written books, and this lady has only to practise compression to become an excellent novelist.   (pp. 596–7)

Sandwiched between notices of two mediocre novels Meredith gives a long account of his own recently published *Farina*. Biographers have all followed Sir J. A. Hammerton in saying of this review that 'George Eliot was again the critic of her friend's work, . . . and in her estimate of the story we can see personal liking struggle with the critical sense, the latter proving the stronger in the result'.[5] A careful reader will observe how trivial the objections are compared with the skilfully insinuated praise of the book's narrative interest.

The Author of 'Farina' has exposed himself to a somewhat trying ordeal. Last year he treated us to a delightful volume of well-sustained oriental extravagance, and we remember our friend Shibli Bagarag too well to be easily satisfied with any hero less astonishing. It was refreshing to leave the actual and the probable for a time, and follow Mr Meredith's lead into the bright world of imagination. The hope of such another enchanted holiday prepared us to welcome his new tale with all due honour and cordiality. It was with something like disappointment, therefore, that we found ourselves brought down to the vulgar limits of time and place, and our appetite for the marvellous entirely spoilt by scenes which challenge prosaic considerations of historical truth and the fitness of things. The title 'Farina: a Legend of Cologne', will naturally carry the reader's mind to those ungainly-shaped bottles, with which the British tourist is sure to return laden from the city of evil smells. Mr Meredith is pleased to bestow a high antiquity on the famous distillation, and his hero, doubtless the first of all the Jean Marie's, is invested with the dubious honours of a dealer in the black art, on account of his suspicious collection of bottles and vases, pipes and cylinders. But when the Devil is beaten in single combat on the Drachenfels, and returns from whence he came, entering to his kingdom under the Cathedral Square, and leaving behind him a most abominable stench, Farina's perfumed water does good service. The kaiser, six times driven back by the offence to his nostrils, is enabled to enter the good city of Cologne, and then and there reward the restorer of a pure atmosphere with the hand of his long-loved bride. For the rest, the story is sufficiently slight. We have the blonde and bewitching heroine, Margarita, and her troop of lovers, who prove their devotion by such strenuous interchange of blows in her honour, that there is not one of them who is not black and blue; and we have *the* lover, Farina, tender and true, brave as Siegfried, and worshipping his 'Frankinne' with such fanatical homage, as 'Conrad the Pious' might have sung. Margarita's father Gottlieb Groschen, the rich Cologne citizen, is a characteristic specimen of the prosperous mediæval Rhinelander, and we cannot give our readers a more favourable specimen of Mr Meredith's style than by introducing the father and daughter, engaged in receiving that nuisance of the middle – as of all ages – morning visitors.   (p. 597)

Three carefully chosen excerpts then give the opening scene, in which a brutal cavalryman, seeing the girl at the window, wagers that he will have a kiss from her within twenty minutes.

How Margarita escapes this indignity, how she becomes the captive of the terrible Werner himself, and how she is rescued, we have not space to tell; much clever and vigorous description is to be found in the narrative, and Mr Meredith has been very success-ful in setting before us a vivid picture of the coarse, rough manners, the fierce, warlike habits, and the deep-seated superstition of the 'good old times' of chivalry. The character of the jovial Squire Guy the Goshawk, is especially well done. As a whole, we think 'Farina' lacks completeness, and the ghostly element is not well worked in. The combat between Saint Gregory and the Devil is made ludicrous by its circumstantiality. It was not as a jeering satirist that the old monkish legends set forth Sathanas, and there is a clumsiness in the whole affair which accords ill with the boldness and skill displayed in other portions of the tale. We must also protest against Father Gregory's use of the nominative case 'ye' instead of the accusative 'you', monk though he be, and privileged doubtless to speak bad grammar at will; nor can we admire many passages, in which the Author has sacrificed euphony, and almost sense, to novelty and force of expression. With these blemishes, 'Farina' is both an original and an entertaining book, and will be read with pleasure by all who prefer a lively, spirited story to those dull analyses of dull experiences in which the present school of fiction abounds.   (pp. 598–9)

This pleasant tribute to his own novel Meredith follows with an account of Thomas Mackern's *Lucian Playfair* unappetising enough to show which of them a reader was certain to enjoy the more.

Meredith next turns to foreign novels with some interesting paragraphs on *Madame Bovary*.

A great change is coming over French works of fiction. The miserable intrigues and villanous [*sic*] dog-loves which have till recently formed the staple of every French novel, and disgusted the world by the exhibition of a state of corruptness bordering on profanation of all that the mind holds most sacred, are gradually disappearing. . . . Intrigue continues, but does not minister to depraving excitement: the systematic seducer takes his proper criminal rank, and the fair and frail are not so enchantingly lovely as to dazzle us into forgiveness, and throw goodness and purity into the background.

In 'Madame Bovary', the husband is a fool to his wife. To the reader he is a simple apothecary, a weak, everyday sort of character, who loves his offspring and adores the wretched woman that deceives him. She is about equal to him in station: his superior in intellect. Living in a provincial town, and sighing for the unknown delights of Paris and splendour, her whole nature cries out to be seduced. Of course she does not go to her grave without being satisfied. As the German poet writes –

'Ein Thor ist immer willig,
Wenn eine Thorin will.'

The old blandishing graces of Dumas, Sand, and De Balzac, are quite excluded from this story. All is severe matter of fact painfully elaborated. We flung the book to the four corners of the room; but we took it up again, and finished it. The Author is uncompromising: he gives Madame Bovary successive lovers. She has not even the excuse of love and its poor consolation when the end comes. She endeavours to persuade both lovers to elope with her; she begs money of both. She plunders her husband; ruins him; finally the discovery of her treason kills him. The Author is right: if an adultery is to be treated of at all (and England cannot deny that such things really are in France), it should be laid bare – not tricked out in meretricious allurements: subjected to stern analysis – not made solely to present the passion, thereby to awake the sympathies of a vulgar prurience. No harm can come from reading Madame Bovary; but it is physic for adults, as the doctors say. The Author has no more love for her than an anatomist for his subject. He does not preach. He allows her patiently to make her own wickedness manifest, and leaves us to contemplate the picture at our leisure. M. Gustave Flaubert is a singularly powerful writer. (pp. 600–1)

The novels of Amédée Achard may have provided Meredith with some glances at his own crumbling marriage.

Madame Rose has left her husband, but not her duty. She is prepared to sacrifice her heart and her life to him still, and wins the man who loves her to a similar devotion. What may not women do? (p. 601)

Maurice de Treuil is the story of a young artist of genius who 'has the misfortune to love his wife' and must choose between her and his art.

The latter part of the story is told with great pathos, and the contrast to the fate of Maurice is well brought out in the characters of Philippe, his friend, and Laura, who loved him, and whom he might have married and lived a happy man. We thank M. Achard for not sullying the wife. French writers have evidently only to be decent to be delightful.   (p. 602)

Commending the moral tales of J. T. de St Germain for 'awaking in us the same kind of tender and loving emotion in all that is holy in domestic uses, and reverent in family bonds and religious senti-ment' (p. 603), Meredith does not expect them to influence French literature.

There is no doubt that a healthy revolution in the moral tone of fiction must proceed from fiction itself: criticism may bring the plough and the harrow, and improve the ground; but the fruit of the soil is dependent on conditions beneath the surface, and slight as they are, we welcome these little works, and the stories gener-ally of the Bibliothèque des Chemins de Fer, as flowers out of the rank, fermenting earth, indicating an impulse and a power for purer and better things.   (p. 603)

IV

Though no receipt has been found for the Belles Lettres and Art section of the *Westminster* in January 1858, the style is unmistakeable. Like the preceding articles it begins with general reflexions on

the increasing influx of volumes self-christened 'Poems' on the title-page, and as guiltless of kinship with the Muse as the alder-man's wife with royalty, though their names may be similar, and they wear dresses of the same silk pattern.   (vol. LXIX, p. 291)

Most of these attempts he passes in silence, hoping that the evil will work its own cure,

as possibly it might do if the ambitious youth were only fortunate enough not to fall into the hands of one of those so-called critics who are ready with a bellows to inflate any aspiring conceit, and puff it till it burst; though generally, we must say, it is found to possess an extraordinary power of expansion, and for a time largely imposes on the public. But the public is a wise old beast, and if it has a trick of gaping at air-bags, it will not be satisfied by only swallowing wind. When the cheat is discovered, it has less mercy than we in the critical chair should have; for we can see some germ of good in the attempt to please, but the public in its hatred of disappointment ignores every minor consideration. (p. 291)

Robert Story's volume of poetical works

stands out like Leviathan in bulk from among its smaller compeers, and, like our Leviathan, we fear it will not take the stream. The songs are very well worthy the poet's corner of a provincial newspaper; they are gentle, and exhibit good feeling. We are not acquainted with Mr Story's antecedents; he seems to have laboured in a humble position, and to have found patrons. He deserves every credit for the culture he has obtained, and we regret not to be able to say more.   (p. 291)

The Arabian Nights had been one of Meredith's favourite books since childhood, and from it he drew much of the atmosphere of *The Shaving of Shagpat*. Reviewing a translation of Oehlenschläger's *Aladdin*, he calls the choice of subject extremely infelicitous.

This Aladdin does not breathe East. He is a hybrid, and comes to us, who knew him so well in youth, like a half-resuscitated wretch whose end should in mercy be near. Then, again, old remembrance is outraged by our finding the names altered. . . . 'Gulnare' is now the name of the beautiful princess we slept with, [now] the sword of the Genie dividing us. We know nothing of Gulnare but as a Corsair's mistress. . . .

The gallant English lieutenant chose to forget for the time that he was an Englishman, and he reached the shrine of Mecca. This the poet must do who deals with an Eastern subject. He must not only look on, his imagination must have sufficient strength of sympathy and imagination combined to cast themselves loose from the West, and start fairly; and moreover it requires a subtle dramatic and a mimetic power not common. Göthe succeeded; Rückert in a less degree. Freiligrath and Tom Moore conjured up pretty pictures, one with fire, and one with tinsel. No impediment of personal feeling stood in the way of Moore, and his industry enabled him to get together vast hoards of costume. He lacked the genius to give his stories more than artificial life. There is a cold glitter in 'Lalla Rookh', rendered sickly at times by clap-trap side-appeals to purely Western sentiments.

Moore had not full faith in the East. Beckford had, and his 'Caliph Vathek' is as superior to 'Lalla Rookh' in truthfulness as it is unrivalled in grandeur of outline. The Arab is a passionate animal expressing himself in wild fancies: like a fire lit among rocks, striking up the oddest reflections alike from by-nooks and broad slabs and tumbled blocks; yet if you examine each, you will find it a perfect image of the flame. Moore was fanciful enough, and danced and tripped from simile to simile, but the central fire was wanting, the solid core of heat which burns in the Arab bosom. Oehlenschläger seems to have felt his own deficiencies, for he summons fairies to his assistance, and Aladdin sleeps lulled by the singing of Zephyr and Lympha! The singing is not bad, we must allow; but although everything is possible to the fairy world, we are still inclined to ask how this classic young gentle-man and his lady-love arrived there, and are not satisfied that Oehlenschläger should have been the means of their introduction. (pp. 291–3)

Felix Meldred's *Leonilda* provokes some remarks on the Spenserian stanza:

We think the author ill-advised in selecting it as the vehicle for narrative. Spenser, Byron, Keats, and Shelley, who mastered it and made it their own, were all poets depending on treatment rather than story. It is the grand gala-coach of the Muses – not a chariot in the race-course. Pegasus in his most rampant state will not help it to move briskly; and therefore it is the measure to which a garniture of philosophical reflection, or rich imaginative ornament – cumbrous elsewhere – may, and should, be added. (p. 293)

The Spasmodics come in for another drubbing in the dismissal of Robert Buchanan's *Poems*:

We must hand over Mr Buchanan to Mr Alexander Smith, that he may see his own image in a distorting mirror, to which let this quotation, from 'Poems and Love-Lyrics', bear witness:–

> 'The wrinkled sea lies foaming at the mouth,
> In a fierce fit of agonizing wrath
> 'Gainst the pale partner of his bed, the land,
> Whose locks, the tufted forests, stand on end,
> Or, damp with mangled flesh, uprooted are
> Beneath his tyrant hand, the clutching wind . . . .'

O Scotia! O Muses! North of Tweed we are surpassed in every-thing – even in spasmodism! (p. 294)

Meredith's opinion of Pope may be deduced from his comment on Gilfillan's *Library Edition of the British Poets*:

> We were curious to see how he would deal with Pope, and, as might have been imagined, he is altogether Bowlesian in his judg-ment on that perfect artist. As to typography, the edition is ex-cellent, and will form, when complete, the cheapest extant. Those who think Pope a poet, and Crashaw not a 'transcendant' genius – those, in short, who object to Mr Gilfillan's standard of criticism in poetics – will have nothing to do with it. (p. 294)

Some of the liveliest pages must have made stinging reading for Charles Reade, whose *White Lies*, Meredith says, is written with his 'usual dash'.

> A rattling fire of italics and interjections, backed by a great artillery of capitals and short paragraphs, distinguish his style. He adopts French idioms freely, and defends his system in a preface. In spite of his affectation and bumptious arrogance, he is really an artist. He has French characters, and he makes them thoroughly French. They talk, think, and act French. This story is remarkable for its ingenious exposition of a few of the endless intricacies of female character. Mr Reade would have us think that he knows women offhand. He marshals Madam before us, and turns her in and out with a juggler's ease of legerdemain; and after it is over, has the air of posturing to an astonished people to ask them what they think of that for a show? Adam could not have done so much, 'tis certain.
>
> Mr Reade is never bewildered by his Eve. He labours to expose the original woman bare of all her shifts, for the benefit of noodles. We should possibly think more of what he does, if he would allow

us to fancy that he thought less of it. Few writers of the present day know women so well. Their inconsistencies are consistent to him. But he seems as yet solely to have studied them on the side that's next the sun. He is only surpassed by Mr Thackeray – how immeasurably need not be said – in this branch of his art. We intend by this to speak high praise, but it does not say much. What other living novelists seem to have any idea of the character of one real woman? We are at a disadvantage in England, owing to the stiffness of Society and the small natural intercourse that takes place between women and men; but something better than dolls and stiff-backed passionless puppets should be given us by novelists who have seen the world and tried their luck in the marriage-lottery. Is the sympathy of such novelists with women defective? or, worse, is it only a sentimental sympathy? Real women abhor that in art, as they learn to do in life. Mr Reade gives himself up to them heart and soul, and the consequence is that they candidly tell him something of what they are. That something he has erroneously taken for all the secret. We who are more humble, think we see how far he has gone wrong, and may be pardoned a smile at his airs . . . .

We must protest against Mr Reade, as an artist, writing down such exclamations as, 'Oh! oh!' 'Ha! ha!' 'He! he!' 'Sh! sh!' so frequently. They are very good stage directions, but read flat and pointless in print. He promises us now a German story. We shall be curious to see how he adapts his style to the rolling, long-winded, cumbrous Teutonic model. Hitherto, when he speaks in person, he has been the same in English, Scotch, and French stories. Mr Reade has the reputation of a gentleman who makes war on his critics, and appeals from them to the public – a sort of literary demagogue. It is a silly thing to do, and time lost. We have spoken what we think of his work, and cannot help his displeasure because our praise is not without reserve.   (pp. 296–7)

Georgiana M. Craik's *Riverston* and Matilda Betham Edwards's *The White House by the Sea*

introduce us to two governesses who are the daughters direct of Miss Jane Eyre. The governess in an autobiographical novel is pretty sure to be the heroine and authoress thereof. She is the family dissector – the social anatomist; she is a manager of women, and of men. She represents principle, as opposed to impulse. She is generally, therefore, even in her own picture, more upright than agreeable – indeed, she is quite unbending. For the purposes of autobiography, she is compelled to hear strange things; she 'finds herself listening' to many conversations, and 'accidentally over-hears' much that serves the story. It is in the nature of things that she should marry an old, broken, if not blind, gentleman, at the close of the third volume. Young men do not appreciate principle as opposed to impulse. We confess for ourselves, that we do not greatly care for these ladies in books. In actual life they are admirable; in books they are tedious, morbid, distasteful. They have a terrible deal of temper, too. They can 'fire up', and upon occasion, fire off.   (pp. 297–8)

It is delightfully ironic to hear the author of *Richard Feverel* and *Evan Harrington* hoping that Miss Craik

will not be autobiographical in her next novel. The tendency is not healthy, and she can write so sweetly and well, that it will be a pity to see such powers marred at the outset. Of these heroine-governesses, one can only wish that England may have more of them, and the circulating libraries less.   (p. 298)

So far Meredith has filled only eight of the sixteen pages usually allotted to this section. As obvious padding he inserts two-and-a-half pages of excerpts from C. A. Murray's trashy *Hassan; or, the Child of the Pyramid*, which he is betrayed into praising by his fondness for the 'oriental'. He uses half a page in commending Heine's poems to save himself the trouble of saying anything about Hebbel's, which he was supposed to review. Heine had been the subject of George Eliot's brilliant article in the *Westminster* two years before, to which Meredith alludes:

As a humourist, he is known to the pages of this Review; as a poet, the scattered attempts to translate him have not been the means of a favourable introduction to the English public. We will only say of him here, that there are more qualities combined and condensed in his verse than will be found in any European poet since Göthe; and that in variety and tenderness of song, in spontaneity and suggestive beauty, in richness, naturalness, and colour, he, as a lyrist, surpassed that great master.   (p. 302)

The article ends on the fourteenth page with a perfunctory notice of Eugène Baret's *Espagne et Provence*, which interests Meredith chiefly for its 'exposure' by parallel passages of Victor Hugo's modelling Esméralda on Cervantes's Jitanilla [i.e. Gitanella].

This is the last of the four articles that Meredith is known to have written. His heart had never been in the work, and the flashes of style and idiosyncrasies of opinion that distinguish it were scarcely suited to the sober pages of the *Westminster*. After reading this article George Eliot wrote to the editor John Chapman, 12 January 1858:

> I wish you could get the Belles Lettres better done, though it is troublesome to say so to you just now. This number seems to me worse done than the previous ones – the tone is so flippant and journalistic. I only mention it in this letter that, if you have any intention to make a change in that department, I may contribute towards confirming that intention.[6]

Evidently in response to his reply she returned to the subject two weeks later:

> It is so difficult to get a satisfactory writer! One can never judge à priori. For example, you had good reason to believe that the Belles Lettres would be well done by the present writer (Meredith, is it not?); yet he turns out to be unfit for that sort of work.[7]

Meredith's successor proved to be far worse. One has only to read a few of the clumsy, dull, pedantic sentences in the April Belles Lettres to lament the loss of the sparkling prose with which Meredith enlivened the pages of the *Westminster* for a whole year.

Notes

This essay first appeared in the *Modern Language Review*, vol. 53 (January 1958) pp. 1–16.

1. *A Catalogue of the Altschul Collection of George Meredith in the Yale University Library* (privately printed, 1931) p. 19.
2. Lionel Stevenson, *The Ordeal of George Meredith* (New York, 1953) p. 58.
3. *Fortnightly Review*, vol. xi (1 May 1869) p. 628.
4. Cf. *Letters of George Meredith*, 2 vols (London, 1912) vol. i, p. 11.
5. J. A. Hammerton, *George Meredith: His Life and Art in Anecdote and Criticism*, rev. edn (Edinburgh, 1911) p. 142.
6. *The George Eliot Letters*, ed. Gordon S. Haight, 7 vols (New Haven, Conn., and London, 1954–5) vol. ii, p. 421.
7. Ibid., p. 427.

11

Tennyson's Merlin

The Victorians' curious reluctance to face the facts is nowhere more clearly illustrated than in their writing of biography. The candid self-revelation of Rousseau, Hume, Gibbon, Franklin and of course Casanova found no imitators in the nineteenth century. Lockhart, publishing his *Scott* in the year Victoria ascended the throne, was the last to follow the model so magnificently established by Boswell; and Froude's effort in the 1880s to revive intimacy without accuracy raised a storm of public protest, and not a little cold fear among the Great who were possible future subjects. Most of them regarded biography as a posthumous task of piety left to one's family, or those vaguer 'friends', who could be trusted to publish nothing but conventional and laudatory remarks. The need of some account to perpetuate one's memory was universally recognised. But the Victorians' pious effort to insure fame more often than not added the lethal weight of three thick volumes to sink forever the subject's claim on posterity. In their zeal to present a marmoreal ideal to the world, they did not hesitate to suppress facts. Many a scholar who has spent his nights sifting Victorian biographies for some stray straw of information that the author has neglected to remove cries a hearty Amen to Carlyle's exclamation: 'How delicate, decent is English Biography, bless its mealy mouth! A Damocles' sword of *Respectability* hangs forever over the poor English Life-writer (as it does over poor English Life in general), and reduces him to the verge of paralysis.'[1]

None of the great Victorians was more reticent about his private life than Lord Tennyson. Just after accepting the peerage he wrote in a letter to Gladstone a story about an old lady who had corresponded with all the great men of her time.

> When Froude's *Carlyle* came out, she rushed up to her room, and to an old chest there wherein she kept their letters, and flung them into the fire. 'They were written to me,' she said, 'not to the public!' and she set her chimney on fire, and her children and grandchildren ran in – 'The chimney's on fire!' 'Never mind!' she

said, and went on burning. I should like to raise an altar to that old lady, and burn incense upon it.[2]

It is more probable that he would have burned his own letters if he had. But realising the inevitability of some account of his life, he entrusted the task to his son Hallam. In the Preface to the *Memoir* Hallam remarks that his father 'disliked the notion of a long, formal biography'; he was willing to have the incidents of his life given 'as shortly as might be without comment, but that my notes should be final and full enough to preclude the chance of further and unauthentic biographies. For those who cared to know about his literary history', the Preface continues, 'he wrote "Merlin and the Gleam", which he thought 'would probably be enough biography for those friends who urged him to write about himself'.[3] How much mistaken he was is obvious in the thousand or more pages his son saw fit to add. Yet this poem, one of the most riddling that Tennyson ever wrote, deserves particular attention because, though usually resenting any identification of himself with his characters, he has here expressly sanctioned it.

Tennyson told his son: 'In the story of "Merlin and Nimue" I have read that Nimue means the Gleam, – which signifies in my poem "the higher poetic imagination".[4] To understand how Nimuë (or Vivien, as he later called her), the most licentious lady in the *Idylls*, could also represent 'the higher poetic imagination' we must examine the source of the legend and Tennyson's earlier use of it. Her name is found in the opening chapter of Book IV of the *Morte D'Arthur*, where Malory tells how Merlin 'fell in a dotage' on 'one of the damsels of the lake, which hight Nimuë', apparently the same benevolent lady who gave Arthur his sword Excalibur, protected Sir Pelleas all his life, and, in one account, served as Launcelot's foster-mother. In her relations with the lecherous old magician this Nimue (whom Malory found in the French *Suite de Merlin* in some manuscript closely akin to the Huth *Merlin*)[5] is afraid of Merlin because 'he was a devil's son'; and, at length, 'passing weary' of his importunities, shut him up under a stone by means of a charm he had taught her.

Except for their names there is no resemblance between this odd pair of lovers and Tennyson's lascivious Vivien, winding like a snake about her moody reluctant victim. The enchantment is wrought, not as Malory has it in Benwick, but in the forest of Broceliande, and upon a Merlin far different from the too-eager wooer of the French sources. Tennyson's Merlin has no joy whatever in love. He has fallen into 'a great melancholy' because of it, distressed to see 'the meanest having power upon the highest'.[6] His journey to Brittany was undertaken not in pursuit of, but to escape Vivien, who gets into the same boat unheeded by the brooding old man, and follows him through the forest for days until she can learn the charm, which she instantly uses to quench his greatness.

The version of the legend closest to Tennyson's idyll is found in the Vulgate *Merlin*,[7] one of the prose continuations of Robert de Boron's poem. There is no need to assume that Tennyson read it in the Old French. For the edition of Malory published in 1817 in two handsome quarto volumes contains over a hundred large pages of notes in many of which the Vulgate *Merlin* is extensively translated by the editor, Robert Southey. In these notes Tennyson found the forest of Broceliande, spelled as he spells it.[8] Here he found his melancholy Merlin, who, when Viviane asked him to teach her 'how to enclose and imprison a man without a tower, without walls, without chains, but by enchantments alone', 'shook his head, and began to sigh deeply', knowing full well 'that you are devising how you may detain me'.[9] Tennyson's Merlin had a similar 'dark forethought' that she planned to betray him.

> The vast and shaggy mantle of his beard

that stretches

> Across her neck and bosom to her knee,[10]

as she combs it, seated on Merlin's lap, may have been suggested by the observation in the Vulgate that 'he was swarthy and more hairy than any other man',[11] combined, perhaps, with the account of how he was born covered (appropriately for a devil's son) with thick black hair.

Tennyson's portrait of Vivien also draws a number of details from Southey's notes. Her technique of lovemaking is perhaps less lurid in the Vulgate version, though she does 'fawn' and 'flatter' Merlin to coax the secret from him: 'The better to delude and deceive him', Southey writes, 'she put her arms round his neck, and began to kiss him.' And after he had told her the secret, she 'showed him greater semblance of loving him than she had ever before made; and they sojourned together a long while'.[12] In Southey, as in Tennyson, she is called 'harlot', not by Merlin, to be sure, but by Morgan le Fay.[13] Her serpentine traits, so remarkable in the *Idylls*, also seem to come from

Southey's notes. In a passage he translates from the *Prophecy of Merlin* Viviane refers to herself as 'the white serpent' which Merlin had prophesied would go into the forest 'with the demi-man, and he should remain there, and the white serpent should return with a glad cheer out of the forest'.[14] There are other reptiles in the notes, too. The revolting story of Carados and the serpent from the *Perceval le Gallois*[15] is translated at length and could hardly have escaped Tennyson. Another curious possibility occurs in the text of Malory: the chapter where the Merlin and Nimue story is found,[16] opens in Southey's edition with a grotesque ornamental capital *S* formed by an enormous serpent, apparently ten feet long, winding itself about the ankle and across the knees of a naked man, who clings to a sort of ribbon fastened to the creature's neck – if serpents have necks. There is undoubtedly a recollection of this fantastic ornamental capital *S* in Tennyson's description:

> lissome Vivien, holding by his heel,
> Writhed toward him, slided up his knee and sat,
> Behind his ankle twined her hollow feet
> Together, curved an arm about his neck,
> Clung like a snake.[17]

Tennyson's Merlin is imprisoned forever in a hollow oak, 'lost to life and use and name and fame'.[18] But like all the versions that connect the enchantment with a tree, the Vulgate *Merlin* places it under the shade of a 'white thorn which was laden with flowers'.[19] At the very end of his note, however, Southey cites a Breton legend mentioned by an English traveller that Merlin 'is still alive, enclosed in a tree by the power of a greater enchanter than himself'. The passage is found in Anne Plumptre's *A Narrative of Three Years' Residence in France*.[20] Now, an oak is almost the only tree known to Tennyson large enough to accommodate a pair like Merlin and Vivien. There were many picturesque specimens in England that had stood since the days of the Druids. In the New Forest, close at hand after the family settled at Farringford in 1853, there were some famous ones, which Tennyson made a special journey to see. According to the *Memoir*[21] there are many reminiscences of the New Forest in his woods of Broceliande. From the beginning Tennyson had imagined his Merlin confined in the hollow oak. One of his MS books 1833–40 contains the scenario for an Arthurian drama, in which the Lady of the Lake, under the name of Nimue, plays an important role; Act III is laid at the 'Oak tomb of Merlin', where Mordred and Arthur come to consult the imprisoned magician as Meliadus had in a passage quoted by Southey from the *Prophecies*.[22]

'Nimuë', as Tennyson originally called the poem, was the first Idyll to be written after the 'Morte d'Arthur' was published in 1842. Begun early in 1856, it was finished on 31 March.[23] During the ensuing summer, spent by the Tennysons in Wales, he wrote the 'Enid', which was completed in August. Tennyson discovered that the *E* was pronounced short in *Enid* only after the poem was in proof, and changed the phrase 'wedded Enid' to 'married Enid'.[24] The two poems were then printed together in a trial-copy with the title *Enid and Nimuë: The True and the False*, 1857. A copy with Tennyson's autograph inscription is in the British Museum. In March 1858, while he was working on the third poem, 'Guinevere', a young Pre-Raphaelite named William Morris brought out a volume entitled *The Defence of Guenevere*. On this, as on so many interesting matters, the *Memoir* is silent. Yet there can be no doubt that Tennyson, always conscious of the public taste and busy with the Arthurian legend, read the poem that gave its name to Morris's book. A review in the *Athenaeum* (April 3) made a number of comparisons with 'The Lady of Shalott' which would have piqued his curiosity if necessary. Though the *Memoir* says that 'Guinevere' was 'finally completed' 15 March 1858,[25] it is impossible to know what revisions Tennyson made in it before the end of the year, when, with 'Elaine', written during the summer, it was added to the *Enid and Nimuë*. In the proofs the title read *The True and the False. Four Idylls of the King*.

The pretentious scheme that was to make the *Idylls* a nature myth and an allegory of Victorian morality had not yet entered the Laureate's mind when these four were published. They had their own simple scheme of the true and the false, the good women Enid and Elaine contrasted with the evil ones Nimuë and Guinevere. What allegory there was resolved itself into a mild sort of Paradise Lost: both Merlin, the wisest of mankind, and Arthur, the noblest, have their careers ruined by a woman, a new Eve. In the frame he had placed round the 'Morte D'Arthur' in 1842 Tennyson confessed to 'some modern touches here and there'; in his dreams he saw

> King Arthur, like a modern gentleman
> Of stateliest port.[26]

But there is little for modern application in the story of Bedivere's failure to throw the sword; Tennyson has followed Malory closely. In his earliest sketch of Guinevere he also stayed close to the character he found in the sources. A fragment published in 1842 as 'Sir Launcelot and Queen Guinevere' was, I believe, originally a part of 'The Lady of Shalott'. Here in the same stanza form there is a detailed description of Guinevere's costume with plumes, golden clasps and jingling bridle reins to match those that Lancelot sports in the Lady's mirror, but the knight himself hardly appears in the fragment. Perhaps the description of the Queen was to follow the similar one of Lancelot, which Tennyson wisely decided to use as the sole subject of Part III of 'The Lady of Shalott'.

However that may be, Tennyson's early Guinevere is the great lover of the romances:

> A man had given all other bliss, –
> And all his worldly worth for this,
> To waste his whole heart in one kiss
> Upon her perfect lips.[27]

By the time the 1859 *Idylls* appear she has been metamorphosed into the guilt-laden Victorian matron, the original sinner of a modern allegory whose theme is adultery. Her physical inferiority has become a symbol of that deadly moral weakness which threatened, unless it were held in check, to disrupt nineteenth-century society as it had the Garden of Eden and the Round Table. Overwhelmed with remorse, realising what she might have made of this fair world had she but loved God's highest creature – for every Victorian woman, her husband – Guinevere withdraws into the cloister to prepare herself to be a worthy mate in heaven, where Arthur, this paragon of manhood, seems assured of his place.

With this attitude freshly in mind, we are better prepared to understand the distress with which Tennyson must have read William Morris's defence of the passionate young Guenevere, whose only excuse for sin is that she is human:

> the sick
> Sure knowledge things would never be the same
>
> However often Spring might be most thick
> Of blossoms and buds, smote on me, and I grew
> Careless of most things, let the clock tick, tick,
>
> To my unhappy pulse, that beat right through
> My eager body; while I laughed out loud,
> And let my lips curl up at false or true.[28]

'False or true'! That line alone, appearing as Tennyson was working on his proofs of *The True and the False*, would probably have been enough to make him change the title; and one would not be surprised to find that he had revised or added to the text of his 'Guinevere' to counteract the vicious tendency of Morris's. The single mention of Morris in the *Memoir* says: Tennyson 'was not a great reader of William Morris; but he liked *The Life and Death of Jason*'.[29] Between these two meagre lines one may easily read that he did not like *The Defence of Guenevere*, whose frank avowal of her passion,

> When both our mouths went wandering in one way,
> And aching sorely, met among the leaves,

and whose coarse allusion to having been

>   bought
> By Arthur's great name and his little love,[30]

must have shocked the Laureate. Such feelings had no right to disrupt the ordered plan of life. The Victorians had seen so many scientific phenomena reduced to formulae that they were confident marital relations might in time be similarly regulated. It was part of the Practical Ideal to strive towards that noble end. Guinevere realised too late that

> It was my duty to have loved the highest;
> It surely was my profit had I known;
> It would have been my pleasure had I seen.[31]

Thus Tennyson, refuting Morris's defence of his shameless Guenevere, stands forth as staunch champion of the Victorian ideal of marriage. Beside his remorseful Queen, that shallow sensualist Nimuë with her perverse taste for the aged Merlin takes second place among the false.

    The decision to change her name to the more familiar form *Vivien* was made after the trial-copy of 1857 had been printed. It may, I think, be ascribed with some confidence to Tennyson's fear that Nimuë might be mispronounced as a word of two syllables, destroying the rhythm of his carefully wrought lines. He had placed a diacritical mark above the final *e*. But the use of such signs was a practice for which the reviewers of his early volumes had twitted him a good deal, and recollection of their ridicule, reinforced, perhaps, by hearing Nimuë mispronounced by friends to whom he had lent trial-copies, probably induced him to alter it throughout to *Vivien*.

Few names in the Arthurian matter occur with more bewildering variants. It was so easy for scribes to confuse *n* with *u* or the open *a*, *ui* with *ni* or *in*, that the name is found in at least a dozen forms. *Nyneue* as well as *Nimue*, *Ninane*, *Niniene* and *Nynyane* appear; by a misreading of the second *n* it becomes *Nimainne*, *Nimenne* or *Nivienne*; and the transformation is completed by a misreading of the initial *n* as a *u*, resulting in *Vivienne* or *Viviane*. Such variants as *Jumenne* are occasionally noted; and Professor John Rhys shows quite plausibly that Nimuë is identical with a legendary Welsh lady named Rhiannon.[32] After this varied display one is not surprised at Tennyson's remark: 'In the story of "Merlin and Nimue" I have read that Nimue means the Gleam, – which signifies in my poem the higher poetic imagination'. Just where did he read this? Professor Tom Peete Cross who in 1921 surveyed Tennyson's knowledge of Celtic, confessed: 'The fanciful etymology of Nimuë referred to by Tennyson I have been unable to run down.'[33] It can be traced, I believe, very close to the source.

Tennyson's interest in the poetry of the ancient Britons began as early as 1856, when during the summer spent in Wales he learned a little Welsh with the help of local schoolmasters. Though the *Memoir* says that he and Mrs Tennyson 'read together the *Hanes Cymru* (Welsh History), the *Mabinogion* and Llywarch Hen' for the 'Enid', which he was writing at the time, he must have relied principally upon Lady Charlotte Guest's translation of the *Mabinogion* (1849). In 1867 he was reading *Barddas*, a collection of bardo-druidic documents collected and translated by the Rev. John Williams ab Ithel.[34] It is from the titlepage of this work that he took the motto *Y Gwir yn erbyn y byd* (The truth against the world), which he sent in 1869 to a gentleman in Philadelphia who had announced the establishment of a Tennyson Society in that city. 'I have it in encaustic tiles on the pavement of my entrance hall [at Aldworth]', Tennyson wrote; it is 'a very old British apophthegm'.[35] In the 1870s his poem 'The Battle of Brunanburh', based 'more or less' upon his son's prose translation from the Anglo-Saxon, reveals a continuing study of the old metres, to which, finally, he returned late in the 1880s for the unrhymed dimetre line of 'Merlin and the Gleam'.

Many of the Old Welsh poems have exactly the rhythm of Tennyson's haunting

> O young Mariner,
> You from the haven
> Under the sea-cliff,
> You that are watching
> The gray Magician
> With eyes of wonder,
> *I* am Merlin,
> And *I* am dying,
> *I* am Merlin
> Who follow The Gleam.

In *The Black Book of Caermarthen*, for example, Poem xxx begins:

> Lym awel llum brin.
> Anhaut caffael clid.
> Llicrid rid reuhid llin.
> Rÿseiw gur arvn conin.
> Ton trathon toid tu tir.

These lines are quoted from William F. Skene's *The Four Ancient Books of Wales*,[36] a work that Tennyson could hardly have been ignorant of. Here in the 'Avallenau' (the apple trees), the famous poem by Merlin Sylvestris, occurs the word *Hwimleian*, translated 'The Sibyl', which Skene says 'is also written *chwimpleian*, *chwibleian*, and *chwivleian*'. He then quotes the following passage from the Rev. Thomas Price's *Literary Remains*:

> [It] seems evident that it is to his Cwifleian that we are to attribute the origin of the Viviane of the romances of chivalry and who acts so conspicuous a part in those compositions; although it is true there is not much resemblance betwixt the two names. But, if we look into the poems of Merlin Sylvestris, we shall find that the female personage of this name, which by the French romancers might easily be modified into Viviane, is repeatedly referred to by the bard in his vaticinations. It also seems probable, as Chwifleian signifies a female who appears and disappears, and also as the word bears some resemblance in sound to Sibylla, that the bard, by a confusion of terms and ideas, not uncommon in early writers, coined this name as an appellation for some imaginary character, and thus furnished the original of Viviane.[37]

La Villemarqué in his *Merlin l'Enchanteur*[38] also accepts this identification of *Chwifleian* and *Viviane* and invents for a link the hypothetical form *Vivlian*, almost the only possible variant that is nowhere
found, interpreting it as *'nymphe'*. Both the sibyl and the nymph spring
from the same source: in Owen Pughe's *Dictionary of the Welsh Language* (1793–1803) *Chwifleian* is defined as 'a female who appears and
disappears; a fairy'. Unhappily, this charming lady proves to be a
wholly imaginary creation of Owen's Celtic magic; unromantic
scholars like Gaston Paris declare that *Chwifleian* is a proper name
and nothing more.

I have no absolute proof that Tennyson learned from Skene's note
of the link between Nimuë and the female who appears and disappears. He does mention La Villemarqué, on whom he thought of
calling during his trip to Brittany in 1864.[39] But wherever he found
the information, it can doubtless be traced to the original definition
of *Chwifleian* in Owen Pughe's *Dictionary*. There remained in
Tennyson's mind simply the idea of the glimmering Welsh fairy, –
now you see her, now you don't. It is obvious that he was not
thinking at all of his evil and fleshly Vivien when he equated Nimuë
with 'the higher poetic imagination'.

Her metamorphosis into the Gleam can be traced, I believe, still
further. Tennyson used the word *gleam*, not in its primary sense of a
brilliant light, but with the later connotation of a transient or inter-
mittent one. In the 'Elegiac Stanzas Suggested by a Picture of Peele
Castle in a Storm' Wordsworth had used it in relation to the fitful
nature of inspiration:

> Ah! THEN, if mine had been the Painter's hand,
> To express what then I saw; and add the gleam,
> The light that never was, on sea or land,
> The consecration, and the Poet's dream . . . .[40]

Here the word is already connected with 'the higher poetic imagination', and it required nothing more than for Tennyson, in identifying
himself with the bard Merlin, to recall that Nimuë was said to have
had the habit of appearing and disappearing.

The Preface to the *Memoir* declares that 'From boyhood he had felt
the magic of Merlin – that spirit of poetry – which bade him know
his power and follow throughout his work a pure and high ideal,
with a simple and single devotedness and a desire to ennoble the life

of the world'.[41] There were certain coincidental resemblances between him and Merlin. Both had a swarthy complexion and full
beard (Tennyson's was grown during the Crimean war when he was
writing 'Nimuë'); like Merlin, Tennyson was a defender of the Throne
and was acknowledged the greatest bard of his time. Such things
would help make it natural for him to assume the character of Merlin
when at the age of 80 he turned to review his career as a poet.

Adopting his own statement that the poem represents his literary
history, the commentators have been greatly puzzled by its peculiar
chronology. Stanza II they generally interpret as referring to
Tennyson's earliest volumes:

> Mighty the Wizard
> Who found me at sunrise
> Sleeping, and woke me
> And learn'd me Magic!
> Great the Master,
> And sweet the Magic,
> When over the valley,
> In early summers,
> Over the mountain,
> On human faces,
> And all around me,
> Moving to melody,
> Floated The Gleam.

Stanza III is obviously an account of the harsh criticism of the 1832
volume that is often blamed for the 'Ten Years' Silence'.

> Once at the croak of a Raven who crost it,
> A barbarous people,
> Blind to the magic,
> And deaf to the melody,
> Snarl'd at and cursed me.
> A demon vext me,
> The light retreated,
> The landskip darken'd,
> The melody deaden'd,
> The Master whisper'd
> 'Follow The Gleam.'

In the next stanza the reader naturally expects something about the 1842 volumes. Instead he finds The Gleam

> Gliding, and glancing at
> Elf of the woodland,
> Gnome of the cavern,
> Griffin and Giant,
> And dancing of Fairies
> In desolate hollows,
> And wraiths of the mountain,
> And rolling of dragons
> By warble of water, . . .

No single volume of Tennyson's is concerned so exclusively as this with the supernatural. The 1832 volume contains scarcely perceptible traces of fairyland in 'Eleänore' and 'Lilian'; but in 1842 the only poems this stanza could describe are 'The Sea Fairies', 'The Kraken', 'The Mermaid', 'The Merman' and 'The Lady of Shalott', all in the earlier volumes too. Stanza v fits the 1842 *Poems* somewhat better:

> Down from the mountain
> And over the level,
> And streaming and shining on
> Silent river,
> Silvery willow,
> Pasture and plowland,
> Innocent maidens,
> Garrulous children,
> Homestead and harvest,
> Reaper and gleaner,
> And rough-ruddy faces
> Of lowly labor,
> Slided The Gleam –

Tennyson told his son that stanza ɪᴠ is 'the early imagination' and that v 'alludes to the Pastorals'.[42] Though 'Dora' and 'Audley Court' and 'The Gardener's Daughter' appear in the second volume of 1842, it is strange that Tennyson should have selected them while ignoring the finer and more characteristic poems like 'Ulysses', 'The Two Voices', 'The Vision of Sin' and most popular of all, 'Locksley Hall'.

Stanza VI recalls his beginning to use the Arthurian material:

> Then, with a melody
> Stronger and statelier,
> Led me at length
> To the city and palace
> Of Arthur the king;
> Touch'd at the golden
> Cross of the churches,
> Flash'd on the Tournament,
> Flicker'd and bicker'd
> From helmet to helmet,
> And last on the forehead
> Of Arthur the blameless
> Rested The Gleam.

Without too much straining this would pass for an account of the four *Idylls of the King* published in 1859. But the next stanza suddenly plunges us back to the death of Arthur Hallam in 1833:

> Clouds and darkness
> Closed upon Camelot;
> Arthur had vanish'd
> I knew not whither,
> The king who loved me,
> And cannot die;
> For out of the darkness
> Silent and slowly
> The Gleam, that had waned to a wintry glimmer
> On icy fallow
> And faded forest,
> Drew to the valley
> Named of the shadow,
> And slowly brightening
> Out of the glimmer,
> And slowly moving again to a melody
> Yearningly tender,
> Fell on the shadow,
> No longer a shadow,
> But clothed with The Gleam.

Here clearly is a description of *In Memoriam*.

Stanza VIII is not, as the commentators usually say, an account of Tennyson's 'later poetic activity'. Rather, it describes his satisfaction in the comfort that *In Memoriam* had brought to sorrowing minds:

> I saw, whenever
> In passing it glanced upon
> Hamlet or city,
> That under the Crosses
> The dead man's garden,
> The mortal hillock,
> Would break into blossom . . . .

The poem ends with an exhortation to the 'young Mariner', to whom the dying Merlin has been recounting his life-long pursuit of The Gleam:

> Down to the haven,
> Call your companions,
> Launch your vessel,
> And crowd your canvas,
> And, ere it vanishes
> Over the margin,
> After it, follow it,
> Follow The Gleam.

In these lines we hear for the last time the brave voice of his Ulysses, now too old 'to sail beyond the sunset', but with the same indomitable spirit urging the course on younger Mariners.

The confusion that has arisen over the chronology of this poem springs, I believe, from a too-limited interpretation of Tennyson's remark that it represents his 'literary history'. It seems clear that instead of a systematic account of his published volumes it is intended to be a statement of the various forms in which he had found inspiration: his poetic awakening in boyhood; the feeding of his 'early imagination' on tales of gnome and elf and giant; the later interest in common life stirred by Wordsworth's pastorals; the Arthurian matter begun with 'The Lady of Shalott' and 'Morte d'Arthur' and confirmed by the fusion of the King with his ideal of Arthur Hallam; and, finally, Hallam's death, which became his greatest inspiration, when, as sorrow and doubt were conquered,

> a melody
> Yearningly tender,
> Fell on the shadow,
> No longer a shadow,
> But clothed with The Gleam.

The 'shadow', of course, recalls his image of death in *In Memoriam,*
xxii–xxiii.

Every reader sees the allusion to Hallam in Tennyson's ambiguous reference to Arthur. But it has not, I think, been observed that
there are several other personal allusions in this poem. The stanza
beginning 'Once at the croak of a Raven' is rightly understood to
express the effect of the savage attack on Tennyson in the *Quarterly
Review* for April 1833. Professor Lounsbury in his *Life and Times of
Tennyson* (1915) accepted the customary ascription of this article to
Lockhart, and until 1941 all the commentators followed him.[43] Harold
Nicolson,[44] troubled by the chronological position of the stanza, toys
tentatively with the possibility that the Raven represented *Blackwood's*
Christopher North, who had been unappreciative of the 1830 volume
of Tennyson's poems, but rejects the theory immediately because
North's criticism, not altogether an unkind one, had produced little
effect upon the general public and aroused only momentary petulance
in its victim. No people, barbarous or otherwise, snarled at or cursed
him because of it.

The croak of a raven is a raucous and cacophonous sound; it is
sometimes considered ominous; but I know of no instance in history
or fable where it has incited mass persecution of a poet. Aside from
this passage the word *raven* occurs only five times in Tennyson's
poems. *Croak* appears four times, usually describing the unpleasant
noise of a frog or a rook; once the Princess applies it to her mas-
querading lover's falsetto singing of the song 'O swallow, swallow'.
Now, the *Quarterly* article with its sarcastic line-by-line commentary
on 'O Darling Room', cannot by the most charitable interpretation,
be described as a 'croak'. It is a broadside in the full slashing tradition. It opens with a gloating reference to the review of Keats's
Endymion fifteen years before, a less contemptuous and vitriolic
castigation than Tennyson was about to undergo. If Professor
Lounsbury and the commentators who followed him had not over-
looked the *Quarterly's* centenary article on itself in 1909, they would
have known that the attacks on both Keats and Tennyson were
written by John W. Croker.[45] The point of the line

Once at the croak of a Raven who crost it

lies in the pun on Croker's name. Tennyson clearly knew the author
of the review; there is no other reason for his so distorting the
meaning of the word *'croak'*.

Who, then, is the mighty 'Wizard' who first woke Merlin and
started him in pursuit of the Gleam? *Wizard* is another rare word in
Tennyson, used for the most part only of Merlin himself. Tennyson
says in a note he gave his son Hallam in 1890:

> At about twelve and onward I wrote an epic of six thousand lines
> à la Walter Scott, – full of battles, dealing too with sea and moun-
> tain scenery. . . . Though the performance was very likely worth
> nothing, I never felt myself more truly inspired. I wrote as much
> as seventy lines at one time, and used to go shouting them about
> the fields in the dark.[46]

Though the evidence is slim, it is enough to suggest that Walter
Scott, the 'Wizard of the North', may have been the poet who first
inspired Tennyson to follow the Gleam.

The only figure for whom it now remains to propose an original
is the Mariner of the opening stanza:

> O Young Mariner,
> You from the haven
> Under the sea-cliff
> You that are watching
> The gray Magician
> With eyes of wonder,
> *I* am Merlin,
> And *I* am dying,
> *I* am Merlin
> Who follow The Gleam.

There is a vividness in these few lines that I cannot help feeling
reflects some actual encounter. In the autumn of 1888 Tennyson fell
seriously ill; for a time his life was despaired of; Jowett, Browning
and others wrote anxious letters. After a second relapse the doctors
'ordered his removal in an invalid carriage to Farringford',[47] one of
them attending him on the way. During the landing on the Isle of
Wight it is easy to imagine some young sailor, one of the village lads

whom Tennyson had often seen, gazing with awe at the now pros-
trate Laureate, whom he was helping to carry. In this humiliating
position Tennyson must have been more sensitive than usual to
stares of the curious. And in the following August, when he began to
write the poem, the young Mariner's inquiring look may have won
him immortality as Merlin's confidant.

Notes

This essay first appeared in *Studies in Philology*, vol. 44 (July 1947)
pp. 549–66.

1. Thomas Carlyle, 'Sir Walter Scott', in *Works*, Library Edn, 30 vols (London, 1869–71) vol. x, p. 221.
2. Hallam Tennyson, *Alfred Lord Tennyson, A Memoir*, 2 vols (New York
   and London, 1897) vol. ii, p. 301. Hereafter referred to as *Memoir*.
3. Ibid., vol. i, pp. xii, xv.
4. Ibid., vol. ii, p. 336.
5. Gaston Paris and Jacob Ulrich, *Merlin, roman en prose du XIIIe siècle*, 2 vols
   (Paris, 1886) vol. i, pp. xliv–xlvii. See also H. O. Sommer, *Le Morte
   Darthur*, 3 vols (London, 1889–91) vol. iii, pp. 58, 120, and his *Le Roman
   de Merlin* (London, 1894) pp. xxvii–xxix.
6. Alfred Lord Tennyson, 'Merlin and Vivien', ll. 188, 193.
7. H. O. Sommer, *The Vulgate Version of the Arthurian Romances*, 8 vols
   (Washington, D. C., 1908–16) vol. ii, pp. 451–2.
8. *The Byrth, Lyf, and Actes of Kyng Arthur* . . . , ed. with an introduction and
   notes by Robert Southey, 2 vols (London, 1817) vol. i, p. xlvi. Hereafter
   referred to as *Kyng Arthur*.
9. Ibid., p. xlv.
10. Tennyson, 'Merlin and Vivien', ll. 254–5.
11. *Kyng Arthur*, vol. i, p. xli.
12. Ibid., pp. xlv–xlvi.
13. Ibid., vol. ii, p. 464.
14. Ibid., p. 464.
15. Ibid., vol. i, pp. xxxv–xxxviii.
16. Ibid., p. 90.
17. Tennyson, 'Merlin and Vivien', ll. 236–40.
18. Ibid., l. 968.
19. *Kyng Arthur*, vol. i, p. xlvi.
20. Anne Plumptre, *A Narrative of Three Years' Residence in France*, 3 vols
    (London, 1810) vol. iii, p. 187.
21. *Memoir*, vol. i, p. 414.
22. Ibid., vol. ii, p. 124; *Kyng Arthur*, vol. ii, pp. 465–6.
23. *Memoir*, vol. i, p. 414.
24. Ibid., vol. ii, p. 125n.

25. Ibid., p. 424.
26. Tennyson, 'Morte d'Arthur', ll. 329, 345–6.
27. The concluding lines of Tennyson's 'Sir Launcelot and Queen Guinevere'.
28. William Morris, 'The Defence of Guenevere', ll. 71–8.
29. *Memoir*, vol. II, p. 286.
30. Morris, 'The Defence of Guenevere', ll. 136–7, 82–3.
31. Tennyson, 'Guinevere', ll. 652–4.
32. The fullest account of Nimue–Vivien is found in Lucy A. Paton, *Studies in the Fairy Mythology of the Arthurian Romances* (Boston, Mass., 1903) ch. 4. See also Paris and Ulrich, *Merlin*, vol. I, p. xlv; James D. Bruce, *The Evolution of Arthurian Romance*, 2 vols (Baltimore, Md., 1923) vol. I, p. 150; John Rhys, *Studies in Arthurian Legend* (Oxford, 1891) p. 284; Roger S. Loomis, 'Some Names in Arthurian Romance', *PMLA*, vol. XLV (1930) pp. 438–41.
33. Tom Peete Cross, 'Alfred Tennyson as a Celticist', *Modern Philology*, vol. XVIII (1920–1) p. 491n.
34. *Barddas*, trans. John Williams ab Ithel, vol. I (Llandovery and London, 1862).
35. *Memoir*, vol. II, p. 91.
36. William F. Skene, *The Four Ancient Books of Wales*, 2 vols (Edinburgh, 1868) vol. II, p. 47.
37. See Skene, *op. cit.* In the text *Hwimleian* is found on II, 20; in the translation of the 'Avallenau', I, 370; the note quoting Price, II, 336.
38. T. H. La Villemarqué, *Myrdhinn ou l'enchanteur Merlin*, new edn (Paris, 1862) p. 203.
39. *Memoir*, vol. II, p. 50.
40. William Wordsworth, 'Elegiac Stanzas Suggested by a Picture of Peele Castle in a Storm', ll. 13–16.
41. *Memoir*, vol. I, p. xii.
42. Ibid., vol. II, p. 366.
43. Samuel C. Chew, in *Tennyson: Representative Poems* (New York, [1941]) p. 451, was the first to give it correctly.
44. Harold Nicolson, *Tennyson* (Boston, Mass., and New York, 1925) p. 123. This passage is unchanged from the first edition, 1923.
45. The Lockhart legend dies hard. Croker's authorship was suggested by Prothero in the centenary article of the *Quarterly Review*, vol. CCX (April 1909) p. 775n., and accepted by Walter Graham, *Tory Criticism in the Quarterly Review, 1809–1853* (New York, 1921) p. 52. In *The Times Literary Supplement*, 24 April 1937, Sir Herbert Grierson published Lockhart's letter thanking Croker for the article on Tennyson; and Mr F. L. Lucas has recently described the bound volumes of Croker's contributions to the *Quarterly*, which include a proof of it (*TLS*, 30 November 1946). See also M. F. Brightfield, *John Wilson Croker* (Berkeley, Cal., 1940) pp. 349–51, and two letters from Sir John Murray in the *TLS*, 14 December 1946 and 18 January 1947.
46. *Memoir*, vol. I, p. 12. The passage is not indexed under *Scott*.
47. Ibid., vol. II, p. 348.

12

Robert Browning's Widows

Perhaps, no love story is better known than the romance of Elizabeth Barrett and Robert Browning. The meeting of these two poets – she 39, he six years younger; courtship under the handicap of her father's monomaniacal opposition to the marriage of any of his eleven children; the clandestine wedding and flight to Italy: all these and more their letters recorded in detail. 'How do I love thee? Let me count the ways', wrote Elizabeth, and she counted them over and over again in her *Sonnets from the Portuguese*, published four years later, after they had settled into Casa Guidi at Florence. Robert reciprocated her sentiments warmly. His best work is permeated with devotion to his 'moon of poets'. And when she died after fifteen years of notoriously happy married life, the whole world knew that he shared her belief: 'I shall but love thee better after death.' As soon as the funeral was over he took their only child Pen, a boy of twelve, and departed from Florence for ever. But his heart, it was understood, he left behind, buried there with Elizabeth.

Browning was soon established in London in a modest house in Warwick Crescent, not far from Paddington Station and overlooking the Grand Junction Canal, on which Pen could row almost every day. For months he saw few friends except his sister-in-law Arabel Barrett, who lived not far away. He busied himself in preparing a selection of Elizabeth's poems and a new edition of his own work in three volumes, which he dedicated to John Forster. His poems, in spite of their baffling obscurity, were beginning to win wider recognition, especially among the intelligentsia, who regarded Tennyson, the Poet Laureate, as rather obvious. Even people who did not read them wanted to know the husband of the famous author of *Aurora Leigh*. Gregarious by nature, Browning began to find the long solitary evenings after Pen had gone to bed morbid and useless. He was soon accepting invitations to dinner parties and appearing at concerts. He was elected to the Athenaeum, where he met other writers and artists and influential leaders in Church and State.

To those who grew up in the age of Freud the loss of his mother may seem something less than tragic for Pen. When he was twelve she was still dressing him in silk blouses and velvet tunics with lace frills, finely embroidered trousers and hats trimmed with feathers and satin ribbons. His long golden curls hanging below his shoulders, which would be the envy of many a youngster today, annoyed his father. Strangers would sometimes ask him whether Pen was a girl or a boy. One visitor to Casa Guidi described him as 'looking like a fairy born of a lily and a rose'. Nathaniel Hawthorne said that he had never seen a boy

> so slender, fragile, and spirit-like, not as if he were actually in ill-health, but as if he had little or nothing to do with human flesh and blood. . . . I should not quite like to be the father of such a boy [he added]. . . . I wonder what is to become of him, whether he will ever grow to be a man, whether it is desirable that he should.

Before they left Florence, Browning saw to it that Pen's curls were cut.

In Italy Pen had never gone to school. His father and mother guided his reading and got the best teachers for languages and music and drawing. In England Browning continued this plan of education. He had no intention of sending Pen to a public school, where he would be thrown into the company of other boys of his own age. In the summers he took him off to little villages on the coast of Brittany to give him sunshine and fresh air and outdoor exercise. Pen became an excellent swimmer. He never grew as tall as his father, who stood barely five feet eight, but resembled his mother, whom Hawthorne called 'elfin rather than earthly'. Though Browning himself had found the mild discipline of London University intolerable during his single term there in 1828, he was determined to send Pen to Oxford. So in 1865, he made the acquaintance of Benjamin Jowett, then senior tutor of Balliol, to ask his advice about preparing Pen for entrance. Through his efforts the University was persuaded to give Browning the MA degree by diploma, and a little later Jowett got him elected an Honorary Fellow of Balliol.

But nothing that he could do succeeded in getting Pen ready for the college. After their first interview Jowett advised him to study for two years before attempting the examinations. When that moment

arrived, he counselled further postponement with intensive tutor-
ing. One summer he took Pen with his own reading party to Scotland,
where he got on well with the undergraduates but made little progress
in his studies. His Greek was found quite unsatisfactory; his arithmetic
and even his English writing were deemed inadequate. His loving
parents had been so eager to foster what they fondly imagined to be
Pen's creative genius that they never bothered to inculcate the ru-
diments of spelling or grammar. The 'weakness of memory' his
tutors all complained of was simply his indifference to work. After
having failed the examinations twice, Pen – now nearly twenty years
old – had to resign all hope of admission to Balliol.

Through Jowett's influence again he was admitted to Christ
Church. Though he survived there for three terms, his career was
hardly distinguished: he steered the college boat and won a cup for
excellence in playing billiards! In June 1871 it was made painfully
clear that he could not go on towards a degree. His failure was a
bitter disappointment to Browning. From Scotland, where they were
visiting the Benzons, he wrote that Pen was

> assiduously labouring in that occupation to which Providence
> apparently hath pleased to call him, – that is, in shooting, idling
> and diverting himself. . . . I can do little now but watch him and
> watch for him. . . . If I could dispose properly of Pen, see him
> advantageously disengaged from me, I would go to live and die
> in Italy tomorrow.

The next day, however, he went – not to Italy, but to Loch Luichart,
to Lady Ashburton's house in Ross-shire, where Browning proposed
marriage to his hostess! Only a sentimentalist believes that his notable
attachment to the memory of Elizabeth made the idea of remarriage
inconceivable. Rumours of it had been circulating for several years.
In 1865 an unnamed lady was the subject of such reports in Paris: 'I
never supposed you believed any of them', Browning wrote to his
friend Isa Blagden, 'but then, after all, people change their minds,
and I have no right to pass for something above changes even of that
sort.' Friends had been condoling with Browning's sister about the
approaching change to Pen under a stepmother

> whose name, as you don't mention, I shall not: this was my first
> acquaintance with *that* report, just as stupid or spiteful as the rest.
> If there were *not* an intention of being spiteful, there are other
> names of people in houses where I visit, which are those at least

of ladies I *do* occasionally see and converse with, and like well enough, – but you'll never hear of *them*, I think. I suppose that what you call 'my fame within these four years' comes from a little of this gossiping and going out, and showing myself to be alive.

In 1867 the candidate for Elizabeth Barrett's successor was the middle-aged poetess Jean Ingelow. Mrs James T. Fields, the wife of the Boston publisher, wrote in her diary that Dickens 'tells us Browning is really about to marry Miss Ingelow'. To Isa Blagden, who had also reported this gossip, Browning wrote:

No goose tells you I *am* married, – only, that I *shall* be, – and six years hence the same goose can cackle 'so it *was* to be, – only, it was broken off'! – (I never saw Miss Ingelow but once, at least four years ago, at a musical morning party, where I said half a dozen words to her: only heard of her, as I told you, by her writing a note to accompany her new book a day or two before I left London.) It is funny people think I am likely to do nothing naughty in the world, neither rob nor kill, seduce nor ravish, – only honestly *marry* – which I should consider the two last, – and perhaps two first, naughtinesses united, together with the grace of perjury. Enough of it all.

A little later Mrs Sutherland Orr, author of the earliest Browning *Handbook* and pillar of the Browning Society, seemed a plausible prospect. According to Thomas Hardy his friends believed that there 'was something tender between Mrs Orr and Browning'; Mrs Procter had been heard to ask, 'Why don't they settle it?' In 1869 his name was coupled with the peerage. 'There is a curious lie floating about *here* – concerning poor me', Browning wrote:

I am going to marry Miss A. daughter of Lady B. mother also of Lady C. &c. &c. I heard of it three times last week. I never even heard there was such a person as any one of the three, — never heard their names even. You will soon have it retailed you as indubitable fact.

It is an indubitable fact, however, that in October 1871 he proposed to Louisa, Lady Ashburton. From her father, James Alexander Stewart Mackenzie, she had inherited an estate of some 30,000 acres in Scotland worth £6000 a year, and from her husband William

Baring, 2nd Baron Ashburton, who died in 1864, a much larger estate in England valued at £47,000 a year. It included a vast country house called the Grange and Bath House in Piccadilly at Bolton Street.

There Ashburton's first wife, Lady Harriet Montagu, daughter of the 6th Earl of Sandwich, until her death in 1857, presided over one of the most dazzling salons of the Victorian era. Louisa, Ashburton's second wife, tall and majestic, with intense black eyes and hair, a rich musical voice and proud dominating spirit, was more beautiful if less brilliant. Mrs Carlyle, who had been fond of Lady Harriet and was noted for tart comments on people, declared herself in 1858, after her first visit, 'much pleased with the new Lady, who was kindness's self! A really amiable, loveable woman she seems to be; much more intent on making her visitors at their ease and happy, than on shewing off *herself*, and attracting attention.' Louisa ably maintained the Ashburton tradition of hospitality to distinguished guests. Browning, one of her greatest lions, came often to Bath House, and each summer was invited to the Lodge at Loch Luichart in Ross-shire. Pen was naturally included. During the month they spent there in 1869 he enjoyed the shooting and deer-stalking and killed his first stag – a ' "royal": the head of which will glorify his rooms at Christ Church'. In the evenings about the blazing fire Browning would read to the company passages from *The Ring and the Book*, recently published, which one critic calls 'a great monument' raised by the poet to his wife. There in October 1871 Browning made his proposal to Lady Ashburton and was rejected.

Our knowledge of the affair comes from a few sentences in a letter he wrote six months later to Edith Story, who had heard about it from Lady Ashburton's friend Harriet Hosmer, the sculptor:

But I should like to know . . . what business Hatty had with my behaviour to Lady A. in Lady A's house? I suppose that Lady A. did not suppress what she considered the capital point of her quarrel with me when she foamed out into the couple of letters she bespattered me with, – yet the worst she charged me with was, – having said that my heart was buried in Florence, and the attractiveness of a marriage with her lay in its advantage to Pen – two simple facts, – as I told her, – which I had never left her in ignorance about for a moment, though that I ever paraded this in a gross form to anybody is simply false; but had it been true, – does Hatty instantly practise impertinence on any friend of hers who intends to make an ambitious or mercenary marriage?

Without further detail it is impossible to judge this episode fairly. Browning's apologists praise his forthright honesty and seem inclined to blame Lady Ashburton for not having loved enough to accept his humiliating proposal. Yet, from the author of 'Two in the Campagna' one expects a subtler realisation of the effect it would have on a proud and beautiful woman. She never forgave Browning; and, though he pretended to, he could never forgive himself. In a letter to William Story in 1874 he wrote: 'I see every now and then that contemptible Lady Ashburton, and mind her no more than any other black beetle – so long as it don't crawl up my sleeve.' Fifteen years after the event her rejection was still rankling in him when he spoke of 'the calumnies which Lady A. exploded in all the madness of her wounded vanity'. In his 'Parleying with Daniel Bartoli' (1887) he made his spokesman, the Duke, who has resigned a true but humble love, review his mistake one sleepless night:

> as when a cloud enwraps
> The moon, and, moon-suffused, plays moon perhaps
> To who walks under, till comes, late or soon,
> A stumble: up he looks, and lo, the moon
> Calm, clear, convincingly herself once more!
> . . .
> 'Who bade you come, brisk-marching bold she-shape,
>   A terror with those black-balled worlds of eyes,
> That black hair bristling solid-built from nape
>   To crown its coils about? O dread surmise!
> Take, tread on, trample under past escape
>   Your capture, spoil, and trophy! Do – devise
> Insults for one who, fallen once, ne'er shall rise!
> . . .
> 'Some day, and soon, be sure himself will rise
>   Called into life by her who long ago
> Left his soul whiling time in flesh disguise. . . .

So far as we know Browning's 'stumble' into disloyalty to his eternally beloved 'moon of poets' was never repeated. No one, I think, has yet noted a somewhat similar affair that was being gossiped about in 1873, while Pen's future was still Browning's constant anxiety. It involved another very rich woman, the widow of Ernst Leopold Schlesinger Benzon, the steel magnate. Born Schlesinger in Hamburg, Germany, he had assumed the name of Benzon, it is said,

from a fancied connexion with the ancient Italian family of Benzoni.
Emigrating to Boston about 1840, he became the sole American agent
for the Naylor, Vickers Company of Sheffield, receiving 5 per cent
commission on the price of all steel they sent over to the United
States. Among his Boston friends was Mrs Lydia Maria Child, the
Abolitionist, whose cause he supported generously, and to whom he
left a bequest of £1500. In her words: 'The strength of his domestic
affections was one of his most prominent characteristics. His memory
clung with tenacious tenderness to a large family of brothers and
sisters whom he had left in the dear Fatherland.' By persistent pressure he compelled the reluctant English partners to take his young
brother-in-law Frederick Lehmann and his brother Barthold
Schlesinger into the company. Their efforts in keeping it solvent
during the panic of 1857 won for his family a half share in the firm.
The demand for steel used in railways and armament during the
Civil War made them all immensely rich.

Coming to London, Benzon bought a magnificent house at 10
Kensington Palace Gardens, collected fine paintings and sculpture,
bought whole libraries of rare books and manuscripts. His great-
nephew, John Lehmann, in his delightful *Ancestors and Friends*, describes Benzon as 'round as a ball all over, quite fat and enormous –
or abnormous', as he pronounced it in his strong German accent. He
'always said the music was schön when it wasn't, and looked like a
fish out of water, gasping for the ocean of iron and steel again'. This
view must rest on family tradition, since Mr Lehmann never saw
him. He reports that Mrs Benzon was 'very jolly – always'. She was
the daughter of Leo Lehmann, a miniature painter and drawing
master at Hamburg. Her brother Rudolf, also a painter, who had
lately moved to London, was married to Amelia Chambers, the
sister of Mrs Frederick Lehmann; they were daughters of the Edinburgh publisher and writer Robert Chambers. Another brother of
Benzon's, Henry Schlesinger, and a cousin, Felix Moscheles, with his
mother, the widow of the composer Ignaz Moscheles, also belonged
to the large family group to be met at the lavish parties the Benzons
gave. On Christmas Eve, in the fashion imported from Germany by
the Prince Consort, there was always a great tree round which the
Benzons' friends gathered to watch the children open their presents.
The elaborate dinner parties ordinarily saw twenty guests at table,
drawn more, perhaps, from the arts than from society. There one
might meet painters – Leighton, Millais and Landseer; writers –
Thackeray, George Eliot, George Henry Lewes, Browning and John

Forster; or any of the noted musicians of the period. After dinner one might hear Joachim or Mendelssohn or Clara Schumann or Rubinstein play till midnight. The Benzons loved parties.

Browning was one of their most welcome guests. His maternal grandfather, Mr Wiedemann, had been born in Hamburg, and the poet found himself comfortably at home with the Benzons. He was also invited to stay at their country house near Tunbridge Wells and, in the summers, at Allean House on Lake Tummel in Perthshire. There during August and September 1869 he wrote most of *Prince Hohenstiel-Schwangau*. On these visits Pen, of course, accompanied him, passing his days agreeably in 'shooting, riding, and dancing the Highland Reel' with 'his kind friends', as Browning called them. In the summer of 1873 Pen was there alone, his father and aunt having gone to Normandy, when Mr Benzon fell gravely ill. The most famous physicians of the day – Jenner, Quain, Sir Henry Thompson from London, Begbie and others from Edinburgh – were summoned to do their utmost. But on 14 September he died. Pen, who had been keeping his father informed about the patient, had removed to Pitlochry, the nearest town, some miles away, for the house was overflowing with doctors. 'It is hardly necessary to say', Browning wrote, 'that I would have gone to Scotland could there have been any conceivable good to Benzon in the visit.'

He learnt of his friend's death from a newspaper in Paris and left at once for London. The extensive alterations that had begun on the house in Kensington Palace Gardens were countermanded, but it was some time before it was ready to receive Mrs Benzon. When she returned to town, Browning 'saw her at once', and during the early months of her widowhood he was, according to her brother, Rudolf Lehmann, 'an almost daily visitor'. The gossips who had invented so many false tales of Browning's remarriage did not wait to begin broadcasting the new rumour. Only two days after the event, John Forster wrote to Robert Lytton:

> Your little friend Benzon is dead. Quain [Forster's own physician] succeeded James in attendance but too late. Lizzy thinks it possible that Browning may make another Mrs. B. of the widow, but I don't think his love of ease and luxury will bring him to that.

John Forster was for many years one of Browning's best friends. He was the first critic to praise the early poems, and on Browning's return to London after Elizabeth's death took endless pains to find

him a suitable house. In 1863 Browning's *Poems* appeared with this
enthusiastic tribute:

> I dedicate these volumes to My Old Friend John Forster, glad and
> grateful that he, who, from the first publication of the various
> poems they include, has been their promptest and staunchest
> helper, should seem even nearer to me now than thirty years ago.

Forster had long made a profession of befriending celebrities in
order to bask in reflected glory, and had a strangely proprietary
feeling about them. In his forty-fifth year he had married his Lizzy,
the wealthy widow of Henry Colburn the bookseller, and he let it be
known that hostesses who wanted his lion-of-the-moment would do
well to invite Mrs Forster too. As Browning's popularity increased,
he began to grow restive under Forster's demands. One day at the
Benzons' dinner-table, as Browning was telling a story that he had
heard from a certain Lady – 'Forster retorted that he did not believe
it a whit more on account of that authority. Suddenly Browning
became very fierce, and said, "Dare to say one word in disparage-
ment of that lady" – seizing a decanter while he spoke – "and I will
pitch this bottle of claret at your head!"' Benzon, who had been
seeing Sir Edwin Landseer off, returned at this moment. Hurrying
all the other guests from the dining-room, he tried to bring about an
apology, but in vain. The 'grateful old friend' never spoke to Forster
again. We may be quite certain that they met no more at the house of
Mrs Benzon, about whom two or three years later Forster was
gleefully spreading his scandal.

Robert Lytton had owed a great deal to the Brownings since his
first acquaintance with them in Florence twenty years before. During a long fever in 1858 their continuous nursing undoubtedly saved
his life, and his letters to them were effusively affectionate. Yet in
this quarrel with Forster, who had been more than a father to him,
Lytton could not side with Browning; though there was no violent
break, the glamour was at an end; their friendship chilled and
dwindled away, and the correspondence ceased. On 2 June 1874,
nine months after Benzon's death, Lytton wrote to Forster, who had
been busily peddling his rumours about the engagement:

> Your wife's news of the Browning–Benzon engagement seems
> to me too good to be true. I owe it to my recollections of what
> Browning was not to believe the engagement till I hear of the

marriage. If the marriage ever *does* take place, I shall write the epitaph on a lost belief. That such an event should even be generally supposed possible makes a depth of degeneration in the subject of such a report which saddens me.

I spoke to Lady Ripon (whom I like *immensely*) about Browning: as I had heard him boast of his intimacy with *her*. She said she knew him, slightly, that he was extremely antipathetic to her, that she thought him shockingly vulgar and underbred, that he was a snob and a toady, and that the way in which he talked to everybody of his wife *revolted her*. . . . So much for our fine friendships with our fine friends! Adieu! adieu! adieu!

Yours
R.[1]

In his reply, dated 4 June 1874, Forster gave further details, which had been supplied by Dickens's daughter Mary:

The Browning matter stands thus – Many weeks ago (before this bad illness) Mary Dickens told me confidently it *would* be – and I so peremptorily expressed my disbelief, and indeed was so really angry at what I treated as a most unworthy imputation, that she was silent, though unconvinced. I said too, I remember, that if I were conscious of any wrongs unsettled, such a fate as *that*, if it awaited him, would be a discharge in full.

Now comes the denouement, or catastrophe – which Mary Dickens came in eager exultation to tell, and crow over me with, one day when I was very ill. I did not see her – but thus the tragedy runs.

Long before the 'joint-stock-baby' made its appearance, and when it had been despaired of, Benzon adopted a child, who passed as Lily B —, and to this girl, making her of age at 18, and till then making Mrs. B's brother her guardian, he left 70000 £.

The widow appears to [have] taken a violent hatred to her (I suppose for having carried off so much of the spoil) – and this poor girl went the other day to her guardian, said the house was rendered intolerable to her by the conduct of Mrs. Benzon and Mr. Browning (who were to be married in the Autumn), and entreating him to allow her to leave it and go abroad. So there you have the plot of the new Decline and Fall. The explanation given is (for this rich woman taking a man of 62–3) that she wanted, in exchange for her money, admission to the houses and confidences of Great Folks – and here, if what Lady Ripon told you be at all general, she may possibly be deceived.

Forster's obvious malice in this unpleasant letter needs no comment, but some of the allusions may be explained. The 'joint-stock-baby' was Henry Ernst Schlesinger Benzon (1866–1911), who inherited two-thirds of his father's residuary estate – without, alas, any of his cautious business acumen. Coming of age in 1887, Queen Victoria's Jubilee Year, he dissipated the huge fortune so swiftly that it won him the dubious sobriquet of 'The Jubilee Plunger'. He described his exploits in a foolish book called *How I Lost £250,000 in Two Years* (1898). To Lily, his adopted daughter, Benzon bequeathed one-third of the residuary estate – considerably more than the £70,000 Forster mentions in this letter, written six months before the will was probated. I cannot now determine the source of Mary Dickens's gossip. Possibly it came from one of Lily's cousins in the family of Frederick Lehmann or that of Henry Schlesinger, both of whom were executors of the estate. It is quite clear, however, that Lily did not leave home. At Mrs Benzon's parties, which were resumed after a decent interval, she was in attendance as usual. On 9 June, five days after Forster's letter, Browning reported to Story that 'Mrs. B. is very well – doesn't go out, but sees old friends of an afternoon. Lily is quite well, and the boy gets a big fellow; but you may hear of all this and more from herself, perhaps.' In the autumn, when the alleged marriage was to have occurred, we have a glimpse of mother and daughter driving in the park with George Eliot and Lewes, and in March 1877 they both came to the Leweses' to hear Tennyson read his poems.

We can only guess whether Browning really proposed to Mrs Benzon. One thing is certain: they remained good friends always. She was still 'very jolly'. Browning continued to frequent her drawing-room; they were invited to the same parties. One Sunday evening in March 1876, the Leweses met them both at dinner at the Frederick Lehmanns' with Mr and Mrs Joachim, Charles Hallé and his married daughter, the Rudolf Lehmanns, and Henry and Mary Dickens! After dinner the Japanese Ambassador and his wife, Sir Coutts Lindsay, Mrs Baring, the Gordons (Mrs Sartoris's daughter) and others came in. 'Joachim and Hallé played duets of Mozart and Schumann – very delightful', Lewes wrote in his diary: 'Home at 12.15.' In this same year Browning published 'A Forgiveness', a melodramatic monologue of adultery – and revenge three years later; in it he describes one of the collection of oriental swords and daggers, some of them set with precious stones, which Benzon had bequeathed to him in 1873.

When Pen withdrew from the house during Benzon's last illness, he had gone to stay at Birnam with Millais, who shared his enthusiasm for fishing and shooting and spent part of each year in Scotland, dividing his time between outdoor sports and painting. Inspired by watching Millais work on 'The Scotch Firs', Pen decided that he, too, would become an artist. Browning welcomed the prospect heartily and sent him off to Antwerp to study with a teacher recommended by Felix Moscheles. Before he set out, Pen proposed to a rich young American girl, Fannie Coddington, a cousin of Mrs Henry Schlesinger. Nothing came of it. Pen obviously did not press his suit with any vigour. But fourteen years later, in 1887, they happened to meet again. Again Pen proposed, and this time Fannie, now an orphan, accepted him. It was his father who applied for the publication of the banns in the absence of Pen, who, he told the clerk, 'would probably be back in time' for the wedding.

They were married from the Schlesinger house at Pembury, near Tunbridge Wells, on 4 October 1887. They went on their honeymoon to Venice, where Pen was soon to buy the seventeenth-century Palazzo Rezzonico on the Grand Canal. Describing his daughter-in-law's fine qualities, Browning added that 'the means of comfortable life are abundant in this case – indeed Pen might become independent of my own assistance, did either he or I permit of such an arrangement'. At last, two years before his death, Browning could see Pen 'advantageously disengaged' from him and feel relieved of all anxiety about how to support him in the state to which he had been so long accustomed.

Notes

This essay first appeared in *The Times Literary Supplement*, 2 July 1971, pp. 783–4.

1. This letter and Forster's reply that follows are among the Lytton papers deposited in the County Record Office at Hertford. These extracts are here published for the first time with the permission of the Hon. David Lytton Cobbold.

13

George Eliot and Watts's
Clytie

When Burne-Jones and Rossetti came to lunch at the Priory on 9 January 1870, they surprised George Eliot by carrying into the drawing room a bust of Clytie, the gift of its sculptor, George Frederic Watts. Though she had often admired his paintings and may even have seen the original marble *Clytie* exhibited at the Royal Academy in 1868, she had never met Watts. Suffering all his life from vague ill health, he did not go about like his friends Millais and Leighton, whom the Leweses sometimes saw at dinner parties. Yet his enthusiasm for George Eliot's work is clear from a letter he wrote to Charles Rickards in 1866:

> In the belief that art of noble aim is necessary to a great nation, I am sometimes tempted in my impatience to try if I cannot get subscriptions to carry out a project I have long had, to erect a statue to unknown worth – in the words of the author of *Felix Holt*, 'a monument to the faithful who are not famous'. I think this would be a worthy thing to do, and if I had not unfortunately neglected opportunities of making money, I would certainly do it at my own expense. I am at this time making a monumental statue, and feel confident I could execute a colossal bronze statue that should be a real monument. I would give up all other work to be enabled to carry out such an idea, and should be contented if guaranteed against loss; contented to be able to meet the expenses of the undertaking.[1]

Watts had just finished his fine portrait of Rickards, a wealthy patron in the North, whose enthusiasm for colossal statues was apparently not stirred by a book called *Felix Holt, the Radical*. Like some others of his grander projects, this statue never materialised.

Clytie was a water nymph who was so enamoured of Apollo that she followed his course constantly from sunrise to sunset, her love unrequited. According to Ovid,[2] she sat naked on the bare ground, gazing at the face of her god as he went on his way. After nine days her limbs grew fast to the soil, and she was changed into a plant, which in England popular fable identified as the sunflower. Regardless of botanical fact, Tom Moore wrote,

> The heart that has truly loved never forgets,
>   But as truly loves on to the close;
> As the sunflower turns on her god when he sets
>   The same look that she turned when he rose.

Watts's *Clytie*, 28 inches high, shows the head and shoulders of the nymph encased in a cuplike cluster of broad leaves of some plant not much like our common sunflower. Looking downward to catch the last glimpse of the setting sun, her head is bent sharply to the right, the chin resting upon her shoulder, providing a full-length view of the 'neck like a tower' so much prized by the Pre-Raphaelites.

Watts had worked in clay since boyhood, having begun his career as an artist in the studio of a sculptor, William Behnes. In the 1860s he began to accept commissions for sculptures, building a special studio in the garden at Little Holland House where he could do huge equestrian figures. But according to Mary Watts, the *Clytie* was moulded in the greenhouse, because during the winter the cold and moisture of the wet clay aggravated his rheumatism. He carved the marble himself. It was still unfinished when he exhibited it at the Academy in 1868, and he was continuing to work on it as late as 1876, when his friend and neighbour Mrs Russell Barrington watched him carving on it.

> I never realised so strongly Watts' instinctive sensibility for form as when I used to see him chiselling the marble on the *Clytie*. As I watched his subtle conception of the different planes and delicate curves, worked in innumerable facets, which he said would produce, he thought, a better effect of atmosphere and a more palpitating quality of surface than chiselling the form with more direct touches, and saw him strike and guide the chisel, an echo seemed to be awakened in my own sensibility for form. The delight which Watts was feeling himself while chiselling seemed contagious, carrying with it a kind of mesmeric influence.[3]

According to Mrs Watts, he employed several models. The principal one was a woman he always called 'Long Mary', who 'sat to him, and to him only, from the early 'sixties and onwards for several years'. But, 'the muscles for the *Clytie* were carefully studied from a well-known Italian male model of the name of Colorossi, and for this bust also a beautiful little child, not yet three years old – Margaret Burne-Jones – was laid under contribution, and was studied in her mother's arms!' (*Annals*, vol. 2, p. 45). The nymph's well-rounded shoulders, reminiscent of the Demeter group in the Elgin marbles, clearly owe something to Colorossi, but to see anything of Mrs Burne-Jones and her daughter one must study the look of suffering in Clytie's face.

Mrs Barrington believed that the original inspiration for the bust came from the disaster of Watts's first marriage in 1864 to Ellen Terry, thirty years his junior, from whom he separated eighteen months later. Though his Clytie shows no similarity to the lovely features of the seventeen-year-old Ellen, the expression of hopeless yearning may reflect something of Watts's remorse for his unfortunate match. For a subtler expression of the yearning of despised love than 'Long Mary' could assume, Watts may have appealed to Mrs Burne-Jones. At this time she was bravely enduring the pain caused by her husband's turbulent love affair with Mary Zambaco, who had attempted to drown herself when he tried to break if off.[4] Knowing of Mrs Burne-Jones's long ordeal, Watts may have sought in her face the anguished look of his abandoned Clytie. More than once in those desolate years she had taken her two children away from the emotional turmoil. She did not come with Burne-Jones and Rossetti when they brought the bust to the Priory.

Two days later George Eliot wrote this letter of thanks, now in the George Eliot Collection in the Beinecke Library, and published here for the first time:

21 North Bank
Jan. 11. 1870

My dear Mr. Watts

You have sent me the finest present I ever had in all my life, and I wish you knew better than I can tell you how much good it has done me. But Mr. Rossetti was telling me on Sunday that you have long been and still are continually suffering from bad health, and *that* experience is almost sure to include some sadness and discouragement. Therefore, when I tell you that such conditions have made a large part of my history, you will understand how keenly I feel the help brought me by some proof that anything I have done has made a place for me in minds which the world has good reason to value. And this strong proof from you happens to come at a time when I especially needed such cheering.

The Bust looks grander and grander in my eyes now that I can turn to it from time to time. Mr. Burne Jones, who had a generous delight in carrying it, brought me also the message, that we should not be unwelcome if on some fine day we presented ourselves in your studio. Both Mr. Lewes and I desire to have that pleasure, and we shall not forget the permission.

Long ago as one of the public, but now on private grounds also, I can truly call myself

Yours most gratefully
M. E. Lewes

In his reply Watts repeated his invitation:

> I would pay my respects to you and Mr. Lewes, but I am a wretched creature, and dare not go out in the evening, or even in the daytime, unless the weather is perfect; then every moment is required for work. But if – kindly overlooking the apparent want of respect due to you and Mr. Lewes – you would sometimes give me your opinion of the things scattered about in my studio, it could not but be of great service to me. I aim at what is beyond me, and, in a wholly unsympathetic age, struggle with my half-formed conceptions, miserable in the consciousness of my incapacity. You who can not only imagine but give perfect form to your poetry, cannot fortunately realise such a struggle with phantoms. (*Annals*, vol. 1, p. 277)

In this diffidence about his achievement Watts betrays a remarkable parallel with George Eliot. Phrases like 'struggle with my half-formed conceptions' and 'miserable in the consciousness of my incapacity' are very like those that George Eliot used constantly about her writing. There is also a similarity in their liberal views of religion. A friend of Watts called him 'one who without sect or dogma shall answer to the welcoming Infinite with simplicity and calm' (*Annals*, vol. 1, p. 222), a description that could well describe George Eliot in this aspect. A true sympathy between them might have been predicted.

A month after his present of *Clytie*, Watts paid a morning call at the Priory and probably renewed his invitation. A few days later, after stopping at the milliner's and the bank, the Leweses drove to Little Holland House, where they found his studio 'crowded with fine things. Pleasant hour with him', Lewes reported in his Journal (5 and 10 February 1870); and George Eliot wrote to Barbara Bodichon that she had 'just come in from a cold drive, back from Watts's who has wonderful things in his studio'.[5] But two years seem to have passed before they saw him again. While she was working hard over *Middlemarch*, Lewes 'called on Watts to see his Daphne (exquisite purity) and other works', and was introduced to the whole Prinsep family, with whom Watts lived at Little Holland House (Journal, 13 February 1872). On 25 March 1872 he called again to see Watts's pictures and to get him to sign a petition to Gladstone to pension George du Maurier, who had lost the sight of one eye in 1859, and was threatened with the loss of the other. On 13 May 1873 Lewes came again and secured Watts's vote for E. F. S. Pigott as Secretary of the Royal Academy. The Journal notes a few other visits to the studio accompanied by George Eliot and occasional meetings at previews of exhibitions, but no more calls at the Priory.

There were four women whom Watts wanted to include in his series of English notables: Elizabeth Barrett Browning, whom he never met; Florence Nightingale, 'whose portrait he found he was unable to complete'; Josephine Butler, the campaigner for reform of laws concerning 'fallen women', for whose heroism Watts had 'a deep veneration'; and George Eliot, 'whose portrait he was afraid to attempt, perceiving the difficulty that it would have presented' (*Annals*, vol. 2, p. 250). According to Mrs Watts, 'he knew that the features belonged to a type he would have found most difficult; and afraid of not doing the great mind justice, he did not venture to make the attempt' (ibid., p. 276). It is regrettable. Although he had little personal acquaintance with George Eliot, his sympathy for her art would have offered Watts a challenge commensurate with his own, and might have resulted in our truest portrait of her.

Notes

This essay first appeared in *Yale University Library Gazette*, vol. 56 (April 1982) pp. 65–9.

1. Mary S. Watts, *George Frederic Watts: Annals of an Artist's Life*, 3 vols (London, 1912) vol. I, p. 224. The quotation is from *Felix Holt*, ch. 16.
2. Ovid, *Metamorphoses*, Book 4, ll. 256–70.
3. Mrs Russell Barrington, *Reminiscences of George Frederic Watts* (London, 1905) pp. 41–2. The original marble *Clytie* is in the Guildhall Gallery, London. Two others, carved by an assistant, are in the Queens Park Gallery, Manchester, and the Harris Museum and Art Gallery, Preston. A bronze cast from the Tate Gallery is on permanent loan at Leighton House.
4. See Penelope Fitzgerald, *Edward Burne-Jones: A Biography* (London, 1975) pp. 117–31.
5. *The George Eliot Letters*, ed. Gordon S. Haight, 9 vols (New Haven, Conn., and London, 1954–78) vol. V, p. 77.

14

Male Chastity in the Nineteenth Century

On 25 April 1848 John Forster gave a dinner for Ralph Waldo Emerson at his chambers in Lincoln's Inn Fields – the very chambers that Dickens had described in the December number of *Bleak House* as the scene of Mr Tulkinghorn's murder. Dickens was already there when Emerson arrived, deep in consultation with Forster over the final rehearsals of *The Merry Wives of Windsor* for the Shakespeare Fund benefit. Soon Carlyle appeared, greeted with what Emerson called Forster's 'obstreperous cordiality' by the loud salutation 'My Prophet!' Emerson had known Carlyle since 1833, when he sought him out at his remote cottage at Craigenputtock. Urging him to return to England to lecture, Carlyle had promised that 'Pickwick himself shall be visible; innocent young Dickens reserved for a questionable fate'. He should also meet Leigh Hunt ('my near neighbour, full of quips and cranks, with good humour and no common sense') as well as 'blockheads by the million'. Now, as the end of his nine-month visit drew near, Forster had arranged this intimate evening to introduce Emerson to Dickens. Another friend of Forster's, young Pringle, was the only other guest.

Since 'there were only gentlemen present', Emerson wrote in his journal,'the conversation turned on the shameful lewdness of the London streets at night'. Carlyle, in his best fulminating mood, exclaimed: 'I hear it, I hear whoredom in the House of Commons. Disraeli betrays whoredom, and the whole House of Commons universal incontinence, in every word they say.' Emerson had observed the problem at closer range going back and forth to John Chapman's house at 142 Strand, where he lodged while in London, and travelling about other English cities giving his lectures.

> I said that when I came to Liverpool, I inquired whether the prostitution was always as gross in that city as it then appeared to me, for it seemed to betoken a fatal rottenness in the state, and I

saw not how any boy could grow up safe. But I had been told it
was not worse or better for years.

Carlyle and Dickens replied that chastity in the male sex was as
good as gone in our times; and in England was so rare that they
could name all the exceptions. Carlyle evidently believed that the
same things were true in America. He had heard this and that of
New York, etc. I assured them that it was not so with us; that, for
the most part, young men of good standing and good education,
with us, go virgins to their nuptial bed, as truly as their brides.

Dickens replied that incontinence is so much the rule in England
that if his own son were particularly chaste, he should be alarmed
on his account, as if he could not be in good health. 'Leigh Hunt,'
he said, 'thought it indifferent.'

How much of this account are we to believe? No one looking at
the world today can accept such a violent contrast between the
English and the American male. In his biography of Dickens, Professor
Edgar Johnson suggests that Emerson's friends that evening were
deliberately exaggerating the licentiousness to shock 'their prim-
minded American visitor', and he notes that Dickens's eldest son
was then only twelve years old. Yet, I think, Dickens may have been
sincere in his remarks. He had known the streets of London from
childhood and as a journalist had seen a good deal of its seamier
side. At this very moment he was deeply involved with Miss Coutts
in establishing a home for fallen women at Shepherd's Bush; he
drew up the regulations for it, helped select the Matron, and personally interviewed most of the women admitted, inquiring into the
details of their past lives 'to give the Matron some useful foreknowl-
edge of them'. The problem of chastity in the male sex must have
been playing a lively part in his thoughts. Carlyle, too, though he
loved to talk for effect, may have been serious in this argument.
Emerson told Fredrika Bremer that Carlyle had been

very angry with him for not believing in a devil, and to convert
him took him among all the horrors of London – the gin-shops etc.
and finally to the House of Commons, plying him at every turn
with the question, 'Do you believe in a devil noo?'

Of course, the serene philosopher was unconvinced. Though in his
system pure malignity could not exist, the horrors he had seen were
real enough.

On 6 May, two weeks after Forster's dinner, Emerson crossed the Channel to Paris and settled for a month in lodgings on the Left Bank. Louis Philippe had fled in February but Paris was still rumbling with revolution. The mob confronted and occupied the National Assembly and were finally put down by the cannon of the National Guard. A great *Fête de Concorde* was celebrated on the Champ-de-Mars. All of this Emerson saw with his own eyes. Far from interfering with tourism, political tension seemed rather to heighten the life of pleasure for which Paris was famous. Emerson had a new coat cut in the latest mode, went often to the theatre, and dined regularly with his English friends. Chief of these was Arthur Hugh Clough, who had invited him to Oxford in March and had become a warm friend. Unsettled in his religious opinions by the conflicts of the Tractarians and the Liberals, Clough had resigned his tutorship at Oriel and was about to give up his fellowship as well. He was 31, sixteen years younger than Emerson, who found him full of 'interest in life and realities, in the state of woman, and the questions so rife in Paris through Communism, and through the old loose and easy conventions of that city for travellers'.

Clough's conversation about women included 'the *grisette* estate'. Did he perhaps propose that they make a more practical study of the problem? One can only speculate on the meaning of a riddling entry in Emerson's journal for 13 May:

> What can the brave and strong genius of C. himself avail? What can his praise, what can his blame avail me, when I know that if I fall or if I rise, there still awaits me the inevitable joke? . . . But when I balance the attractions of good and evil, when I consider what facilities, what talents a little vice would furnish, then rise before me not these laughers, but the dear and comely forms of honour and genius and piety in my distant home, and they touch me with chaste palms moist and cold, and say to me, You are ours.

The flaming youth whom Carlyle and Dickens were discussing in Lincoln's Inn felt little pressure from the 'chaste palms moist and cold' that restrained the sage of Concord. The purity which Emerson claimed for young men of good standing in America was almost unknown in England. The eighteenth-century novelists show plainly in what indifferent regard male chastity was held in their day. In 1749, Fielding's Mrs Waters, with whom Tom Jones was sleeping when Sophia came to the inn at Upton, assured Squire Allworthy that he was 'the worthiest of men. No young gentleman of his age is, I believe, freer from vice.' Sophia herself upbraids Tom, not for fornication, but for having (as she thought) mentioned her name in public. To any one who doubts that this was a true picture of English manners, Boswell's journals give undeniable confirmation. With the Napoleonic era came the relaxation of morals that wars always bring. The profligacy of the Regency was public scandal for both sexes.

What reform there had been came principally from the rise of the Evangelical Movement initiated by the Wesleys in the Church of England, but extending into every denomination of Dissenters. If their most spectacular victory was the abolition of slavery in the colonies, at home their attacks on intemperance and prostitution were more deeply felt. And after the Queen married Prince Albert, an earnest German Lutheran with lofty ideals of domestic relations, she established a standard of propriety that in popular usage promises to outlive every other sense of the word Victorian. The 1840s saw a marked alteration of manners. But the new respectability was often superficial; human nature changes slowly, and vice was not so much eliminated as huddled out of sight. Young John Chapman, Emerson's publisher, may serve as an example. As a youth in the 1830s, he was called Byron by his friends because of his exploits with women. In 1851 he refused to publish a novel by Eliza Lynn because of the warmth with which it depicted a love scene. Both his wife and his mistress, whom he kept in the house, objected to the 'sensual nature' of the book, and 'as I am the publisher of works notable for their intellectual freedom', he wrote, 'it behoves me to be exceedingly careful of the *moral* tendency of all I issue'.

Emerson's fear that with prostitution so prevalent no boy 'could grow up safe' applied with particular force to the universities. The nineteenth-century novelists for the most part temper their accounts for polite readers, who get only fleeting glimpses of what they refer to as 'gross vice'. In *Tom Brown at Oxford* Thomas Hughes (BA 1845) hardly glances at it. The wealthy fellow-commoner Drysdale, one of the fast set, quotes a saying of his old uncle that 'a young fellow must sow his wild oats', and adds that 'Oxford seems a place specially set apart by Providence for that operation'. He keeps a mistress established in 'a pretty retired cottage' near Abingdon, where he once drives Tom to see her. Needless to say, the reader does not accompany them beyond the door. Less affluent undergraduates were dependent on prostitutes at the edge of town, who of course do not appear in the novel. But the main plot concerns Tom's infatuation with Patty, a barmaid, and the misunderstanding it causes later with his true love, Mary Porter. Her father, Tom says, 'had heard very bad stories of me at Oxford, but he would not press me with them. There were too few young men whose lives would bear looking into for him to insist much on such matters, and he was ready to let bygones be bygones.' None of the other novels laid at Oxford or Cambridge treats this aspect of undergraduate life so frankly. John Gibson Lockhart's *Reginald Dalton* (1823) has faint hints of vice in the gay youth Chisney and his fast friends, but the worst a reader can see is the Town and Gown riot the night Dalton first comes up. Newman's *Loss and Gain* (1848) does not even hint at vice; the serious lapses are not physical, but doctrinal: 'a young man of twenty-two professing in an hour's conversation with a friend what really were Catholic doctrines and usages of penance, purgatory, councils of perfection, mortification of self, and clerical celibacy'. Markham Sutherland, the hero of James Anthony Froude's *The Nemesis of Faith* (1849), has finished his undergraduate career at Oxford before the story opens. His conflict is not over chastity, but over taking orders. When the old scepticism leads to resignation of his living, he retires to the shore of Lake Como, where his technical adultery (for 'they did not fall as vulgar minds count falling') seems less his fault than that of the husband, who, not loving his young wife, invited Markham to move into his house and went off for five months with an unnamed count to a castle in the Apennines. Oxford has failed Markham.

> All along his life he had turned with disgust from every word which was sullied with any breath of impurity; the poetry of voluptuous passion he had loathed. Alas! it would have been better far for him if it had not been so. He would have had the experience of his fallen nature to warn him by the taste of fruit which it had borne in others.

By 1869, when Henry Kingsley published *Stretton*, the jolly under-graduates drink little and are too much absorbed in their reading and boat-racing to give any thoughts to loose women.

The most objective description of undergraduate life in the 1840s is found in *Five Years in an English University*, published in 1852 by Charles Astor Bristed. Bristed's father, son of an English clergyman, was educated at Winchester, studied medicine at Edinburgh, and was admitted to the bar at the Inner Temple before emigrating to the United States. In New York he married the daughter of John Jacob Astor the younger. Charles was born there in 1820. Educated by private tutors, he entered Yale College at the early age of fifteen, and graduated in 1839. After a year of graduate study at Yale, he entered Trinity College, Cambridge, at first as a Fellow Commoner. His five years at Trinity gave him a unique opportunity to compare educational methods in England and America as well as the character of undergraduate life. Those years, 1840–5, coincided exactly with Thomas Hughes's years at Oxford, when the Tractarian controversy was reaching its climax. At Cambridge, which for a generation had been the proselytizing centre for the Evangelicals, the Anglo-Catholics also had an active group in the Camden Society until Newman's reception into the Roman Catholic Church ended it. Bristed's account throws some interesting light on the religious turmoil of those days.

The chapter of his book that concerns us most is entitled 'On the State of Morals and Religion in Cambridge'. After the austere fare of Yale College, where puritan tradition still frowned on pleasure, he was astonished at how comfortably men lived.

> That decanters and glasses should be among the articles directly recommended by the tutor's servant who assists him in furnishing his room – without any objection, too, from the Evangelical friend who assists him in his purchases; that he should be able to order supper for himself and friends out of the College kitchen, and his College tutor, so far from appearing as a bird of ill omen to mar the banquet, will perhaps play a good knife and fork at it himself – all this seems odd to him at first.

Bristed found, in general, two types of undergraduates. 'The reading men are obliged to be tolerably temperate, but among the "rowing" [*row* rhymes with *cow* and has no connection with boats] men there is a great deal of absolute drunkenness at dinner and supper parties.' But what really shocked Bristed was the frank indulgence in both groups of what he calls 'the animal passions'.

> The American graduate who has been accustomed to find even among irreligious men a tolerable standard of morality and an ingenuous shame in relation to certain subjects, is utterly confounded at the amount of open profligacy going on all around him at an English University; a profligacy not confined to the 'rowing' set, but including many of the reading men and not altogether sparing those in authority. There is a careless and undisguised way of talking about gross vice, which shows that

public sentiment does not strongly condemn it; it is habitually talked of and considered as a thing from which a man may abstain through extraordinary frigidity of temperament or high religious scruple, or merely as a bit of training with reference to the physical consequences alone; but which is on the whole natural, excusable, and perhaps to most men necessary.

Bristed discovered that a student would remain chaste or not entirely in accordance with some medical friend's opinion of its effect on his working condition, preserving 'his bodily purity solely and avowedly because he wanted to put himself at the head of the Tripos and keep his boat at the head of the river'. At the lowest estimate, Bristed put the number of known prostitutes in Cambridge, most of them gathered in the Barnwell suburb towards the north, at nearly 100 – a fairly generous provision for the total of 1600 undergraduates.

> One of my first acquaintances at Cambridge, the Fellow Commoner next to whom I sat in Chapel, had not known me two days or spoken to me half-a-dozen times before he asked me to accompany him to Barnwell one evening after Hall, just as quietly as a compatriot might have asked me to take a drink. . . . The proposition made to me in so off-hand and matter-of-course a way might justify the conclusion that the practice was sufficiently common – as indeed subsequent experience fully proved.

In comparing the American with the English undergraduates Bristed conceded that the Cambridge men, 'so inferior to ours in purity, were superior to them in some other moral qualities'. They had less of the envy, malice and uncharitableness of an American college.

> I was personally acquainted with many men who thought no more of committing fornication than a Southerner would of murdering an Abolitionist, and yet were models of honesty, generosity, truth, and integrity: that men are frequent among us, not only in youth but at a more advanced stage of life, spotlessly pure, rigidly abstemious, making great personal and pecuniary sacrifices in the cause of philanthropy, who are nevertheless greedy of scandal, careless of truth, with very loose conceptions of the obligation of contracts or the duty of citizens to the government. I might set off the integrity of one country against the purity of the other, and say, that if the Englishman is apt to forget that his body

is God's temple, the American is equally apt to overlook the assertion, on equally high authority, that what cometh *out* of the mouth defileth a man.

The worst objection Bristed felt was to 'gross vice' practised by men about to take orders.

Many of the men whose undergraduate course has been the most marked by drunkenness and debauchery, appear, after the 'Poll' examination, at Divinity lectures – step out of Barnwell into the Church, without any pretence of other change than in the attire of their outward man. . . . The idea of going into Christ's ministry as a mere business . . . is sufficiently abhorrent to people brought up in our way of thinking, even when the hireling shepherd is a man of correct moral character; but when his life for years has been giving the lie to every word he will preach, *can* language be strong enough to express our emotions of grief and indignation?

He illustrates his point by an ancedote, literally set down as he heard it told, '(except that the real names are changed and the coarse language of the narrator slightly modified)':

You want to know what this row was between Lord Gaston and Brackett – well, it happened this way. Brackett had brought his *chère amie* down from London. Gaston made her acquaintance. Brackett goes there one night and finds the door locked; so he kicked the door open, and gave Gaston a black eye. Then Gaston wanted to challenge him, and said he didn't care whether he was turned out of the University or not [this is the penalty for being concerned in a duel]; but his friends agreed that, *as Brackett was going into the Church*, they had better make it up.

Bristed attributed the differences he noted to neglect in early years of the moral education of English boys. If they

can be made *manly*, that is to say, courageous, honest, and tolerably truthful, the formation of habits of purity and self-denial is altogether a secondary matter. Grown people, old, grey-headed men, encourage boys to drink, and talk before them as the fastest specimen of Young America would not talk before his younger brother. A stranger, with no further knowledge of the subject than he would gain by reading any good sermons addressed to boys, Arnold's at Rugby for example, could not but remark the progress made in vice at an early age by the inmates of a public school, and . . . the admitted theory of their elders, that indulgence in sensual vices is not incompatible with a Christian life.

But a second cause, more deeply rooted in English society, is

the low estimate which men in the upper ranks of life form of women in the lower. The remark has often been made, and with perfect truth, that that spirit of chivalry which makes every man the protector of every woman, is a peculiar feature of American civilisation. . . . That shop-girls, work-women, domestic servants, and all females in similar positions, were expressly designed for the amusement of gentlemen, and generally serve that purpose, is a proposition assented to by a large proportion of Englishmen, even when they do not act upon the idea themselves. You meet the position, either directly expressed or implied (more frequently the latter), both in their conversation and their writings. . . . And in a popular novel[1] published some years ago, I recollect that an old gentleman lecturing his nephew says to him, 'You seduced a servant. I know young men are young men, *and servant maids are not Lucretias.*' Then he goes on to say, that what he *does* blame him for is abandoning his illegitimate child without support.

The English upper classes Bristed considered 'tolerably moral in their own sphere'.

Their women are well brought up. Their young men respect ladies; perhaps it would be more correct to say *they are afraid of them* . . . . But the virtue of a housemaid or a milliner-girl is a thing inconceivable to [a young Englishman]; he has no more conception of it than, I suppose, a native of New Orleans would have of the virtue of a Quadroon. . . . He does not think that a poor man must necessarily be dishonest or mendacious, or may not be altogether a very good Christian. . . . But that a woman from among 'the common people' should be anything but a *common woman* he will be slow to believe. Female virtue he deems a luxury of the wealthy.

The University, Bristed thought, is much to blame for the prevalence of vice in Cambridge. It appoints two Proctors, who on alternate nights with their servants or 'bull dogs'

> make the tour of Barnwell suburb and other suspicious places, and apprehend any women who may be seen openly enticing gownsmen, or any gownsmen detected in improper localities. Now I do not doubt but these gentlemen perform their disagreeable duties with much diligence, that they prevent some vice and detect more; but were I asked honestly my opinion of their practical efficacy, I should say that they were not equal to the amount of police work they took in hand, and that they were more successful in catching small offenders against University rules – pouncing upon a poor fellow like myself for instance, who had crossed the street after candle-light without his cap and gown, and fining him six-and-eightpence – than in checking or punishing men of profligate habits.

If the authorities were seriously inclined to it, they might easily 'put down all disorderly houses and expel from the place all the notorious prostitutes, of whom there are nearly a hundred at the lowest estimate as well known as if they were under a Parisian registration'.

> And if any offence against morals is committed in their own order, how do the Dons treat the delinquent? A tolerably strong case occurred in my time. A young woman of previous good character went to a Fellow of Kings to procure an order of admission to the chapel on Sunday evening. He made her drunk and seduced her. The reader will probably agree with me that if the corporation of Kings had expelled him from their body it would not have been a punishment beyond his deserts. What *did* they do? They suspended him from his Fellowship for two years, which was equivalent to a fine of £400 or thereabout.

Bristed's picture of Cambridge is not all black. He acknowledges that a young man who is disposed to find a truly 'good set' can find one, or indeed have his choice among several sets of really virtuous and religious men. But why such men have not more influence in reforming the evils about them 'is a question easier to ask than to answer'. In general, however, Bristed seems to confirm Emerson's view in his conversation in Lincoln's Inn Fields.

The appearance of *Tom Brown at Oxford* (1861) prompted an article entitled 'English and American University Life' in the *Boston Review* for March 1862, discussing *Tom Brown's School-Days* as well as

Bristed's book, which had been published ten years before. The anonymous reviewer, an earnest Evangelical, a militant teetotaller, probably a Harvard man, attacked Hughes's picture of the 'boating, horse-racing, wine-drinking crowd that congregate at Oxford'. He does not doubt the accuracy of the picture of college life as Hughes saw it; but

> the one decidedly immoral tendency of these volumes seems to us to be that the author has no earnest word of disapprobation for those drinking habits so prevalent among English students. . . . What we complain of is that he appears to take sides with the drinkers, – that he tells us, with an evident relish and gusto, how many bottles were uncorked on this trivial occasion and how many on that.

Hughes is not the only one who thus offends against good taste and morality.

> Dickens cannot go a dozen pages with any set of his grotesque characters without feeling it needful to stop and 'liquor' them. Thackeray has very much the same philosophy; and indeed, from many sources of information, it is evident that the public sentiment of England on this subject is not advanced much beyond what ours was half a century ago.

Three-quarters of the *Boston Review* article is devoted to disapproving comments on Bristed's book. 'The author of *Five Years in an English University* has presented a picture so black and revolting on this subject, that we should hardly dare to exhibit it at full length in these pages.' Yet in the latter part, that is in the chapter on morals, Bristed 'talks like a man and a Christian', though his account shows 'a state of society corrupt beyond anything of which we have knowledge in our American colleges'. Here is further corroboration of Emerson's view of the superior virtue of young Americans of good standing and good education.

Professor Kathleen Tillotson in her *Novels of the Eighteen-Forties* points out that prudery in regard to sexual relations was not an early Victorian phenomenon, but came in the 1860s with the development of the shilling magazines for family reading. Dickens satirises it in *Our Mutual Friend* (1864) with Mr Podsnap, who abhors anything that might bring a blush to the cheek of 'the young person', his daughter Georgiana. In America, however, the Puritan tradition, reinforced by the Evangelical Movement, dominated genteel society during the whole of the nineteenth century. In 1823, the Reverend Nathaniel S. Wheaton, Rector of Christ Church, Hartford, looked with distaste at Westmacott's *Achilles*, recently erected near Apsley House in honour of the Duke of Wellington. In his *Journal of a Residence during Several Months in London* (1830) Wheaton wrote:

> Although erected by his fair country-women, they are said to complain that they are debarred from seeing it – their husbands and fathers alleging, as a reason for the prohibition, certain oversights in the disposition of the drapery, which, scanty as it is, need not perhaps have been *all* suspended from the left arm.

Even at the British Museum Mr Wheaton was ill at ease:

> The gallery of marbles appeared to me not altogether proper for the indiscriminate admission of visitors of both sexes; and it is impossible to say how far the taste of the British fair may have been disciplined among the Elgin statues, for the erection of the monument in Hyde-park to the honour of their heroic countryman. Indeed it was not difficult to perceive that the ladies here felt a little out of place.

In 1830, Miss Emma Willard, the founder of the girls' school which still bears her name, was similarly distressed by the immodesty of the statues in the Tuileries Gardens. In a letter to her pupils she wrote:

> No – my dear girls, I shall not take you to examine those statues. If your mothers were here, I would leave you sitting on these shaded benches and conduct them through the walks, and they would return, and bid you depart for our own America; where the eye of modesty is not publicly affronted; and where virgin delicacy can walk abroad without a blush.

This absurdity was not limited to strait-laced Yankees. There was a loud outcry over the exhibition of nude statues at the Crystal Palace in 1851, about which *Punch* waxed uproarious, and before it was reopened at Sydenham in 1854, a committee of lords and bishops, headed by the Archbishop of Canterbury, remonstrated with the directors on their disregard of public decency. In an open letter dedicated 'To the Fathers of Great Britain', a certain William Peters

objected particularly to Hiram Powers's *Greek Slave*, the most prominent exhibit in 1851, as a work, not of art, but of mechanical skill
made 'by copying from the naked figure and moulding from the
naked form'. If the directors persist in showing it at Sydenham,
Peters will acquaint

> the matrons, and through them the daughters of England, that
> women are habitually hired to expose themselves to the gaze of
> the penciller, and forms selected for their exquisite symmetry and
> beauty are modelled in plastic clay by the hand of the artist – nay
> more, that art has the conceit to attempt improvement on Deity,
> and that a fine female statue may be the connected and consolidated
> model of detached portions, seemly and unseemly, of many re-
> alities – nay more than all this, I am credibly informed, that it is
> not an uncommon practice for young artists to invite their young
> companions who make no pretence of having been trained by
> practice to the modesty of the artists themselves, to be present at
> these 'sittings'.

Even more vehemently Peters objected to statues *not* copied from life
– the fauns and bacchanalians, 'living monuments of drunkenness
and vice . . . *in puris naturalibus*, the exposure of which is contemplated by nearly every male with *unmitigated disgust*'. These works
are more fit for the College of Surgeons than for the 'decoration of a
parterre through which we Englishmen are invited to introduce our
sons and daughters'. Though the Second Commandment, forbidding graven images, troubles him nearly as much as the Fourth,
which clearly forbade opening the Exhibition on Sundays, Peters
would not have it thought that he was opposed to all sculpture:

> There is grandeur and good taste in a colossal statue of a
> warrior or a statesman – a well-clad Cornwallis, an Eldon, and a
> Stowell may be appropriate in colossal bronze or marble. But if
> you can find *any* advantage, in *any* way, in *any* naked alabaster,
> what answer will you give as to the colossal *Nymph of Fontainebleau*?

Peters learns from the handbook that this work of Cellini (now in the
Louvre) was rejected by the mistresses of Francis I and Henry II.
'Away with it then from an Exhibition to which you invite the
women of England!'

One further document may be offered in support of Emerson's belief in the chastity of the American male. One reader of the *Boston Review* article, Elbridge Jefferson Cutler, wrote to the editor commending it. Cutler, a Harvard graduate (1853) and class poet, had taught school for several years and served as tutor preparing boys for college. In 1859–60, he travelled in Europe and, after spending another year abroad in 1864–5, on his return was appointed Professor of Modern Languages at Harvard, a post he held until his death in 1870. He is described as a rather strange young man, shy and reserved, 'temperate, nay almost ascetic, in his habits'. One man who knew him wrote: 'He seemed singularly quickened at the core, and strangely free from all tendencies to practical vice and folly. His atmosphere was pure and bracing, and it seemed impossible to associate anything low or unworthy with him. He was a man whose presence and society befitted a home, and the companionship of pure women.' The only woman in his life was his mother, to whom his life-long devotion was notable. After reading the *Boston Review* he wrote to the Reverend Joshua Thomas Tucker, the editor:

That article in the current number of the Boston Review on English and American University Life contains in my opinion a just view of the relative morality of the English and American Colleges. I suspect however that the superiority runs thro' the whole body of our people.

I spent a week on Lake Leman at Lausanne, almost constantly in the company of an English clergyman temporarily absent from his parish on account of Bronchitis, who seemed to me in every respect a genial, candid man and a Christian. I had at that time in my company a beautiful American of 18, singularly pure in his character, and whom I would have trusted in Sodom. Alluding to him, the Englishman asked if I did not feel great anxiety about him lest he be ruined by foreign influences etc. Our conversation turned upon the licentiousness of young men, and when I expressed this confidence in my friend, the gentleman seemed amazed. He asked me if I pretended to assert that any young American reached the age of 25 a chaste man. I told him that in my college class I felt sure that four in five were perfectly correct on that point, and that two thirds were never the worse for liquor in their lives. He told me that in his opinion (and he allowed me to take his words down in my pocket book) that he did 'not believe that one Englishman in 50 reached the age of 25 a chaste man', and he added 'I condemn myself'. You may have the means of identifying my interlocutor, when I say that he was the son of the English Bishop who founded an Episcopal Chapel in the Vale of Chamounix.

. . .

Within two hours after my young friend and I put up in Liverpool at a very nice hotel, an attaché of the house offered to conduct us to a house of prostitution. Many other young travellers who put themselves (as I tried to do) on terms of ease with everybody of whatever grade in order to learn the people have reported similar experiences. Probably your age protected you from such contact.

While the older generation's faith in a higher level of chastity among American males is well documented, we should like to know whether it was really shared by the young. What would we give for the travel journal kept in 1859 by that 'beautiful American youth of 18' whom Mr Cutler 'would have trusted in Sodom'? Shielded from the vices of corrupt foreign societies, did he return to Yale or Harvard to be similarly guarded until, after graduation, he went virgin to his nuptial bed as truly as his bride? Did he leave college in 1861 to join the colours, and in the army among men of lower station and little education find his ideal of chastity considered exceptional, even unnatural? The Kinsey *Report* in 1948 revealed to the most incredulous moralist the revolution wrought by two World Wars in the attitude towards chastity. In the permissive era of the 1970s, the Pill has doubtless reduced still further the number of young men and women of good standing and good education who had no sexual experience before marriage. Among the lower-middle or 'working-classes' conditions are probably much as they have always been on both sides of the Atlantic.

Notes

This essay first appeared in *Contemporary Review*, vol. 219 (November 1971) pp. 252–62.

1. G.H. Lewes, *Ranthorpe* (London, 1847) pp. 200–1.

Checklist of Articles, Notes, Letters to Editors and Book Chapters by Gordon S. Haight

The following checklist includes 57 scholarly articles, notes, letters to editors and book chapters published by Gordon S. Haight between 1930 and 1982. The list does not include books, book introductions or book reviews. Items are arranged in chronological order by year of publication. Those preceded by an asterisk are reprinted in the present edition.

'Longfellow and Mrs Sigourney', *New England Quarterly*, vol. 3 (July 1930) pp. 532–7.

'Johnson's Copy of Bacon's *Works*', *Yale University Library Gazette*, vol. 6 (April 1932) pp. 67–73.

'The Publication of Quarles's *Emblems*', *The Library*, vol. 15 (June 1934) pp. 97–109.

'Lydia Huntley Sigourney', in *Dictionary of American Biography*, vol. XVII (New York: Charles Scribner's Sons, 1935) pp. 115–56.

'Francis Quarles', *The Times Literary Supplement*, 11 April 1935, p. 244.

'The Sources of Quarles's *Emblems*', *The Library*, vol. 16 (September 1935) pp. 188–209.

'Francis Quarles in Ireland', *The Times Literary Supplement*, 17 October 1935, p. 652.

'Francis Quarles in the Civil War', *Review of English Studies*, vol. 12 (April 1936) pp. 147–64.

'The John William DeForest Collection', *Yale University Library Gazette*, vol. 14 (January 1940) pp. 41–6.

'The Author of "The Address" in Quarles's *Shepheards Oracles*', *Modern Language Notes*, vol. 59 (February 1944) pp. 118–20.

'St Nicholas's Clerks (*I Henry IV*, II. i)', *The Times Literary Supplement*, 16 September 1944, p. 451.

* 'Tennyson's Merlin', *Studies in Philology*, vol. 44 (July 1947) pp. 549–66.

'George Henry Lewes', *New Statesman and Nation*, 20 September 1947, p. 232.

'Realism Defined: William Dean Howells', in *Literary History of the United States*, ed. Robert E. Spiller, Willard Thorp, Thomas H.

Johnson, Henry Seidel Canby *et al.*, 3 vols (New York: Macmillan, 1948) vol. II, pp. 878–98.

'The Heritage of Culture', *The Times Literary Supplement*, 12 February 1949, p. 105. Library service for scholars visiting Great Britain.

'George Eliot and Bedford College', *The Times Literary Supplement*, 3 June 1949, p. 365.

'Cross's Biography of George Eliot', *Yale University Library Gazette*, vol. 25 (July 1950) pp. 1–9.

'Cross's Marmoreal Image', *CEA Critic*, vol. XII (November 1950) p. 6.

'George Eliot's Royalties', *Publishers' Weekly*, 7 August 1954, pp. 522–3. Reprinted in *Bookseller*, 2 October 1954, pp. 1140–1.

'Department of Correction and Amplification', *New Yorker*, 6 November 1954, pp. 109–11. Response to Anthony West's review of *The George Eliot Letters*.

'The Tinker Collection of George Eliot Manuscripts', *Yale University Library Gazette*, vol. 29 (April 1955) pp. 148–50.

* 'Dickens and Lewes on Spontaneous Combustion', *Nineteenth-Century Fiction*, vol. 10 (June 1955) pp. 53–63.

* 'Dickens and Lewes', *PMLA*, vol. 71 (March 1956) pp. 166–79.

* 'George Eliot's Originals', in *From Jane Austen to Joseph Conrad*, ed. Robert C. Rathburn and Martin Steinmann Jr (Minneapolis: University of Minnesota Press, [1958]) pp. 177–93.

* 'George Meredith and the *Westminster Review*', *Modern Language Review*, vol. 53 (January 1958) pp. 1–16.

'H. G. Wells's "The Man of the Year Million"', *Nineteenth-Century Fiction*, vol. 12 (March 1958) pp. 323–6.

'George Eliot', *Victorian Newsletter*, no. 13 (Spring 1958) p. 23. A guide to manuscripts.

'The George Eliot and George Henry Lewes Collection', *Yale University Library Gazette*, vol. 35 (April 1961) pp. 170–1.

'George Eliot', in *Encyclopaedia Britannica* (London and Chicago, Ill., 1962) vol. VIII, pp. 283–4.

'George Gissing: Some Biographical Details', *Notes and Queries*, vol. 209 (June 1964) pp. 235–6.

'"All Deliberate Speed"', *New York Times*, 9 March 1965, p. 34. Scott's use of legal phrases in *Rob Roy*.

'Robert Frost at Yale', *Yale University Library Gazette*, vol. 40 (July 1965) pp. 12–17.

* 'George Eliot's Klesmer', in *Imagined Worlds: Essays on Some English Novels and Novelists in Honour of John Butt*, ed. Maynard Mack (London: Methuen, 1968) pp. 205–14.

'Unpublished George Eliot Letters', *The Times Literary Supplement*, 30 May 1968, p. 553. Identifies current holder of copyrights.

'George Eliot and John Blackwood', *Blackwood's Magazine*, vol. 306 (November 1969) pp. 385–400.

'Lydia Huntley Sigourney', in *Notable American Women*, 3 vols (Cambridge, Mass.: Radcliffe College, 1971) vol. III, pp. 288–91.

'A New George Eliot Letter', *The Times Literary Supplement*, 12 February 1971, p. 187. Reprinted in *Yale University Library Gazette*, vol. 46 (July 1971) pp. 24–8.

* 'Robert Browning's Widows', *The Times Literary Supplement*, 2 July 1971, pp. 783–4.

'The George Eliot and George Henry Lewes Collection', *Yale University Library Gazette*, vol. 46 (July 1971) pp. 20–3.

* 'Male Chastity in the Nineteenth Century', *Contemporary Review*, vol. 219 (November 1971) pp. 252–62.

'New George Eliot Letters to John Blackwood', *The Times Literary Supplement*, 10 March 1972, pp. 281–2.

'Letters as Literature: 2. To Whom It May Concern – and Others', *The Times Literary Supplement*, 26 January 1973, pp. 87–9.

'Letters from George Henry Lewes to Richard Hengist Horne', *Books at Iowa*, no. 18 (April 1973) pp. 18–25.

'Dorothea's Husbands', *The Times Literary Supplement*, 1 June 1973, pp. 616–17.

* 'Poor Mr Casaubon', in *Nineteenth-Century Perspectives: Essays in Honor of Lionel Stevenson*, ed. Clyde de L. Ryals, John Clubbe and Benjamin Franklin Fisher IV (Durham, N. C.: Duke University Press, 1974) pp. 255–70.

'Original Mss Bound In', *The Times Literary Supplement*, 15 March 1974, p. 264.

* 'George Eliot's "Eminent Failure", Will Ladislaw', in *This Particular Web: Essays on 'Middlemarch'*, ed. Ian Adam (Toronto: University of Toronto Press, [1975]) pp. 22–42.

*'The Carlyles and the Leweses', in *Carlyle and His Contemporaries: Essays in Honor of Charles Richard Sanders*, ed. John Clubbe (Durham, N. C. : Duke University Press, 1976) pp. 181–204.

'Professor W. K. Wimsatt', *The Times*, 2 January 1976, p. 12.

* 'The Heroine of *Middlemarch*', *Victorian Newsletter*, no. 54 (Fall 1978) pp. 4–8.

'The Publication of Motley's *Rise of the Dutch Republic*', *Yale University Library Gazette*, vol. 54 (January 1980) pp. 135–40.

'Gordon Haight's Speech in Westminster Abbey on 21 June, when a

Memorial Stone to George Eliot Was Unveiled', *London Review of Books*, vol. 2 (17 July–6 August 1980) pp. 16–17.

* 'George Eliot's Bastards', in *George Eliot: A Centenary Tribute*, ed. G. S. Haight and Rosemary T. VanArsdel (London: Macmillan, 1981) pp. 1–10.

'Strether's Chad Newsome: A Reading of James's *The Ambassadors*', in *From Smollett to James: Studies in the Novel and Other Essays Presented to Edgar Johnson*, ed. Samuel I. Mintz, Alice Chandler and Christopher Mulvey (Charlottesville, Va.: University Press of Virginia, [1981]) pp. 261–76.

'Journals and Jottings', *The Times Literary Supplement*, 9 January 1981, p. 32. An account of the George Eliot Exhibition in the Beinecke Library, Yale University, November 1980–January 1981.

'The Reader's Convenience', *Browning Institute Studies*, vol. 9 (1981) pp. 137–9.

* 'George Eliot and Watts's *Clytie*', *Yale University Library Gazette*, vol. 56 (April 1982) pp. 65–9.

Index

Deutsch, Emanuel, 20
Dexter, Walter, 133, 145
Dickens, Charles Culliford, 211
Dickens, Charles, 3, 10, 14, 22, 49,
    51, 54, 84, 117–33, 134–45, 195,
    210–11, 212, 220, 221
  works:
    Barnaby Rudge, 144; *Bleak House*,
    3, 84, 122, 134–5, 137–41, 143–4,
    145, 155, 210; *David Copperfield*, 3,
    14, 22; *Dombey and Son*, 84;
    Martin Chuzzlewit, 155; *The
    Mystery of Edwin Drood*, 127; *The
    Old Curiosity Shop*, 131, 132;
    Oliver Twist, 54, 119; *Our Mutual
    Friend*, 51, 220; *Pickwick Papers*,
    10, 118, 119, 210; *A Tale of Two
    Cities*, 124, 126; *The Uncommercial
    Traveller*, 127; *see also All the Year
    Round*
Dickens, Mrs Charles, 131
Dickens, Henry Charles, 119, 138
Dickens, Henry Fielding, 202
Dickens, Mary, 201, 202
Dictionary of National Biography, 19,
    86
Dictionary of the Welsh Language, 183
Dido, 49
Dilke, Sir Charles, 32, 33–4
Disraeli, Benjamin, 210
Donne, John, 31, 48
Dostoevski, Feodor, 3
Drayton, Michael, 31
Duffy, Sir Charles Gavan, 111, 116
Dumas père, Alexandre, 166
du Maurier, George, 208
Dupuytren, Guillaume, 140

Ebdell, Bernard Gilpin, 5
Ebdell, Mrs Bernard Gilpin, *see*
    Shilton, Sally
Eckermann, Johann Peter, 101
Edel, Leon, 49
Edinburgh Review, 115
Edinburgh, University of, 138, 214
Edwards, Matilda Betham, 171–2
Eldon, John Scott, 1st Earl, 222
Elgin marbles, 59, 206, 221
Eliot, George (Marian Evans)

  works:
    'Art and Belles Lettres' [review
    of Ruskin's *Modern Painters*, vol.
    III], 151; 'Contemporary
    Literature of England' [review of
    Carlyle's *Life of John Sterling*], 91–
    2; Journal, 22, 75, 99; 'Miss
    Brooke', 22, 58; quarry for
    Middlemarch, 43; 'Silly Novels by
    Lady Novelists', 23; 'Thomas
    Carlyle', 91–2, 113–14, 116;
    'Worldliness and Other-
    Worldliness: The Poet Young',
    110; see also *Adam Bede*, 'Amos
    Barton', *Daniel Deronda*, *Felix Holt
    the Radical*, 'Janet's Repentance',
    Middlemarch, *The Mill on the Floss*,
    'Mr Gilfil's Love-Story', *Romola*,
    Scenes of Clerical Life, *Silas Marner*
Eliot, T. S., 65
Elizabeth I, Queen, 155
Elliotson, John, 137–8
Elton, Sir Arthur Hallam, 157
Elton, Oliver, 40
Elwes, Alfred, 151
Emerson, Ralph Waldo, 210–13,
    219, 220, 223
Emerson-Tennent, Sir J., 97
Espinasse, Francis, 94, 96, 97, 111,
    114, 115, 116
Euripides, 31
Evangelicalism, 5–6, 7, 33, 79, 80,
    82, 213, 215, 220, 221
Evans, Christiana (Chrissey), 9, 17–
    18
Evans, Isaac, 9, 14–15, 17
Evans, Robert, 9, 10, 11, 12, 15, 17
Evans, Mrs Samuel, 9, 11–12
Evarard, John, 17
Evarard, Mrs John, 16–17

Fechter, Charles Albert, 112
Fedele, Cassandra, 23
Felix Holt the Radical, 19, 78, 84, 204,
    209
  characters:
    Felix, 19; Matthew Jermyn, 78;
    Rufus Lyon, 19; Harold
    Transome, 78; Mrs Transome, 84